S0-AYX-653

Hegemony

John Agnew is Professor of Geography at the University of California, Los Angeles. He is the author or co-author of *Place and Politics*, *The United States in the World Economy*, *The Geography of the World Economy*, *Geopolitics*, and *Place and Politics in Modern Italy*, among other titles, as well as the co-editor of *American Space/American Place*.

Hegemony

THE NEW SHAPE OF

GLOBAL POWER

John Agnew

 Temple University Press

PHILADELPHIA

56531265

For Felicity

Temple University Press
1601 North Broad Street
Philadelphia PA 19122
www.temple.edu/tempress

Copyright © 2005 by Temple University
All rights reserved
Published 2005
Printed in the United States of America

⊛ The paper used in this publication meets the requirements of the American
National Standard for Information Sciences—Permanence of Paper for Printed
Library Materials, ANSI Z39.48-1992

Library of Congress Cataloging-in-Publication Data

Agnew, John A.
    Hegemony : the new shape of global power / John Agnew.
        p.   cm.
    Includes bibliographical references and index.
    ISBN 1-59213-152-2 (cloth : alk. paper) — ISBN 1-59213-153-0 (pbk. : alk. paper)
    1. United States—Foreign economic relations.   2. United States—Economic policy.
3. Consumption (Economics).   4. Globalization.   5. United States—Foreign relations.
6. Civilization, Modern—American influences.   7. World politics—21st century.
8. Geopolitics.   I. Title.

HF1455.A6155 2005
337.73—dc22

                                                                2004058896

2 4 6 8 9 7 5 3 1

RIDER UNIVERSITY LIBRARY

Contents

Preface

As a child, I understood American "influence" in the world differently than that of the "high politics" of diplomacy and economic policy that I had heard about on the radio or from my parents and teachers. The first time I saw an American car taking up both sides of the main street in my home village in northwest England—brought there for display, not to drive, by a vacationing native son usually employed by Chevrolet (GM) somewhere "over there"—I understood something of the pull exerted on the rest of the world by the American cornucopia.

I was disabused of all this as a university student. I was taught in international politics that the only important American influence was that exerted by the U.S. government as a result of its military strength and the capacity of the economy it governed. But apart from that, all states were more or less the same in striving for global primacy. The fact that the United States had "replaced" countries like Great Britain at the top of the global state-heap was attributed to its amazing industrial capacity, a dose of luck, and the support of such stalwart allies as the British, whose time as a world power had finally run out. My more positivist social science instructors were particularly dismissive of the idea that anything "unique" about American history might have anything to do with anything. The "rise" of the United States was due to rational actors exploiting the universal conjunctures associated with spurts of technological change and the outcomes of wars (predetermined by who had most war materiel). The United States was just another "case" like all of the others.

In the years since, the world seems to have changed beyond all recognition. Much of this change is put down to "globalization," although quite what that means remains elusive. It is partly about "time-space compression"—the reduction in the importance of distance for a wide range of transactions—but it is also about significant changes in the geographical scope and the temporal speed of economic transactions and the rapid transmission of cultural messages. Certainly, the old theories of world politics of states bumping up against one another now seem not just antiquated but positively misleading.

This book ties globalization to that American influence on the rest of the world that I had inchoately recognized so many years ago. A paper I wrote previously, "Globalization Has a Home Address," lays out some of the main strands of my thinking. That expresses well one of the main arguments that I make in this book: globalization is to a significant degree "Made in the U.S.A." But now I want to go beyond this idea to make the further argument that globalization under American influence has initiated change in the very spatial ontology of world politics. By this I mean that the geography of power is decreasingly organized on a singular territorial basis by reference to states as we have known them since the eighteenth century. In its place we are seeing a world with an increasingly complex spatiality of power, as localities, global city-regions, regions, and trading blocs connect or network with one another to challenge the primary state-based territorial divisions. So, if the twentieth century was the American century, the twenty first is not likely to be. American hegemony has set in motion a world that can no longer be dominated by any single state or its cultural fruits.

Yet, one of the most common ways of addressing American influence today is to refer to the United States as an actual or incipient "empire." With the disappearance of the Soviet Union as a competing superpower, the U.S. government certainly seems to have no peer. Indeed, particularly since September 11, 2001, the U. S. government has confronted the rest of the world with the hubris and noblesse oblige that are associated with the imperial purple. But the term empire usually implies much more than this. It implies a high degree of territorial organization, effective centralized power, and a directing intelligence. These traits do not seem to match the ways that an essentially improvising American government currently relates to the rest of the world. Perhaps history misleads us in looking for repetition in the behavior of powerful governments. If states with the largest military establishments or GDPs per capita in the past became or tried to become empires, then surely the United States must, too? I think that the empire designation is fundamentally misleading in understanding the current situation and influence of the United States in world politics. In its place I propose the concept of hegemony—not simply in the sense of dominance or equivalence to empire, but as a confluence between a globally dominant position on the one hand and a set of attributes that that dominance has created, enabling it to spread and be imposed around the world, on the other: what I call "marketplace society."

Hegemony, therefore, has had a specifically American content, if one open to adaptation as it travels and enrolls others in its operations. This is not the same as modernization or the conversion of people to modernity in an American guise—that is, the adoption by individuals of a set of modern values in opposition to so-called traditional ones. Rather, it is about the adoption of rules of economic and political life that reorient and reorganize world politics. Globalization and the new geography of power that this entails have been the outcome. The temptation of empire, however strongly felt in some quarters in Washington, reflects the negatively charged reverberation of the success of what I am calling American hegemony on the United States itself rather than a coherent forward-looking strategy that grows out of either American experience or the main course of recent world history. Making the case for a new shape to global power that has developed from American hegemony but which now points to a world increasingly outside the direct control of the United States or any other state is the purpose of the book.

Acknowledgments

I would like to thank a number of people who have helped with this book and the thinking behind it. James Anderson and Gerard Toal encouraged me to develop my argument about empire versus hegemony. Tom Mertes made me clarify my criticisms of empire as a useful concept in the current world situation. David Lake introduced me to how a thoughtful political scientist considers questions of anarchy and hierarchy in international politics. Leslie Sklair questioned my consumption model of American hegemony and encouraged me to spell out my argument. Dennis Conway has tolerated my obsession with the need to understand the "American experience," while understanding that this does not entail indulging in the exceptionalism that incites such hubris along the Potomac. Steve Legg provided me with a careful reading of Chapters 1 and 2. Mat Coleman made some pivotal suggestions that helped clarify the argument of Chapter 5. Jo Sharp and I worked together on many of the ideas in Chapter 4. Chase Langford conceived and drafted the map of the "Coalition of the Willing" that appears as Figure 9.1. He also drew all of the other figures. Finally, Leslie Sklair and Felicity Nussbaum read the manuscript with great care, saving me from a number of errors and misstatements. Any that remain are my responsibility alone. Felicity also offered kind encouragement at difficult moments. Peter Wissoker has smoothed the way with Temple University Press. I am particularly grateful to him. A much earlier version of Chapter 2 previously appeared in *Antipode* 35 (2003), and Chapter 3 appeared as follows: *Millennium: Journal of International Studies;* sections of this chapter first appeared in *Millennium* (vol. 28, no. 3, 1999), and are reproduced here with substantial alterations with the permission of the publisher. I am grateful to Yale University Press for permission to reproduce (as Figure 4.1) the map from Donald Meinig, *The Shaping of America. Volume 1: Atlantic America* (1986), Figure 67, p. 402.

1 Introduction

Words matter. Currently, there is much talk and writing about *empire* or *American empire*—words used to describe the dominant force in world politics today.[1] I want to challenge this creeping consensus by proposing a different word to describe the current state of affairs. This word *hegemony* is often confused with empire and frequently appears with such ancillary words as *imperial*, *imperialist*, and so on, as if they all meant the same thing. Of course, they can be made to mean the same thing. But what if the consensus is fundamentally mistaken about what is actually unique about the current situation? And, by way of substitution, what if the word hegemony is given a meaning distinctive from that of empire, a meaning it has long had, thus providing an alternative conception of contemporary world politics? My task is to convince readers that the word hegemony, at least in the usage I give it, is a much better term for describing the historic relationship between the United States and the rest of the world than is the word empire. This is not an aesthetic choice; it is an analytic one. Words can help understanding—or they can obscure it. In this regard, loose use of the word empire fails to fulfill the theoretical duty it has been given.

In brief, I argue that the main thrust of contemporary world politics is the result of the particular hegemony exercised by American society in the rest of the world through the agency of both the U.S. government and a wide range of other institutions, corporate, philanthropic, and inter-governmental—whose basic structures and norms are those of the marketplace society that developed in the United States in the nineteenth and twentieth centuries. Hegemony, therefore, is more than the simple domination implied when it is equated with empire or, as in other conventional accounts, when it is seen simply as the identity of a dominant state without inquiring into the nature of that identity and how it affects that state's relationships with others.[2] In my usage, hegemony is the enrollment of others in the exercise of your power

1

by convincing, cajoling, and coercing them that they should want what you want. Though never complete and often resisted, it represents the binding together of people, objects, and institutions around cultural norms and standards that emanate over time and space from seats of power (that have discrete locations) occupied by authoritative actors. Hegemony is not, therefore, simply the exercise of raw military, economic, and political power by the latest in a long line of "hegemons" as if the exercise of power had remained unchanged through the centuries. Neither is it a simple continuation of military and political power exercised territorially as implied by use of the word empire, whether or not qualified by such terms as *formal* or *informal*. Such usage simply shifts the intellectual "territorial trap"—meaning seeing power as invariably territorial—from the level of the state to that of a global empire.[3]

If empires have a core feature it is that they exercise power territorially through effective centralized command. The Roman Empire, sometimes taken as analogous to the contemporary American empire, was an *imperium* in which all roads led (figuratively and literally) directly to Rome. American hegemony, however, even though it obviously has coercive attributes that have been very apparent in recent years, is fundamentally not imperial in its goals or territorial in its organization.[4] Indeed, I will claim that *globalization*, in its fragmentation of existing state territories and its increasingly predominant networked geography of power, is the necessary outcome of American global hegemony, not some sort of empire. Globalization today and under American hegemony represents a dramatic quickening and geographical reformulation of the progressive universalization of capitalist commodification and accumulation.[5] But globalization is not an abstract process of imperialism. Neither is it reducible simply to technological change or firm reinvestment strategies. Globalization is a hegemonic project intimately connected to the geopolitical calculus of the U.S. government and economic interests during the Cold War and to the incorporation of the entire world into its grip in the years since the demise of the Communist project in the former Soviet Union and China by a myriad of U.S.-based agents. From this viewpoint, globalization is not the same as liberalization. Globalization refers to the increasing pace and scope of economic and cultural activities across space. Liberalization refers to a mix of government-enacted policies that tend to expose states to the external pressures that attend technological change and policies that invite the guidance of world-level institutions such as the IMF, WTO, and World Bank through the privatization of state assets, reduction of state spending on popular welfare, and increased openness to trade and foreign direct investment. Liberalization has been an important mechanism increasing the intensity of globalization, but it is not at all the same thing.[6]

The trend of the U.S. government since the 1980s toward unilateral military and economic action—from refusal to engage in global environmental treaties or participate in the International Criminal Court to the invasion and occupation of Iraq—represents, rather than its burgeoning strength, the weakness of the United States within the very world order that the country has done so much to create. To associate the contemporary United States with the word empire is to imply the exact opposite.[7] An imperial strategy, whatever its short-term successes might possibly be, and few are immediately apparent, runs against the grain of what American society has brought to the world during the past century in terms of ideas and practices about the centrality of marketplace society to social life: from mass consumption and living through commodities, to hierarchies of class hidden behind a cultural rhetoric of entrepreneurship and equal opportunity, to limiting the delivery of what elsewhere are thought of as public goods and sponsoring an essentially privatized vision of life.[8] This "central market" paradigm is not simply a package of ideas but a set of social practices in which instrumental (market) behavior tends to displace customary (communal) and command (state-mandated) behaviors as the social standard. It is also more demotic or popular than elitist in its idiom. It presumes that physical force is a very unstable, if sometimes necessary, form of rule.[9]

It was in the United States that this marketplace society first took root as a mass as opposed to an elite phenomenon.[10] Indeed, the argument could be made that American independence was itself an early manifestation of the rumblings of an emergent marketplace society against an imperial or extensive command system.[11] In this regard, Karl Marx's famous phrase in his *Critique of Hegel's Philosophy of Right* comes to mind: "Theory ... becomes a material force as soon as it has gripped the masses."[12] From this viewpoint, the content of American hegemony owes much more to American society, therefore, than to the machinations of an often incoherent, incompetent, corrupt, and bewildered American state. In other words, it is much more the American Main Street (and shopping mall) than Washington D.C. that has provided the social norms and practices that others around the world have come to emulate and that has provided much of the basis to American hegemony.

Much writing about empire and hegemony as well as being excessively state-centric rests on a peculiarly productivist view of power. This is the case with both the more state-centered and the more class-centered accounts.[13] According to this approach, because value is created in the production process everything else is traced back to that process. This is mistaken because value is only realized in *consumption* when (at least for Marxists) the M-C-M' circle is closed.[14] Conventional Marxism has lost this "parallax perspective" in which production and consumption play equivalently important roles. To all too many commentators, exchange and consumption are still regarded as illusory spheres in which speculation and commodity fetishism distract potential revolutionaries from taking over their places of employment. But consumption is not merely a "buying off" of workers or an alienating exercise in bourgeois mystification but an essential moment in capitalism itself. In this view, therefore, it was within the vast territory of the United States that capitalism first realized its full potential. People had to be free to consume as well as to labor for the circle of capital to close. With American hegemony this potential has globalized.

The standardization of space that accompanied European settlement and incorporation into the United States in the nineteenth century by, among other things, the township-and-range system of land division, railroads and their timetables, and the logistical innovations of national businesses after the Civil War provided a framework for the birth of the first large-scale consumer economy. The absence of barriers to trade and the presence of a common currency created a massive space within which economies of scale could be captured to realize the liberal dream in which calculation and rationality would provide the basis to realizing the desire to better one's material condition. The United States was the first modern capitalist economy as its avatars such as Adam Smith understood it.[15]

At home and abroad, however, American hegemony is much more of a mixed bag in its consequences than either its proponents or its critics tend to claim. In particular, the cultural logic of marketplace society has politically progressive as well as negative effects. For example, it can refocus male emotional commitment around business deal-making rather than warrior dreams. Edith Wharton memorably declared that, for the Gilded Age (late nineteenth century) upper-class American male, "the real *crime passionnel* is a 'big steal.'"[16] American hegemony can also liberate people from the hold of traditions that disempower various groups, not the least women, whose independent subjectivity (as citizens and consumers rather than solely as mothers or potential mothers) and parallel participation in society as individual persons have tended to increase with its spread.

Marketplace society also has provided the necessary context for the growth of a public sphere in which social, political, and cultural norms can be debated outside the control of absolutist authority. At the same time, its promise of "Paradise Now or Soon" obviously threatens those political (and theological) projects that put Utopia into the indefinite future. Unremitting critics of the culture of consumption, certainly one of the most important components of marketplace society, often tend to operate with a rosy view of the societies the consumption-based society undermined. Clothing the past with the image of artisans lovingly making goods without desire for monetary profit and consumers as connoisseurs of things-in-themselves is historically problematic to say the least. Karl Marx for one was alive to the paradox of capitalist modernity. At the same time it promised more to greater numbers, it also made them increasingly dependent on the nexus of the marketplace without the kinship and familial resources to compensate for their new vulnerability. From this viewpoint, simple romantic anti-consumerism is a backward-looking or conservative utopia.[17]

What the coming of marketplace society did was to democratize desire; to make it possible for the multitude to consume goods in ways previously available only to the rich. Of course, doing so invariably disrupts local ties and dependencies and replaces them with longer distance ones. The "local" sounds good to many American ears, but most of American history has been spent incorporating the local into the national and increasingly into the global. For example, food and information once circulated largely within local confines. This is obviously no longer the case. More significant socially, removing people from preexisting local statuses and giving them new ones in wider spatial divisions of labor required new measures of social value. Goods and people were "shorn of the luminosity of place and the spirit of reciprocity in a full-fledged commodity market."[18] As a result, new measures of value and status were attained through *commodification* of people and goods. As reciprocity and authority retreated as dominant modes of social exchange, they were replaced by social valuations based on position in the marketplace as signified by income and consumption.

But this commodification is best regarded as neither a simple "top-down" process, nor, in functionalist terms, a deliberate trick to make people conform to what their betters desire. People actively demand distinctions from one another.[19] Thus, the demand for distinction in the absence of customary and command mechanisms endows persons and things with their particular values in a marketplace society.[20] In such a society, therefore, people and things are always actually or potentially commodifiable. Whether this process can continue to be sustainable at a global level, economically and environmentally, may be problematic, particularly now that the growing Chinese and Indian middle classes, hundreds of millions of them, aspire to follow in the consumer path blazed by the Americans, Europeans, and Japanese. As its most prized goods are often positional ones, whose social value lies in their relative scarcity, the whole enterprise ends up rather like a dog chasing its own tail. That, however, does not make it any less central to the way the modern world works.

Perhaps commodification's most negative impact is political. Marketplace society is one in which the role of citizen is increasingly eclipsed by that of consumer. Indeed, notwithstanding an early association with the development of a public sphere, its spread is clearly associated with a redirection of popular political energies from meaningful and effective debate over "the good society" into competition between politicians promising "more."[21] If the early narratives about what was later called "the American Dream" were predominantly about religious and political freedom, the more recent ones are all about upward social mobility, home ownership, and achieving fame and fortune.[22] The quantitative character of the American promise and its link to the benevolence of providence is put brilliantly by Immanuel Wallerstein when he writes: "I think that Americans tend to believe that others have *less* of many things than we have, and the fact that we have more is a sign of grace."[23] This "less-ness" is not just about consumption but also about the relative efficiency of economies, the scope of social aspirations, and the wide range of technological accomplishments. During the Cold War, the American promise constituted the kernel of the American entry in the "ideological geopolitics" of that epoch.[24] In this regard, while clothed in the rhetoric of democracy versus totalitarianism, American ideology represented the victory of the promise of ever-increasing consumption over open and deliberative democracy. What De Tocqueville presciently called "the charm of anticipated success" turned workers and employees into consumers whose self-image was of individuals whose fate lay in their own hands not in collective action or solidarity with the poor or the materially less well endowed.[25] The shadow of marketplace society has been cast far and wide even if often challenged by residual and emergent hegemonies. The former would include the republicanism that inspired in part the American political experiment but which was rapidly eclipsed by a socially more powerful liberalism and various religious fundamentalisms urging a return to traditional ways. The latter would include the various socialisms, fascisms, social–democratic experiments, and communitarianisms that have arisen to resist and question marketplace society's inevitability.

For now these alternatives seem largely quiescent, with the notable exception of religious fundamentalisms. Marketplace society is in a period of absolute ascendancy around the world.[26] In late-1980s China, for example, the contemporary leader, Deng Xioaping, at a time of widespread calls for greater democracy, supposedly announced that "to get rich is glorious" and redirected the country toward full-fledged adoption of the marketplace model, with important adaptations to Communist China. In 1989, Deng successfully challenged the Tiananmen Square protesters for democracy, who paraded with a replica of the Statue of Liberty, not just with tanks but with the promise of more consumption. Likewise, the Bharataniya Janata (BJP) political party in India opened up the country to the world economy when it came into national office in the mid-1990s. Representing a largely middle class (and high caste) constituency, it boldly adopted a liberal model of economic development in place of the state-centered model of the dominant post-Independence Congress party. As in China, a major consequence was a growing polarization in economic growth and incomes between regions and across social classes. This allowed a return to power of the Congress party and its allies in 2004 with the support of those excluded from the fruits of consumption. Its commitment, however, is to spread around the benefits of a burgeoning economy not to retreat to its old model. In present day Italy, the electoral popularity of the Prime Minister, Silvio Berlusconi, is based entirely on selling himself (through his fortuitous control over much of Italian television) as a symbol of the rise of an Italian marketplace society that in its crassness eclipses even that of the United States. That Berlusconi has acquired his position as Italy's richest person largely through political manipulation and close calls with the law is seen only as evidence of his *sagacia* (astuteness) and *fortuna favorevole* (good fortune)—in other words, the (hopefully positive) magic of the marketplace. This is an Italian adaptation, not simply a wholesale adoption as a word such as *Americanization* would imply. Part of the genius of American hegemony is its ability to adapt as it enrolls. When the Moslem festival of Ramadan becomes the orgy of consumption that is the American Christmas, then we will know that the hegemony of marketplace society has captured one of its last holdouts. Adopting Christmas itself is not required.

The widespread appeal of consumer sentiments, of course, can be put down to universal "animal spirits" that have inspired consumption for its own sake from the Stone Age to the present. What seems much less arguable than whether marketplace society has at least some local content, however, is that American hegemony by means of enrollment in marketplace society has had a dual aspect to it. On the one hand, U.S.-based institutions have had the power to enact globally a dominant vision of "the good society." On the other hand, this vision has been one of ever-increasing mass consumption. The hegemony of marketplace society, therefore, is what lies at the center of contemporary world society. In William Leach's words: "Whoever has the power to project a vision of the good life and make it prevail has the most decisive power of all."[27] From this viewpoint, thinking about contemporary world politics in terms of classic or mutant empires simply obscures the actual mechanisms through which power is exercised in a world no longer reducible to territorial states and empires bumping up against one another in a competition for primacy.[28] The contemporary geography of power is too complex for this reduction. In particular, global commodity chains, financial networks, and cultural exchanges linking together the global marketplace have local roots but exercise global reach. This is a networked and fragmenting topology of power rather than a territorializing and homogenizing one. Hence, building global or supranational policies or alternative political positions on outdated images such as that of empire could have mistaken if not catastrophic consequences.

This book is a response to the proliferation of publications adopting the empire motif as if it offered the most powerful purchase on contemporary world politics. So, I begin in Chapter 2 with a discussion of the words *empire* and *hegemony* in relation to recent U.S. involvement in world politics, particularly the invasion of Iraq in 2003. Chapter 3 moves beyond the immediate situation to consider the long-term theoretical connections among hegemony, globalization, and the geography of power. I argue that world politics is not set in stone for all time but has evolved well beyond the "field-of-forces" model of territorial states that still dominates so much discussion of world politics. I provide some intellectual tools to help understand how this evolution has happened, emphasizing how crucial to the process the particular form taken by American hegemony has been. I challenge the view that U.S. hegemony is simply the outcome of an ad hoc dialectic between conjunctural constraints (e.g., German and Japanese defeat in the Second World War, the revolt of colonies against European imperialism, etc.) and universal processes (such as the pursuit of primacy between Great Powers or class struggle). Instead, I emphasize the historical development of a set of sociological and cultural features that by the late nineteenth century differentiated the United States from other national-capitalist societies and the rest of the world in general but that have become increasingly the "standard" or norm around the world under American hegemony. From this perspective, the place that comes to exercise hegemony matters, therefore, in the content and form that hegemony takes. In other words, a spatial dialectic between the United States and the rest of the world rather than a conjunctural/universal historical dialectic with only incidental geographical features has done most to shape contemporary world politics.

Chapter 4 takes up the specifics of the case for the United States as the first fully fledged marketplace society in which an emphasis on popular mass consumption—largely new in human history—prevailed and from which many of the features associated with globalization have tended to evolve. From this point of view, the growth of popular mass consumption developed first in U.S.-based capitalism and diffused elsewhere, not mere changes in production, has made possible the perpetuation and deepening of capitalism by scaling it up to the global. Within and outside the United States, the emergent marketplace society has had episodic crises of credibility. Particularly in the 1930s, it came close to collapse in the United States itself. But its resurrection after the Second World War was bolstered significantly by its central role in the ideological conflict with the Soviet Union.

In Chapter 5, I argue that the spread of marketplace society defines the core attributes of American hegemony, not the mimesis or restructuring of world politics around a political division of labor redolent of American constitutionalism, as alleged by some theorists of empire, particularly Hardt and Negri.[29] It is the dominant character of American society rather than a scaled-up version of the American political structure that has provided the basis to American hegemony. Indeed, this character makes it possible to think of a global hegemony no longer attached to its American roots through the actions of the U.S. government. Indeed, such political actions could be seen, at least in light of recent events such as the invasion of Iraq, as having become adversarial to American hegemony rather than serving its purposes. Marketplace society may need institutional supports, but these need no longer be identifiably American ones. But the U.S. government itself is now so severely constrained by its constitutional structures, I also argue, to be singularly ineffective in responding to many economic, military, and political challenges. If it is the monster that is so often alleged, the U.S. government is nevertheless a seriously incompetent and incoherent one.

With Chapter 6, I provide a narrative account of contemporary globalization, tracing it back to the achievement of global power by the U.S. government after the Second World War but with older substantive roots (as I argue in Chapter 4) and link this to an emerging geography of power in which long-distance networks are helping to fragment existing territorial arrangements for the organization of societies and economies. Such networks are hardly new (in Chapter 3 their historical rootedness is emphasized). But the ability of the governments of territorial states to direct and limit them—including the U.S. government—is increasingly problematic. Chapter 7 describes the consequences of this new geography of power for global patterns of development. After detailing dominant views among geographers on the new global economy, I use empirical evidence about trends in global income inequalities to show how the new geography of power explains why at the same time inequalities between states have been decreasing (particularly among developed countries and to a certain extent among all countries because of economic growth in China), inequalities within countries have risen considerably.

In Chapter 8, I bring the case full circle: back to the United States itself. Rather than the fearsome imperial force portrayed in so many recent accounts of world politics, I emphasize the vulnerability of the United States to the very forces of globalization that successive U.S. governments and businesses have helped unleash. Inside the United States, the same social and geographical shifts are under way that can be seen elsewhere with increasing polarization of incomes, a declining middle class, and a re-territorialization of the economy around certain regions. The decreasing share of product markets in the United States held by U.S.-based businesses and massive fiscal imbalances bode ill for a ready reversal of social and geographical polarities. Chalmers Johnson has memorably referred to this process as "blowback," which is "shorthand for saying that a nation reaps what it sows, even if it does not fully know or understand what it has sown."[30] A brief conclusion summarizes the overall thrust of the book by raising in a different way the whole issue I raised previously: Which word—empire or hegemony— best describes the role of the U.S. in contemporary world politics? If it is an empire, it is a peculiarly incoherent and increasingly hollow one. It is better seen as increasingly subject to pressures from the very hegemony it has released on the world.

2 Hegemony versus Empire

The United States brought into existence the first fully "marketplace society" in history. This is a territorial society in which politics and society operate largely in terms of exchange value rather than use value. A distinction first made by Adam Smith but developed in various ways by later thinkers such as Karl Marx and Karl Polanyi, exchange- versus use-value revolves around the idea that social and political relationships can be based predominantly on either their instrumental value (i.e., as if a price could be placed on them) or their intrinsic/consummatory value (i.e., as if they had unique qualities). Previous societies had elements of both, but with the rise of capitalism, exchange value increasingly eclipsed use value. Only in the United States were there so few barriers to the spread of exchange value into all areas of life and so many new incentives for acceptance of the market norms that accompanied this. In particular, the nascent country had none of the feudal-monarchical remnants that were important to modern state formation in Europe. In the United States, the "state" was designed to be the servant of society, in particular its property owners and entrepreneurs, not the instrument for perpetuating aristocratic rule in an increasingly capitalist world economy. The country's size and increasing ethnic diversity combined with the peculiarity of its form of statehood to create material and ideological conditions propitious to exchange value as the basis for all social and political, *not just economic*, relationships. So, even as the United States expanded territorially into North America and through trade and investment into the rest of the world, its process of exercising power has been through bringing places to market, both materially and ideologically, rather than through simply coercing control over territory. That has been supplementary, if episodically, highly significant.

Yet much scholarly and popular discussion of the U.S. role in the world insists that the United States is either simply just "another state" (albeit a bigger, more powerful one) or an empire, by stretching the manifestly territorial meaning of "empire" to include nonterritorial influence and control. Neither approach is satisfactory. First, the present-day world is significantly different, especially in its geography of power, from previous epochs. The present day is often considered the time of "globalization" to signal the rise of actors (multinational firms, global nongovernmental organizations [NGOs], international institutions, etc.) and processes of development (globalized financial markets, global commodity chains, etc.) that cannot be linked to a single territorial address. This is a world that the United States has helped to bring about, both by design and through unintended consequences. If this were an "empire," then it would be the only decentered one in history, which seems to suggest that it is something else. Second, this world has not been brought about predominantly through direct coercion or by territorial rule, but rather through socio-economic incorporation into practices and routines derivative of or compatible with those first developed in the United States. The best word to describe these processes is "hegemony."

Hegemony and empire offer profoundly different understandings of American power and its contemporary manifestations, not the least in terms of how such power can be challenged. Interestingly, in much usage the two terms are not readily distinguished from each other; either way an Almighty America is seen as recasting the world in its image. From this viewpoint, hegemony is simply the relatively unconstrained coercive power exercised by a hegemon or seat of empire. I suggest that this usage is problematic, both historically and analytically. More specifically, the terms hegemony and empire have distinctive etymologies and contemporary meanings in English and other languages. When used analytically they can help to give precision to what has happened to U.S. relations with the world as a consequence, for example, of the 2003 war on Iraq. Taken together, they provide a take-off point for the historical relationship between U.S. hegemony and globalization, which is considered in the rest of the book.

It is possible to have empire without hegemony. For example, neither sixteenth-century Spain nor Portugal had much control over world politics after 1600, but they did have territorial "possessions" left over from their early roles in European world conquest. It is also possible to have hegemony without empire, such as when the U.S. government after the Second World War exerted tremendous influence over world politics but with little or no contemporaneous territorial extension. The U.S. government, in line with its own republican and anticolonial origins as well as a newfound material interest in free trade, identified itself largely with anticolonial movements around the world. The distinction between hegemony and empire can help today in addressing whether securing U.S. hegemony after the end of the Cold War requires increased reliance on seeking empire. Will continued U.S. hegemony depend on creating an empire somewhat like how Britain ruled at the end of the nineteenth century, as opposed to continuing to work multi-laterally through international institutions and alliances, particularly when U.S. economic troubles raise the possibility of a globalized world order in which the United States is no longer paramount? The hegemony/empire distinction also enables us to see two distinctive impulses within U.S. geopolitics that have historically characterized American national self-images and their projection outwards: what can be called "republic" and "empire."

I begin the chapter with a brief discussion of the republic versus empire motif in U.S. political history. I then offer contemporary definitions of "hegemony" and "empire" to orient a subsequent analysis of recent academic usage, including contributions from Niall Ferguson, Joseph Nye, and Michael Hardt and Antonio Negri. Following an overview of U.S. geopolitics since the end of the Cold War, I identify the current moment as a critical one for U.S. hegemony, with a possibly decisive shift toward reliance on empire as the key characteristic of emerging U.S. government geopolitical reasoning. One limitation of this strategy, however, is that the institutions and mores of U.S. marketplace society do not readily support the imperial mantle. U.S. hegemony, it is crucial to point out, is not congenial to a reinstatement of an explicitly territorial empire. It has created a new geography of power associated with the term globalization. Therefore, by way of conclusion, I emphasize the likelihood that empire will fail and, as a result, globalization will become increasingly free of an independent U.S. hegemony to be regulated by a complex of markets, states, and global institutions rather than by a single hegemon.

Republic or Empire?

The makers of the first constitutional state, which was founded in revolt against British colonialism, balanced popular sovereignty against the rule of law. This republican model required carefully constructed rules about the conduct of representation and the limits of government intervention. The fear that public virtue would be corrupted by private interests, however, was difficult to assuage once the revolution against Britain was over and the essentially liberal political economy inherited from the past proved more significant in integrating the vast new country than did the institutions of republicanism.[1] Geographical size and cultural heterogeneity worked against the popular participation and public virtue promised by the republican model implicit in the U.S. Constitution. The United States proved too big to be governed by such tenets. The republican model also necessitated formally breaking with the dynastic tensions and balance-of-power politics of eighteenth-century Europe. Raison d'état was widely seen as antithetical to the American experiment in democracy, as leading to foreign entanglements, and as increaseing the role of the military in domestic politics. Yet, at the same time, the fledgling United States had to adjust to a world that worked according to different rules and made decisions about its territorial shape in North America and the character of its internal political economy that pointed away from the republican ideal.

Though distant from Europe, the United States was immediately implicated in European power politics, not least in how to respond to European claims to territory in the continental interior of North America. Likewise, the republican model offered little by way of how to direct or limit private economic activities within and beyond American borders, not least because it was premised on both limiting government powers and seeing the United States as a fixed territorial enterprise without "interests" beyond its immediate geographical confines. In practice the republican model has always failed to contain the expansionist impulse. Though claiming impeccable republican credentials and therefore requiring assent, cooperation, and consent from those governed by its actions, the U.S. government has consistently expanded its grip territorially and economically beyond the juridical limits of the United States itself. This "urge to empire" initially took a largely territorial form as in continental expansion, but in the twentieth century has been mainly based on constructing alliances (such as the North Atlantic Treaty Organization [NATO]), building international institutions (such as the United Nations [UN] system, the International Monetary Fund [IMF], World Bank, the World Trade Organization [WTO], etc.), and using economic and military leverage (such as the U.S. dollar and the threat of nuclear weapons). Given the origins of the United States, however, explicit territorial control over other places, at least those judged as moral and political equivalents (unlike the native Indian groups of

North America), has been considered problematic unless it could be placed in some positive relation to the republican model.

This is where "hegemony" arose, as a solution to the American dilemma. Exercising power beyond national boundaries does not require territorial control. Indeed, it can be enabled and pursued through the cooperation, assent, and acceptance of others as a result of their socialization into seeing it as right, proper, and rewarding. This required a shift in the geography of power from a strictly absolute territoriality (bounded, absolute space) to a functional, relational spatiality involving command over the rules of spatial interaction (trade, capital flows, etc.). Intended or not, this fundamental alteration in the practice of foreign policy is what laid the foundation for later globalization. By the 1940s, the United States was particularly prepared for this transformation by its worldwide business interests, the centrality of international finance capital to the U.S. economy, the perception that territorialized economic blocs had deepened the depression of the 1930s, and the need to square its republican tradition with a global role. A global role had long been problematic in American domestic politics because of the threat it posed to the ideal of a "new" sort of polity. The Mexican-American War had been condemned by then-congressional representative Abraham Lincoln because it favored territorial expansion at the expense of "good honest government" in the country, as it then was.[2] Lincoln was particularly exercised by President James Polk's fabrication of a pretext for going to war with Mexico, a scenario remarkably similar to that of the build-up to the 2003 war in Iraq involving claims about Iraq's possession of "weapons of mass destruction" that turned out to be specious. Again, between 1890 and the 1920s, as the national economy soured, the "solution" of territorial expansion again became popular.[3] The clear failure of this strategy by the time of the Wall Street crash in 1929 suggested that some other path was necessary to resolve the contradiction between "the bounded national spiritual [republican] landscape and the unbounded, materialistic marketplace."[4]

The idea that *republic* and *empire* are inherently contradictory was "resolved" after the 1940s by attempting to practice and portray the expansionist impulse as conforming to at least minimal republican principles, both abroad and at home: bringing "good government," building "international community," and achieving "global consensus."[5] This was particularly the case after the United States was faced with an especially potent global foe representing a very different model of government and political economy: the Soviet Union. There is evidence that the U.S. government was beginning to orient itself to hegemony as a global political strategy as early as 1934.[6] The presence of a powerful global competitor, however, meant that it had to tread carefully for fear of alienating potential allies from its "republican promise." The end of the Cold War has removed this constraint. At the same time, the U.S. government has become impatient with international ties and more willing to exercise its military power in pursuit of its "interests" without the backing of the "international community." The terrorist attacks of September 11, 2001 provided a more immediate impetus to unilateral action, by signifying that the U.S. "homeland" is not as geographically distant and sheltered from the rest of the world as many Americans had come to think. But the temptation to go it alone has much deeper historic roots. It has been present since the founding of the United States.

The tension between republic and empire has been recurrent in U.S. relations with the rest of the world. How it has been worked out, however, has changed both as the world and as U.S. domestic politics have changed.[7] It seems clear that the institution-building internationalism of the immediate post–World War II period—supported by most of the major political factions in the United States—came to an end with the debacle of the Vietnam War and the U.S. unilateral abrogation of the Bretton Woods Agreement in 1971. Since then, but particularly since the end of the Cold War, the U.S. government has been divided over the best course for continuing to secure U.S. hegemony. The evidence for the range of options both considered and pursued indicates the problem with seeing no difference in policies between and within U.S. administrations or insisting that there is a master design in U.S. foreign policy that has remained unchanged through the years, save for increased military power relative to other states. This realist reading of U.S. foreign policy, popular on both the far right and far left, leaves little room for analysis of actual policies.

By way of example, the rise to national power of a southern-dominated Republican Party with the election of George W. Bush in 2000 was marked by an initial reluctance to be drawn into "international affairs," including little, if any, interest in "humanitarian interventions" or in international agreements. This may well have remained the case if not for the events of September 11, 2001, which triggered a reaction that drew upon the deep-seated fears and previously articulated attitudes of those who surrounded Bush and had brought him to office. The Bush administration's regional origin in the southern and mountain states of the United States is very important to understanding both its policies and its style of government.[8] Not only are the white populations of these states the ones most likely to benefit from military spending and committed to service as officers in the military, but they are also the ones in which the credos of macho bravado, rentier capitalism, vigilantism, and apocalyptic Christianity are most deeply rooted.[9] Not surprisingly, in his post–September 11, 2001, reincarnation supervised by election advisor Karl Rove, President Bush has thrived as commander-in-chief of "good" in the war with "evil," rather than as the chief executive of the federal government. It is little exaggeration to say, "The American President—though not of the United States—whom George Bush most nearly resembles is the Confederacy's Jefferson Davis."[10]

In the immediate aftermath of Bush's contested election in November 2000, the Bush administration made it a priority to try to reorganize the U.S. political economy by giving a freer hand to business and redistributing incomes to the rich on the supply-side premise that this would produce a national investment bonanza. But after September 11, 2001, this focus was largely eclipsed from public view by a fiercely aggressive and militarist foreign policy that played into the hands of a neoconservative group of officials and advisors. This group included such figures as Donald Rumsfeld, Paul Wolfowitz, and William Kristol, who were already eager to pursue an overtly imperial strategy against states seen as aiding, abetting, or providing moral support to terrorist networks opposed to U.S. policies in the Middle East and elsewhere and held responsible for the terror attacks of September 11, 2001.[11] Whether Iraq, the main target of this policy, was actually such a state remains, at best, moot and probably unlikely. Certainly no credible evidence exists, or ever existed, linking Saddam Hussein to Osama bin Laden's al-Qaeda network. Nor does evidence exist proving that Saddam's putative weapons programs posed a threat directly or indirectly (through terrorists) to the security of the United States.[12] As seems obvious to many observers, the essence of al-Qaeda is that it consists of a series of loosely connected terrorist cells without either open or clandestine support from Iraq, Iran, Syria, or any other state. Indeed, it represents a prime example of the new geography of power with a reticular or non-hierarchical network of global reach beyond the control or influence of territorially based actors. What seems more important in motivating the U.S. invasion of Iraq is that Iraq's dictator, Saddam Hussein, has long flouted U.S. designs in the Middle East and that Iraq had the potential resources (in the form of oil) to subsidize its own liberation by

U.S. forces. In other words, it was Saddam's lack of acceptance of American hegemony, his resistance to U.S. norms of political and economic conduct, along with the other "rogue states" of Iran and North Korea in what President G. W. Bush called the "axis of evil" in world politics, that singled him out for special treatment.

In the aftermath of September 11, 2001, the Bush administration largely abandoned the multilateral institutionalism, which, it is important to reiterate, the U.S. government had largely invented and put into place after World War II, for an aggressive and unilateral militarism. This was justified by claiming that because the terrorist attacks of September 11, 2001, were directed at targets in the United States, the U.S. government had the right to police the globe in pursuit of all those it decides may have a connection to future terrorism potentially directed at the United States. This license to operate an endless War on Terror comes with a high price on both the domestic and external front. This policy puts the U.S. government at odds with many other governments, including many of its nominal allies in NATO and with international organizations. It also puts the United States at odds with itself, domestically, having led to the Patriot Act and other antisubversive legislation similar to policies against which the American settlers rebelled in pursuit of independence and the creation of the republican form of government symbolized by the Declaration of Independence and the U.S. Constitution.[13] The fact that the U.S. Congress went along with President Bush's fervent wish to attack Iraq without questioning the shaky "secret" intelligence upon which it was based suggests how much appeals to hypothetical, exaggerated, and imaginary threats, going back even before the "bomber gap" between the United States and the Soviet Union claimed by John Kennedy during the 1960 presidential election, have corrupted the American body politic. "A Congress so easily manipulated has in effect surrendered its role, allowing presidents to do as they will."[14]

As imperialisms go, the American attempt at empire is also singularly inarticulate and inchoate.[15] This is revealed above all in the disinclination to know much of anything about its dominions. Unlike the erstwhile colonial enterprises of the British and French, which assiduously desired to understand those they conquered, even if on largely Orientalist assumptions, the U.S. enterprise is entirely devoid of cultural curiosity. The American historical experience of defining its republican polity in opposition to the rest of the world is crucial here. From this point of view, there is literally nothing much to be learned about or from others that could possibly challenge what is known already. This leads to a hands-off style of administration and policing, seen to lethal effect in postconquest Iraq, that involves the repetition of slogans about "bringing democracy" and "defeating terrorism" but with absolutely no strategies in place to do either. Such an autistic approach to empire inspires no confidence in its longevity. The tension between republic and empire in American political life has never been so clearly visible at any time since the Mexican-American, Indian, and Spanish-American Wars of the nineteenth century.

Hegemony and Empire

Like so many "technical" political words in European languages, "hegemony" and "empire" have Greek and Roman roots. Hegemony is from a Greek word signifying domination or leadership, particularly of a state or nation in a league or confederation, but without clear commitment to whether this is the result of coercion, consensus, or a mix of the two. Undoubtedly, however, the domination or leadership exercised is not necessarily either territorial or contiguous. It can be diffuse and widespread or concentrated geographically. Typically it involves more than simple military and economic coercion and relies on active assent and cooperation. Common "rules," institutions, and values form the core of the hegemony, backed up by the superior economic, cultural, and military position occupied by the state or social group exercising hegemony. The word "hegemony" is thus also a purported solution to the dilemma of either singular economic or cultural determination by positing an "integral form of class rule which exists not only in political and economic institutions and relationships but also in active forms of experience and consciousness."[16] In the context of world politics, the two senses of hegemony can be fused profitably: that of state hegemony, as in much world-systems and international relations literature, or direction by the state that anchors the world economy; and that of consensual domination, in the sense of Antonio Gramsci and the Frankfurt School, in which direction relies on enrolling others into practices and ideas that come out of the experience of the dominant state or social group. Because of its reliance on marketplace society, American hegemony is a form of social domination that has become increasingly transnational in operating beyond formal state sponsorship and control. Even so, empire still could be one geographical form that hegemony might take. But it is not only analytically and historically distinct; it is basically incompatible with the trajectory of American hegemony over the past fifty years.

"Empire" is Roman/Latin in origin, signifying supreme rule, absolute power, and dominion. Typically it is a polity in which many peoples and territories are united administratively under a single ruler or single administrative apparatus. An empire may be a contiguous territory (as with the ancient Roman and modern Russian empires) but can be a maritime or overseas empire (as with the Spanish, Dutch, French, and British empires). Many territorial states have an "empire" aspect to them as a result of the conquest of adjacent territories (e.g., England in Wales and Ireland; the United States to the west of the original colonies), but once populations are sufficiently homogenized, culturally this fades in significance. It is the unification of multiple peoples under a single ruler that is the main distinguishing feature of empires. Or, to put it somewhat differently, "Empire is the rule exercised by one nation over others both to regulate their *external* behavior and to ensure minimally acceptable forms of *internal* behavior within the subordinate states. Merely powerful states do the former, but not the latter."[17] Often, the term is used more metaphorically[18] to indicate domination or hegemony, but this departs from most historic usage and loses the analytic capacity that comes from having different words for different political-geographical constellations of power.[19]

Etymology only takes us so far. Although it allows for clarification of what terms might actually mean in common usage, it does not focus explicitly on how they are actually used in political and academic circles. It is best to survey recent ways in which "hegemony" and "empire" have been used in accounts of contemporary world politics. Usage seems to differ along two dimensions of power: type of power (hard or soft) and geographical organization of power (strong or weak). Obviously, these are continua or ideal types rather than discrete categories and, therefore, any real-world example might be a mix of all tendencies rather simply located one on one between extremes. The two dimensions and associated examples in recent writing are provided in Table 2.1. If hard power is anchored by military coercion and soft power by cultural values, tastes, and preferences, the geographical organization of power ranges from the strongly territorial to the extremely diffuse or networked.

The categories that these dimensions define are necessarily overdetermined in the sense that they leave out how, in any real-world context, one can lead to another. They are not necessarily in total opposition to

TABLE 2.1. Categories of Hegemony and Empire

Territorial concentration of power	Type of power	
	Hard	Soft
Strong	Classic empire (Ferguson, *Cash Nexus*)	Hegemony (Agnew and Corbridge, *Mastering Space*)
Weak	Neo–empire (Hardt and Negri, *Empire*)	Leadership (Nye, *Bound to Lead*)

one another but appear so when put into juxtaposition as in Table 2.1. The categories are also inherently normative in that those who use them can see them as preferred or progressive states of affairs, or as goals or situations that resolve political problems or are at least better than the alternatives. Thus, there is still nostalgia for a benign image of the British Empire in certain circles in England and in the United States (as if self-sacrifice, afternoon tea, cricket, rugby, and political order were all that the British Empire had to it). British bestseller lists in 2003 had any number of books devoted to telling stories about those who had sacrificed themselves for empire. At its most apologetic the position seems to be that empire is not *necessarily* a bad thing. More stridently, it marks the revival of the old Roman idea of *homo sacer*: we Brits, Americans, etc., are capable of self-rule, and others are not; they need our savoir faire and we will impose it on them.[20] Yet, at the same time, the war that now must be fought on "terrorism" is global, without spatial limits or singular territorial goals, and involves the collapse of the distinction between sea, air, and land arenas.[21] There is a major mismatch here between a commitment to "inside/outside" thinking, on the one hand, and the reality of a contemporary world that is no longer divisible into neat territorial blocs or containers, on the other.[22]

In a similar vein, hegemony achieved by means other than empire can be portrayed in either a positive light, involving relatively benign (or even sacrificial) "leadership," or a negative light, involving profoundly exploitative relationships based on steep power gradients between a hegemon and its subordinates in a hierarchy of power. Hegemony's difference from empire, however, lies in (1) its lack of explicit commitment to the territorial or geographical bloc organization of power per se and (2) its reliance on persuading or rewarding subordinates rather than immediately coercing them (though even empire as "absolute hegemony" is never reliably achieved purely by coercive means). If we can give at least some credibility to evidence from experimental games in psychological laboratories, this suggests that "Almost Hegemons [are] even less solicitous of the interests of the junior partner(s) than is an absolute dictator, who needs no allies. . . . [W]hen we have absolute power over others, we take *some* account of their interests, as a matter of moral principle."[23] But when others also have power, "the appearance of having to 'bargain with others' gives an Almost Hegemon license to ignore the interests of others."[24]

The European Union (EU) offers a good contemporary example of a form of hegemony without empire, if only within one world-region.[25] The U.S. neoconservatives who planned the 2003 war on Iraq, of course, famously dismiss the EU rather like Stalin dismissed the Pope: "How many battalions do they have?" They miss the point entirely, however. The EU has immense legal and moral reach. While expanding to cover more countries and more aspects of political regulation, the EU has insinuated itself into the very fiber of everyday life, not just in member countries but also in those that would like to join and in those that trade with it. First, the EU spreads stealthily. Its influence works largely through existing institutions by creating and imposing common standards. Second, the EU "franchises" its legislation by implicitly threatening firms and countries outside its boundaries with isolation. U.S. businesses, for example, must follow EU regulations to gain access to European markets. Third, the EU works as a network rather than as a command-and-control system. Henry Kissinger once complained that Europe didn't have a single telephone number that he could call when faced by a foreign-policy "crisis." It still does not. The EU is, rather, a network of centers united around common goals and policies that can, consequentially, expand both in the scope of what it does and in the geographical area it covers without collapsing. This can be disadvantageous in reaching rapid consensus in crisis situations, but it allows for relatively light administration by encouraging political and economic reform through existing channels rather than centralizing power in a single center.

The various categories of empire and hegemony, however, can be best understood with respect to some specific examples from contemporary usage. The ones that follow are by no means the only ones available, but they are ones that seem to define some of the main features of current debate over empire and hegemony in relation to U.S. government ideology and action.

In Niall Ferguson's *The Cash Nexus*, for example (and also in his more recent book to accompany the BBC television series of the same title, *Empire*), world politics is viewed as *best* ordered by "classic" empires (such as Britain's in its heyday).[26] Ironically, those on the political left who see the U.S. government as the political face of a purely national U.S. capital also see the necessity for the United States to adopt an increasingly imperial approach to guarantee resources (particularly oil) and send bellicose messages to possible challengers for global domination (such as China).[27] This reflects the same imperialism diagnosed by Lenin. Though acknowledging the sacrifices made for empire—largely those of its servants more than its victims—Ferguson wants to recuperate the order that empire brought to disordered and "dangerous" regions. In his view, the present-day world is in disarray in large part because of the United States' refusal to take on its imperial destiny and drag the world into line. Of course, this is similar to the refrain of those neoconservatives in the United States associated with the Project for a New American Century (Gary Schmitt, Richard Perle, William Kristol, Robert Kagan, et al.) and their agents in the Bush administration, such as Paul Wolfowitz. In their construction, there are parts of the world where U.S. hegemony does not currently prevail but where hard power has to be applied to prevent possible future military threats from materializing, to secure fundamental resources for the world economy, and to eliminate rulers who refuse to play by the rules laid down under the current hegemony.

Writing long before September 11, 2001, Ferguson and others argued that for the world to successfully diminish military threats and to enhance U.S. economic interests, the United States *must* become an imperial power rather than continue as a traditional nation-state. From this viewpoint, there is little or no danger of "imperial overstretch" in the sense popularized by Paul Kennedy.[28] The economic threat to the United States does not come from its military budget but from the costs of domestic welfare and pension programs. Its American advocates, however, believe that empire does not necessarily mean direct rule but more a system of informal or indirect rule through surrogates who openly accept U.S. political and economic dominance. Unlike Ferguson, who emphasizes the role of political persuasion and cultural interchange as well as military coercion in empire building, the American advocates of empire tend to place all of their emphasis on military power as the single leg for the construction of empire. Indeed, the 2003 Iraq "coalition" of the United States, Britain, and Australia perhaps suggests something of a WASPish cultural predisposition to empire as a hegemonic strategy when multilateral routes are judged as requiring too much diplomacy, consultation, and compromise.[29]

The other most important recent usage of the term "empire" comes from a very different source (Michael Hardt and Antonio Negri in their book, *Empire*) and has a very different meaning (they are its critics rather than its proponents). In their usage, "empire" is essentially synonymous with contemporary globalization: a world of networks and flows that may have arisen under American sponsorship but that is increasingly diffuse, decentered, and placeless.[30] This "neo–empire," then, bears little or no resemblance to any empires in previous history. It is a set of practices associated with capital accumulation and labor exploitation without any "homeland." It is imperialism without an emperor. But it can also be liberating in the possibilities it offers for releasing ordinary people (the "multitude") from the territorial reifications (states and places) that have long held them in thrall. This could be construed as hegemony without a hegemonic power, and this does seem to be what Hardt and Negri actually do have in mind. Their choice of the word "empire" to describe this phenomenon, however, is misleading, if attention getting. An original and provocative melding of Marxist and poststructuralist thought, *Empire* is a serious attempt to come to terms with what is different about the contemporary world and to avoid slipping back into political vocabularies about imperialism, colonialism, etc., that are firmly stuck in the late nineteenth and early twentieth centuries. Of course, whether this approach bears a one-to-one relationship to the actual organization of the contemporary world economy, which still seems strongly divided geographically between states and places, is very doubtful. Their image of empire seems to be a mirror version of the view of globalization found among its most exuberant proponents: that the Internet and air travel have created a whole new world as opposed to a radically changing one. Politically it also seems problematic in that, even within their framework, the defense of places may be more potent in contesting empire's logic than simply endorsing the virtues of movement and the nomadism it entails. Of course, the challenge then becomes finding mutually intelligible and supportable collective strategies for a "multitude in place." But the discovery of some sort of commonality across places seems a more realistic basis to countervailing action in contemporary globalization than does a "multitude in movement." *Empire* contains more than a whiff of Georges Sorel and Rosa Luxemburg's spontaneism.

Quite what this "empire" has to do with historical ones or with hegemony is not entirely clear from the text except that it notes that hard economic power (control over capital) is seen as making the world go around, if increasingly without any identifiable national-territorial sponsor but within a "constitutional" framework of "separation of powers" between various institutional forms analogous to that of the United States. Where the U.S. invasion of Iraq might fit into this account is not entirely clear, except perhaps as a throwback to "old ways" increasingly anachronistic in a global era. More important, however, their overemphasis on the transcendence of place under globalization perhaps leads Hardt and Negri to underemphasize the degree to which empire, in the Roman sense, is still very much an available option for attempting to secure hegemony and, hence, for protecting their "empire" from the threat posed to it by the multitude. However, in a recent volume that consists of an interview with and a number of clarifying essays by Antonio Negri on themes from *Empire*, Negri makes an argument to the effect that "Bush and the political-military apparatus he uses should not be confounded with the government of the *Empire*. Rather, it appears to me [Negri] that the current imperialist ideology and practice of the Bush government will rapidly begin to collide with the capitalist forces that at the global level work for the *Empire*. The situation is completely open."[31]

The term "hegemony" figures prominently in the account of modern geopolitics proposed by Stuart Corbridge and me in *Mastering Space*.[32] This account sees the modern world as experiencing a succession of hegemonies associated with different dominant states but with recent American hegemony slowly giving way to a hegemony without a hegemon, or hegemony exercised increasingly through global markets and international institutions by a growing transnational class of business people and bureaucrats. In this construction hegemony is absolutely *not* equivalent to simple domination (territorial or otherwise) but refers to widespread assent to principles of conduct that are the "common sense" of world politics and that emanate from distinctive cultural-economic sites with potentially global reach.[33] It sees the transformation of U.S. hegemony as pre-dating the end of the Cold War but intensifying thereafter. It views increased U.S. unilateralism since 1970, beginning with abrogation of the Bretton Woods Agreement governing fixed-currency exchange rates in 1971, as evidence for a crisis in rather than a strengthening of *American* hegemony. Unwittingly, however, this and other unilateral acts by the U.S. government have had the net effect of spreading and deepening the impact of globalization. For example, U.S. recognition of Communist China in 1972 has had the long-term effect of bringing China into the world economy as a major producer and consumer. Also, the support for Islamic fundamentalists in Afghanistan during the period of Soviet occupation helped create the global terrorism that relies on the technologies of globalization. And, the imposition of import controls on Japanese cars in the 1980s brought Japanese car companies to produce in the United States. In this construction, American hegemony is extremely reliant on soft power, the active assent to and agreement with international standards of conduct governing economic and political transactions, even as the U.S. government rails against the very institutions and rules (such as the UN, for example) it first sponsored. Osama bin Laden and al-Qaeda know this very well, and it is why they behave as they do.

In contradistinction to the *Empire* of Hardt and Negri, the post–Cold War geopolitical order is still organized geographically. No longer does the geographical structure consist of U.S. and Soviet blocs and a Third World in which the two central powers compete. Rather, it consists of a profoundly uneven or fragmented global economy with a patchwork of local and regional areas connected together through or marginally to the control centers in the world's major cities and governmental centers. But states are, if anything, even more important to this economic hegemony without centralized political control, to paraphrase Wood,[34] than they were to the Cold War geopolitical order. From this perspective, recent U.S.-government actions post–September 11, 2001, can be seen as an attempt to reestablish the United States as central to contemporary hegemony by using the one resource—military power—in which the United States is still supreme. Though it can be construed that the attacks of September 11, 2001, were directed as much at the values and practices of the world economy in general as at the United States specifically, the Bush administration has chosen to see them in a nationalist light. To a significant degree this response is related to the fact that the Bush administration is dominated by people with business and political ties to U.S. defense industries as well as to the militarist attitudes of the American South.[35] Unfortunately, it is not clear that the United States can economically afford to prosecute a war without end on terrorism or its perceived cultural and political opponents without the active cooperation of its previous allies and without sacrificing the very values and interests that its war is supposedly all about.[36] In the end, empires always seem to undermine exactly what it was they were initially supposed to sustain.[37] From this perspective, empire is both unsustainable and counterproductive as a strategy for resecuring U.S. hegemony.

Finally, U.S. hegemony can be construed as a positive and benign leadership responding to the "collective action" problem of a world in

TABLE 2.2. Leading States and Their Power Resources, 1500–2000

Period	State	Major resources
Sixteenth century	Spain	Gold bullion, colonial trade, mercenary armies, dynastic ties
Seventeenth century	Netherlands	Trade, capital markets, navy
Eighteenth century	France	Population, rural industry, public administration, army, culture (soft power)
Nineteenth century	Britain	Industry, political cohesion, finance and credit, navy, liberal norms (soft power), island location (easy to defend)
Twentieth century	United States	Economic scale, scientific and technical leadership, location, military forces and alliances, universalistic culture and liberal international regimes (soft power)
Twenty-first century	United States	Technological leadership, military and economic scale, soft power, hub of transnational communications

Source: Joseph S. Nye Jr., "Limits of American Power," Table 1, p. 555. Reprinted by Permission from *Political Science Quarterly*, 117 (Winter 2002–03): 545–559.

which most actors have no incentive to work together to craft international agreements and institutions. This account is offered by Joseph Nye in his book *Bound to Lead*. He argues for the necessity of U.S. leadership in a world in need of "public goods"—direction on issues of global importance, a global currency, global enforcement of norms of conduct, intervention on behalf of "human rights", etc.—that can only be provided by the last remaining superpower.[38] From this point of view, the United States has tended to favor soft over hard power in a world that is culturally pluralistic and politically fragmented. In this respect it differs fundamentally from previous "hegemons" in that it *depends* upon soft power (Table 2.2).[39] This goes back to the essentially liberal image that the U.S. government claims to have of its role in world order, in which the absence of spontaneous international collective action requires a leader willing to take on the task of organizing international institutions and agreements. Absent such a role, under conditions of international anarchy collective action will not take place. Because there must be limits to U.S. power, the United States must be a self-denying and benevolent leader and deal with the global collective action problem: the inability to coordinate action across multiple actors. If the United States does not take on this role, the world will become a desperately unstable and dangerous place for all. That the U.S. government did not gain UN backing for its invasion of Iraq might be seen as a failure to fulfill this role. But the war could also be interpreted as taking on that leadership role, albeit one that must be followed quickly by recourse to international coordination rather than by the U.S. administration fully fledging a "liberated" postwar Iraq. The danger to the United States is that its recourse to war will further weaken its hegemony, given that this, more than with any other hegemony in history, depends on the deployment of soft power. This soft power requires at least the appearance of assent and acceptance; recourse to coercion and an urge to empire could be construed as signs of American weakness rather than strength.

After the Cold War

These perspectives on hegemony and empire should be examined in light of trends in the United States and the U.S. relationship to the world since the end of the Cold War in the early 1990s. I will identify four trends that are critical:

1. The first is the obvious military superiority of the United States relative to other countries and alliances. In absolute terms, the United States in 2000 spent just under $300 billion on its military. NATO Europe, the next largest, spent around $152 billion, with Russia third at $50 billion. But in relative terms, the United States spends just under 3 percent of its GDP (as of 2000), whereas France (part of NATO Europe), second at around $40 billion, spends around 2.5 percent of its GDP. In other words, the United States is absolutely superior in defense capability to the next five countries taken together but manages this with only 0.5 percent more of its GDP spent on defense than the second biggest spender. But given the vulnerability of the United States to everyday technologies, such as passenger airplanes, being turned into weapons, it is not clear quite what absolute advantage all of this defense capacity gives in a war against shadowy networks of terrorists.

2. The United States needs foreign capital to finance both its government spending and its high-mass consumption. Because the national savings rate is so low, imports of capital consistently and increasingly outweigh exports in dollar terms. Except for a few years around 2000, the U.S. government has had a large deficit between what it collects in revenues and what it spends on defense, social security, and other services. The United States relies on attracting investment

from around the world to finance the national economy. There is nothing necessarily problematic economically about this balance of payments deficit if, *ceteris paribus*, the world is seen as benefiting from this state of affairs by those who control the inflows of capital. Nevertheless, it does mean that the United States increasingly depends on the good will of foreign investors, including foreign governments, notwithstanding its stellar military capacity.

3. The United States also has a high level of dependence on certain imported resources, particularly oil. Approximately 20 percent of U.S. oil comes from the Middle East. This means that the availability of oil from that region is an important consideration in U.S. foreign policy. It also means, however, that given the vulnerability of oil supplies to political instability and terrorist threats, the United States has historically supported despots and authoritarian regimes to keep the oil flowing in the parts of the world it depends upon for oil. It is important to note, however, that some other countries, such as Japan and China, are even more dependent on Middle Eastern oil than is the United States.

4. Finally, without the Soviet Union or another global threat of similar proportion, it is increasingly difficult for the U.S. government to "discipline" allies into following its lead or accepting its unilateral decisions (ones taken without consultation, negotiation, and agreement). During the Cold War the common danger perceived as coming from the Soviet Union kept allies in line. Absent such a threat they have tended to drift away from hewing to the American line on a wide range of issues. As a result, major fissures have opened up between the United States and its allies in Europe and Asia.

Overall, since the end of the Cold War, the United States has acquired a dominant global military position as far as military spending is concerned. Whether this is sustainable economically depends as much on the willingness of foreigners to finance the U.S. economy (and federal government) as it does on the economic capacity of the United States itself. This and the absence of an external disciplining force on allies would counsel caution in undertaking unilateral action. Increased dependence on foreign, particularly Middle Eastern, oil might suggest the need for unilateral action. But again, others have similar levels of dependence. Either joint action with allies to promote stable supplies or attempts to reduce the demand for oil at home might make more sense as national strategies than engaging in unilateral military action.

The War on Iraq: A Crucial Moment?

The present moment is a crucial one for the direction of U.S. geopolitical reasoning over the next decade or so. It is fair to say that the U.S. geopolitical position since World War II has been based largely on hegemony secured through multilateral and market mechanisms, though this has weakened considerably since the 1970s.[40] But this form of hegemony has had numerous benefits and relatively few costs for the United States. The benefits have included:

1. What could be called "empire lite": a relatively low level of defense spending as a share of GDP.[41] Full empire or Absolute Hegemony would be much more costly
2. The ability to use the U.S. dollar to export domestic economic problems to the rest of the world through manipulating the exchange rate and the money supply
3. The ideological capacity to play up the republican heritage of the United States while reaping material advantage around the world

The costs have involved:

1. Securing agreement with allies
2. Accepting the need to engage in diplomacy that might not always turn out as desired

The temptation of empire is that allies no longer need to be consulted with or taken seriously. The Bush administration's contempt for the "so-called international community" is symptomatic of this appeal.[42] Direct rule or the enforced appointment of surrogate regimes would also give the U.S. government much more freedom to pursue a doctrine of preventive war against states, such as Iran, Syria, North Korea, and Cuba, seen as threatening in one way or another to the United States. This doctrine, of course, is not generally accepted by the "international community," but if empire actually seems to work then allies can also be excluded from the fruits of victory. The costs, however, are likely to be high. They include the following:

1. Much less sharing of military and administrative costs (as was the case with the Gulf War of 1991)
2. Setting of precedent for others to take preventive or preemptive action (e.g., India against Pakistan or China against Taiwan)

3. Undermining the institutional basis to the "rules" of international behavior that have laid the basis for contemporary economic globalization largely under American auspices
4. The hollowness of claims to impose democratic practices on others by force
5. Vulnerability of the United States to both economic and asymmetric military reprisals
6. Limits on domestic dissent and criticism of imperial adventures, undermining what is left of the republican model at home
7. Failure to note that the destruction of secular regimes in the Arab world, such as that of Iraq, is a stated objective of the al-Qaeda terrorists behind the attacks of September 11, 2001; in attacking and conquering Iraq, the United States is doing their work for them

Beyond U.S. Hegemony

The costs and benefits of empire need placing in the context of the times. States and other actors in world politics are increasingly part of global arrangements that point beyond both U.S. hegemony and U.S. empire. The world economy today is truly global to a degree never seen before in its geographical scope, in the pace of transactions between widely scattered places within it, and in its hollowing out of simple territorial forms of political authority across a wide range of issue domains (economic, social, and political). It has become so in this way, subsequent chapters will argue, because of the nature of U.S. hegemony. That hegemony, however, has made itself increasingly redundant. The influence of capital is now mediated through global financial markets, the flow of trade within multinational firms, and the limited capacities of global regulatory institutions. Its benefits and costs now fall on all parts of the world. If they still fall unevenly, the unevenness is no longer on a country-by-country or bloc-by-bloc basis. Geographical variation in economic growth is increasingly local and regional within countries. But it is not the "global" that is new in globalization so much as it is a changing geographical logic to the world economy. In other words, it is not its "globality" that is new but, rather, its combination of global networks and localized territorial fragmentation. Under the "previous" global, the world economy was structured largely (but never entirely) around territorial entities such as states, colonial empires, and geopolitical spheres of influence. The main novelty today is the increasing role in economic prosperity and underdevelopment of *cross-border flows* in relation to national states and to networks linking cities with one another and their hinterlands and the *increased differentiation* between localities and regions as a result of the spatial biases built into flow-networks.

Rather than the "end" of geography, globalization entails its reformulation away from an economic mapping of the world in terms of state territories toward a more complex mosaic of states, regions, global city-regions, and localities differentially integrated into the global economy. There is a geopolitics of contemporary globalization, therefore, both with respect to its origins and with respect to its continuing operation. Culturally, the world is also increasingly "creolized" rather than simply Americanized.[43] This is not surprising given the increasing cultural heterogeneity of the United States itself and the need for businesses, be they from America, Europe, or elsewhere, to adapt their products to different markets at home and abroad. Crucially, for the first time since the eighteenth century, the "cradle of capitalism"—Western Europe and the United States—"has as much to fear from the rapidity of change as does the periphery."[44] More specifically, the most important political change is the dramatic decline in the autonomy of even the most powerful states in the face of the globalization of production, trade, technology, and communication.

Modern state power always has had two aspects to it: despotic power and infrastructural power.[45] If the former refers to the power exerted by the socio-economic elites who occupy political office, then the latter refers to the power that the state accrues from its delivery of infrastructural or public goods to populations. Historically, the rise in relative importance of infrastructural power, as elites have been forced through political struggles to become more responsive to their populations, led to a territorialization of political authority. Until recently, the technologies for providing public goods have had built-in territorial bias, not least relating to the capture of positive externalities. Increasingly, however, infrastructural power can be deployed across networks that, though sited in discrete locations, are not necessarily territorial in the externality fields that they produce. Thus, currencies, systems of measure, trading networks, educational provision, and welfare services need not be associated with exclusive membership in a conventional nation-state. New deployments of infrastructural power both deterritorialize existing states and reterritorialize membership around cities and hinterlands, regions, and continental-level political entities such as the European Union.[46] There is a simultaneous scaling-up and scaling-down of the relevant geographical fields of infrastructural power, depending on the political economies of scale of different regulatory, productive, and redistributive public goods. Consequently, "the more economies of scale of dominant goods and assets diverge from the structural scale of the national state—and the more those divergences feed back into each other in complex ways—then the more the authority, legitimacy, policymaking capacity, and policy-implementing effectiveness of the state will be eroded and undermined both within and without."[47] In the United States' case, this is exacerbated (as I argue in Chapter 5), by the difficulties of coordination of purpose and direction within the governmental system.

Using the example of currencies, the United States has encouraged the use of the U.S. dollar in world trade and finance since the collapse of the Bretton Woods system in the early 1970s. Initially designed by the Nixon administration to make U.S. exports more competitive and to staunch the U.S. balance-of-payments deficit, the floating of the U.S. dollar against other currencies has been a major if unintended stimulus to globalization, both in facilitating trade and in encouraging the explosion of global finance.[48] The U.S. government, insofar as it can influence the Federal Reserve (the U.S. central bank), can use its currency to manipulate the world economy to benefit its producers and consumers. However, there are real limits to this when the United States depends on massive inflows of foreign-originated investment, when such a large proportion of U.S. currency is in circulation outside the territorial boundaries of the United States, and when other governments (such as China) peg their currencies closely to the dollar and build up large reserves that they can use to maintain the peg and thus keep the prices of their exports competitive in the U.S. domestic market. As a result, the United States' dollar and other currencies of wider circulation (such as the Euro and the Japanese yen) have slowly eroded the independent monetary infrastructural power of both the states in which they circulate and themselves. This puts these countries, and not just the bearers of less potent currencies, on the receiving end of currency shocks from "outside." Global markets increasingly determine the relative values of what are still nominally national-state currencies. Indeed, the "inside" and the "outside" of the state are increasingly in question as to their material significance. Thus, in a major area in which the United States has previously exercised economic hegemony there are increasing signs of hegemony—that of global currency markets—without a singular state hegemon that can *effectively* intercede in them.

Conclusion

The 2003 war on Iraq brought into focus the long-standing contradiction in U.S. geopolitical reasoning between republic and empire. With the American rise to global power after World War II, this contradiction was managed by an emphasis on securing hegemony without empire: by recruiting allies and building international institutions. Though U.S. hegemony entered into crisis beginning in the late 1960s and the behavior of the U.S. government thereafter became increasingly unilateral, the United States has nevertheless continued to benefit from the world order that its hegemony helped to build. The post–September 11, 2001, tendency of the Bush administration toward an increasingly brazen imperial strategy, taking off from its systematic attempts at disabling a number of international initiatives that were very much in conformity to previous U.S. attempts at managing world affairs multilaterally, is undoubtedly the fruit of a new ideological commitment to empire rather than to other means of securing hegemony. The problem is, as the American artist Thomas Cole portrayed it in his 1836 painting, "The Course of Empire: Destruction," that empires are remarkably fragile enterprises. Even if they appear to offer total control, this proves illusory as they must expend considerable resources to maintain their moral legitimacy.[49] Other means of securing hegemony are cheaper and longer lasting, particularly when power resources are limited.[50] Empires also invite organized opposition from both subordinate states and from defecting allies.[51] For the United States in particular, empire promises a further erosion of an already badly weathered republic. If either Hardt and Negri or Agnew and Corbridge are correct, if in obviously different ways, then empire American-style may also be largely irrelevant to the world-in-the-making of hegemony without a hegemon. Whatever the long-run prognosis about moving into global empire, Paul Starr puts the current U.S. government dilemma in light of the war on Iraq very clearly from an American point of view:

> When the dust clears over Baghdad, we will likely find ourselves no safer from terrorism than before, but our alliances will be battered and our true enemies will be more convinced than ever that what they need to prevent themselves from becoming another Iraq is a real nuclear arsenal. If this war is easy, it may be no indication of what's in store in the future.[52]

The next chapter considers the three-cornered relationship between geographies of power, globalization, and American hegemony. It does so by providing a more theoretical approach to the geography of power than the comparison of empire and hegemony entailed by this chapter. I return empirically to the nature and global impact of American hegemony in Chapters 4 and 6.

3 American Hegemony and the New Geography of Power

In mainstream theories of world politics, the workings of political power are usually seen as a historical constant. They share the view expressed so clearly by Paul Ricoeur that "power does not have much of a history."[1] At the same time, political power is overwhelmingly associated with "the modern state," to which all states are supposed to correspond, but which is usually a version of France, England, or the United States regarded as a unitary actor equivalent to an individual person. Political power is envisioned in terms of units of territorial sovereignty (at least for the so-called Great Powers) that exercise power throughout their territories and vie with one another to acquire more power beyond their current boundaries.[2] This chapter disputes these contentions and offers an alternative based on the concept of "hegemony." First, I show that political power does in fact have a history. Second, I demonstrate that this history is revealed in the changing spatiality of power under the influence of a specific hegemony. (By the spatiality of power I mean the historically changing character and spatial structure of power.) Hegemony in this usage refers to the mix of coercion and consent that allows a state or group of actors to set the rules for political, economic, and military interaction and movement over space and through time.[3] What has been problematic is a transhistorical understanding of political power in which power is invariably exercised territorially by more or less equal states containing and channeling the circulation of people, goods, money, and weapons.

The objective of this chapter is to construct a historicized understanding of the workings of political power for world politics by mapping it from four different perspectives: (1) in terms of ideal types of the dominant spatiality of power in different historical epochs; (2) with respect to the ontological and moral assumptions about statehood that presume an identity between political power and statehood; (3) in terms of the role of U.S. hegemony in giving a particular inflection to the contours of contemporary political power and as a stimulus to globalization; and (4) with regard to the empirical conditions of movement that reinforce or undermine the association of political power with territorial statehood.

The chapter has six sections. The first offers a brief critical review of definitions of political power and the ways in which they direct understanding of the spatiality of power toward or away from an emphasis on states as exclusive sites for the accumulation and exercise of power. The second section is devoted to one perspective on mapping power. Four models of the spatiality of power are identified, which can be used to characterize the spatiality of power in different historical epochs. In this framework, the pooling of power in territorial states is seen as historically contingent. The third section approaches the mapping of power from a second angle. It questions the ontological privileging of "the state" as the singular nexus of political power and secure political identity by drawing attention to the critical geographical assumptions that make this possible: the identity between statehood and personhood, the neglect of the social rules of statehood, and the territorializing of power. In the fourth section, I argue that in place of the state-based ontology, U.S. hegemony has fundamentally altered the practices of world politics to produce a trend toward a dispersed or networked geography of power. The fifth section discusses the third and final perspective on the mapping of political power beyond state boundaries. It introduces contemporary examples of movement or circulation into the equation of state territoriality and stable political identities in three ways: the impact of population migration on concepts of citizenship, the changing geography of money, and the impact on states of new military technologies in an emerging global economy. Each of these examples points to a dynamic spatiality of power not well captured by the conventional territorialized image of political power. Finally, the sixth section provides a brief conclusion.

Political Power and the Territorial State

Current critical thinking about political power identifies two fundamental types of power: instrumental and associational.[4] The former involves the capacity to make others do our will in relation to objectives that involve access to and control over goods that must be provided collectively because of their character (e.g., infrastructure, security). The latter involves the power to do things by acting in concert or using institutional mediation. This facilitative view of political power is the centerpiece of much recent thinking under the influence of such diverse thinkers as Hannah Arendt, Michel Foucault, Gilles Deleuze, and Bruno Latour even as each of these thinkers also tries to deal with questions of domination.[5] Each of the two views grasps a dimension of political power that the other lacks. The first dimension is the ability to control, dominate, co-opt, seduce, and resent. This can be called negative power. The second dimension is the capacity to act, resist, cooperate, and assent. This can be called positive power. Taking these two together, political power can be considered the sum of resources and strategies involved in struggles over collective goods in which parties act with and upon others to achieve binding outcomes.

Political power never appears to be exercised equally everywhere. This is partly because power pools up in centers as a result of the concentration of resources, but it is also because of the discursive and practical ascription and secondment of power to higher levels in political-power hierarchies by people and institutions at lower levels. Historical configurations of political power, based on the distribution of economic, political, and military resources, give rise to hegemonies (mixes of coercion and consent) exercised by dominant states or social groups.[6] Through these, rules of conduct, public goods, and structures of expectation are established that orient world politics to certain expected behaviors rather than others. But political power also strengthens or weakens geographically because the transmission of political power across space involves practices by others that lead to its transformation as it moves from place to place. Political power, therefore, is exercised from sites that vary in their geographical reach. This reach can be hierarchical and network-based as well as territorial or contiguous in application. Sometimes power flows indirectly from one place to another through clients or intermediaries; at other times it short-circuits hierarchies and moves directly.[7] Thus, today localities or regions are seen as interacting directly with a global economy without so much of the state-level mediation that once dominated such linkages. The balance between levels in hierarchies of power determines the spatiality (or geographical configuration) of political power at any given time.[8]

In much mainstream international relations theory, three crucial conventions about the relationship between political power and the state reduce the possibility of picking up on this geographically informed view of political power. The first is the rigid territorial conception of the *spatial context in which power operates*: that of a system of territorial states. A richer conception of spatial context sees the state's territory as only one of many geographical frameworks in which political power is operative.[9] Imperial, global-network, alliance, and continental framings are all more or less appropriate depending on issue, time period, and world region. The particular importance of different geographical frameworks to the workings and impact of power changes historically in connection with the evolving spatial structure of economic, cultural, and political activities.[10]

The second convention is the dyadic (person-person, person-state, state-state) definition of *the nature of power relationships*. This abstracts power from the sociological contexts in which it originates and operates into a set of isolated individual relationships.[11] It also views power as solely a quantitative capacity of self-evident and preexisting entities: the ability of a person or a state to direct others or expand its range of influence despite resistance.[12] From this point of view, power is a *possession*. The apparent pervasiveness of power in all social relationships might reinforce this idea. Because power is always manifested in its effects rather than simply as a capacity or possession, however, power relationships are better thought of in terms of territories of power and dispersed power networks in which individual persons, states, and other actors (local governments, interest groups, businesses, nongovernment organizations, etc.) are embedded and located spatially relative to one another.[13] But the relative importance of territories and dispersed networks continually changes as a result of the evolving geographical conditions under which political practices take place and with respect to the issue in question.[14]

The third convention is the homology that is drawn between individual persons and states: *states are treated as if they are the ontological and moral equivalents to individual persons*. This both familiarizes the state and gives it a moral/political status equivalent to that of a person.[15] Regarding states as unitary and singular actors is an important feature of many orthodox views of political power and the state. This assumption privileges the territorial state by associating it with an individual person's character and moral agency, an intellectually powerful feature of modern Western political theory. In medieval European political thought, for example, the state did not have such an exalted status.[16] This points again to the historicity of the relationship between political power and the state.

Historical Spatialities of Political Power

The conventional understanding of the geography of political power is underpinned by three assumptions that are invariably related to one another. I have discussed these at some length in a paper entitled the "Territorial Trap."[17] The first, and most deeply rooted, assumption is that modern state sovereignty requires clearly bounded territories. The modern state thus differs from other modes of political organization by its claim to total sovereignty over its territory. Defending the security of its particular spatial sovereignty becomes the primary goal of the territorial state. At one time sovereignty was vested in the person of the monarch or other leader in a hierarchy of "orders," from the lowest peasant to the warriors, priests, and nobles; now sovereignty is vested in territory.

The second crucial assumption is that there is a fundamental opposition between "domestic" and "foreign" affairs in the modern world. This rests on the view common to modern political theory (dealt with later in more detail in relation to the putative personhood *of* states), that states are akin to individual persons struggling to acquire power and wealth in a hostile world. A state's gains always come at the expense of others. Only inside the boundaries of the state are civic life and political debate possible. Outside, reason of state rules supreme. This fixes political competition at the level of the system of states.

The third assumption is that the territorial state is seen as acting as the geographical "container" of modern society. Social and political organization is defined in terms of a particular state. Thus, we speak and write unself-consciously of "American," "Italian," or "Canadian" society, as if the boundaries of a state are also invariably the boundaries of whatever social or political process in which we are interested. Other geographical scales of thinking or analysis are thereby precluded. Often this is because the state is seen as the guarantor of social order in modern society. The state thus substitutes its boundaries for the self-regulating cultural order that is found in so-called traditional societies.

Taken together these assumptions underpin a timeless conception of statehood as the unique source and arena of political power in the modern world. The first assumption dates from the period in European history when sovereignty shifted from the person of the monarch to the state and, eventually, its citizenry. In Europe this process lasted from the fifteenth to the nineteenth centuries. The other two assumptions date from the past 100 years, although the domestic/foreign opposition has roots in seventeenth-century mercantilism. Together they serve to put the modern territorial state beyond history in general and the history of specific states in particular. Geography hides history, so to speak, because the world is seen as divided up among similar territorial actors achieving their goals through control over blocks of space.

The spatiality of power, however, need not be invariably reduced to state territoriality. At least four models of the spatiality of power can be identified. I draw here on the work of the French geographers Marie-Françoise Durand et al. and Jacques Lévy, who have used idealized models of economic and cultural patterns and interaction to understand long-term shifts in world politics.[18] Each of their models is closely associated with sets of political-economic/technological conditions and associated cultural understandings. The logic of these models is that the dominant spatiality of power will change as material conditions and associated modes of understanding of them change. Such processes of change are not construed as entirely spontaneous. Rather, the historicity of spatiality implies that both material forces and intellectual perspectives or representations interact in a dominant set of practices or hegemony to produce the spatiality of power predominant within a given historical era.[19] But each spatial model also has a synchronic validity in the sense that political power in any epoch can never be totally reduced to any single model. This approach is equivalent to Karl Polanyi's discussion of market society in terms of the emergence of market exchange at the expense of reciprocity and redistribution as principles of economic integration, as one model comes to predominate, other models are not so much eclipsed as placed into subordinate or emerging roles.[20] The models offer, then, not only a way of historicizing political power but also of accounting for the complexity of the spatiality of power during any particular historical epoch (Figure 3.1).

In the model of an "ensemble of worlds," human groups live in separate cultural areas or civilizations with limited communication and interaction between them. Each area in this model has a sense of a profound difference beyond its own boundaries without any conception of the particular character of the others. Communal forms of social construction take place within a territorial setting of permanent settlement, with flows of migrants and seasonal movements but with fuzzy exterior boundaries. Time is cyclical or seasonal, with dynasties and seasons replacing one another in natural sequence. Political power is largely internally oriented and directed toward dynastic maintenance and internal order. Its spatiality rests on a strongly physical conception of space as distance to be overcome or circulation to be managed.

In contrast is the geopolitical model of states in a "field of forces." It revolves around rigidly defined territorial units in which each state can

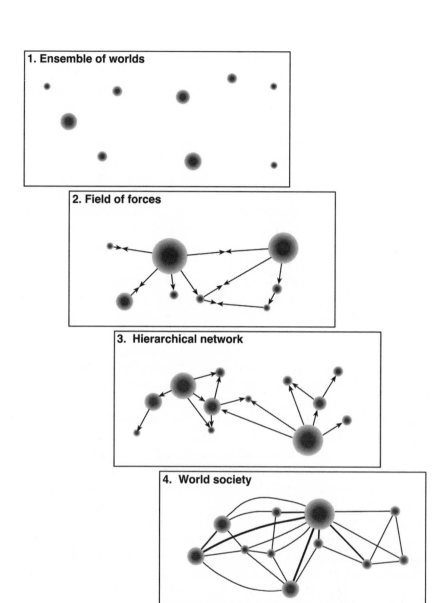

FIGURE 3.1. Alternative Spatialities of Power
Source: Based on M-F. Durand et al., *Le monde, espaces et systèmes* (Paris: Dalloz, 1992), 18.

gain power only at the expense of others and each has total control over its own territory. It is akin to a field of forces in mechanics in which the states exert force on one another and the outcome of the mechanical contest depends on the populations and resources each can bring to bear. Success also depends on creating blocs of allies or clients and identifying spatial points of weakness and vulnerability in the situation of one's adversaries. All of the attributes of politics, such as rights, representation, legitimacy, and citizenship, are restricted to the territories of individual states. The presumption is that the realm of geopolitics is beyond such concerns. Force and the potential use of force rule supreme beyond state boundaries. Time is ordered on a rational global basis so that trains can run on time, workers can get to work on time, and military forces can coordinate their activities. The dominant spatiality, therefore, is that of state-territoriality, in which political boundaries provide the containers for the majority of social, economic, and political activities. Political elites are state elites and they mimic each other's discourse and practices.

A third model is the "hierarchical network." This is the spatial structure of a world-economy in which cores, peripheries, and semiperipheries are linked together by flows of goods, people, and investments. Transactions based largely on market exchange produce patterns of uneven development as flows move wealth through networks of trade and communication thereby producing regional concentrations of relative wealth and poverty. On the local scale, particularly that of urban centers, hinterlands are drawn into connection with a larger world that has become progressively more planetary in geographical scope over the past 500 years. Political power is a function of where in the hierarchy of sites, from global centers to rural peripheries, a place is located. Time is organized by the geographical scope and temporal rhythm of financial and economic transactions. The spatiality results from networks joining together a hierarchy of nodes and areas that are connected by flows of people, goods, capital, and information. Today, such networks are particularly important in linking together the city-regions that constitute the nodes around which the global economy is increasingly organized. In some circumstances, networks can develop a reticular form in which there is no clear center or hierarchical structure. This is the case, for example, with the networks implicit in some business models, such as strategic alliances, in which partnership over space rather than predominance between one node and the others prevails. More notoriously, this is also the case with some global terrorist and criminal networks.

The fourth and final model is that of the "integrated world society." This conforms to the humanistic ideal of a world in which cultural community, political identity, and economic integration are all structured at a global scale. But it also reflects the increased perception of common global problems (such as environmental ones) that do not respect state borders, the futility of armed interstate conflict in the presence of nuclear weapons, the advantages of defense over offense in modern warfare, and the growth of an international "public opinion." This model privileges global-scale communication based on networks among multiple actors that are relatively unhierarchical or reticular and more or less dense depending upon the volition of actors themselves. The sproutlike character of these connections causes them to be compared to plant "rhizomes" (a term popularized by Gilles Deleuze), which spread by casting out shoots in multiple but unpredictable directions. Time and space are defined by the spontaneous and reciprocal timing and spacing of human activities. Real and virtual spaces become indistinguishable. This model obviously has a strong utopian element to it but also reflects some emergent properties of the more interconnected world that is presently in construction.

In the contemporary world, there is evidence for the effective co-presence of each of these models, with the former territorial models somewhat eclipsed and the latter network models somewhat resurgent after a 100-year period in which the field of forces model was preeminent (if hardly exclusive).[21] If the trend toward regional separatism within existing states portends a fragmentation that can reinforce the field of forces model as new states emerge, then economic globalization and global cultural unification work to reinforce the hierarchical network and integrated world society models. At the same time, movement toward political-economic unification (as in the European Union) and the development of cultural movements with a strong territorial element (as with Islamic integralist movements) tend to create pressures for the reassertion of an ensemble of worlds.

Historically, however, there has been a movement from one to another model as a hegemonic or directing element. In this spirit I propose a theoretical scheme drawing from the work of Durand et al. in which the "ensemble of worlds" model slowly gave way to the "field of forces" model around A.D. 1500, as the European state system came into existence (Figure 3.2). Hegemonies tended to vary geographically, so by the nineteenth century a *balance-of-power hegemony* was dominant in Europe. *Imperial hegemonies*, however, were uppermost in much of the rest of

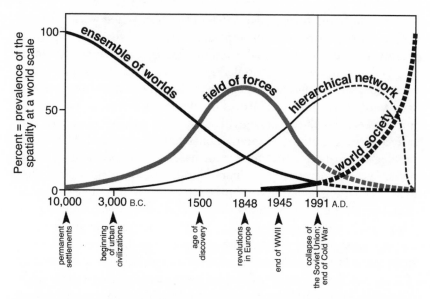

FIGURE 3.2. Diachronics of Spatialities of Power
Source: Based on M-F. Durand et al., *Le monde, espaces et systèmes* (Paris: Dalloz, 1992), 28.

the world save for the *public goods hegemony* exercised by Britain through its roles as upholder of the gold standard and entrepôt in a multilateral trading system that unified an emerging world economy. As this model was establishing its dominance, the modern "hierarchical network" also began its rise in and around the framework provided by the state system. Under European colonialism, the part of the world in which states recognized one another as legitimate actors (what is now often called the Global North) was divorced from the regions in which such status was denied.[22] With independence after the Second World War, numerous new states, irrespective of their relative political efficacy, spread to cover most of the world's land area. But many of these new states were either clients of the United States or the Soviet Union—parts of *sphere-of-influence hegemonies*—or violent zones of conflict between them. In the "field of forces" they were hardly equal forces. Since 1945 the hierarchical-network model has become more and more central to the distribution of political power as a result of the increased penetration of state territories by global trade, population, and investment flows under American hegemony. This is now a truly planetary hegemony—the first in history—with respect to both its potential geographical scope and to the range of its functional influence based on the tenets of marketplace society, even as its primary agent, the United States, may itself become less central to it. With the end of the Cold War, which had produced an important reinstatement of the field-of-forces model among the most powerful states, the hierarchical-network model is ascendent, with signs of the beginning of a trend toward an integrated "world society" model. But this is still very much in its infancy. This framework is, of course, only suggestive of long-term tendencies. It provides a sense of the historical spatiality of political power, associated in different epochs with different dominant modes of spatiality and the copresence of others. Ideal types are a way of thinking about the world, not substitutes for the world's actual complexities at any moment in any place.

The Geosociology of Political Power

The narrow definition of political power has faced considerable challenges in recent years.[23] Political power is typically thought of as showing itself in its effects—in the ability to produce an effect through the application of certain capacities and resources.[24] This often leads to an emphasis on its quantitative possession by self-evident, preexisting actors, usually individual persons or states, that apply power against one another. To account for the indirect or impersonal effects of power in addition to, or in counterpoint to, the traditional idea of power as the *direct* action of one individual or state on another, notions of *structural power* or *metapower* have been suggested.[25] By this extension, the concept of political power can serve to account for the emergence of collectivized and higher-order systems of authority (e.g., regimes), governance (e.g., international institutions), and nonstate transnationalism (e.g., transnational firms, epistemic communities, and issue-networks) that regulate or provide the rules for the relations between the unit-actors in the system of structural power.[26] This kind of power analysis moves the understanding of power relationships "up-scale," beyond the dyadic conception characteristic of conventional political and international relations theories. But it is still lacking a thorough grounding in the social-geographical conditions for the creation and operation of power relationships. In particular, the state is still treated as a given, an ontological and moral actor equivalent to the individual person of classical liberalism, without any of the sociological context needed to explain why the geographical shapes of power change historically. I will provide something of that grounding here.

First of all, exalting the state as the singular font of political power has involved equating the identity of the state with the apparently autonomous identity of the individual person. This does not mean that personhood and statehood are not analogous as social constructions. Rather, it is to deny the atomized understanding of both states and persons that conventional approaches in political and international relations theories take to personal and to state agency. Not only is this a desocialized view of the person or state, implying an essentially transcendental persona, but it also turns sovereign states into naturalized abstract individuals inscribed with the ontological and moral authority of their own personhood. Modern statehood is thus underwritten by modern individualism. A moral claim equating an individual person's autonomy with the state's is masked by the natural claim that is made on behalf of the state as an individual.[27]

The appeal of this conceptual strategy is twofold and reflects an intellectually powerful aspect of the modern social construction of statehood.[28] For one thing, it allows, as the seventeenth-century English philosopher Thomas Hobbes has been regarded as licensing, identification of a historic "state of nature" in which a set of primitive individuals, liberated from social conditioning, can compare their natural condition with that offered by a specified set of social-political conditions associated with statehood. Actual power relationships of dominance and subordination can thus be ascribed to the need for security and/or wealth in a world that no individual person has created. The separation and isolation of individual persons as basic units produces a logically compelling case for the pooling of power in the hands of a single sovereign.

For another thing, the unrelenting suspicion and hostility with which persons regard one another in the state of nature, yet also, and paradoxically, the humanistic tendency to privilege the self-aggrandizing person in other currents of Western thought, underpin the projection of an idealized personhood's qualities onto statehood. At the same time, therefore, the state can be seen as embodying the two sides of the modern ontological and moral coin. The state represents (as in dominant readings of Hobbes) the territorial solution to the problem of human aggression among a discrete group of persons, displacing aggression into the realm of interstate relations. The state is also constructed as equivalent to a person with unique abilities, particularly with reference to its ability to specialize within a spatial division of labor (as in most readings of Adam Smith), that potentially maximize output and thereby increase the wealth and satisfaction of all. These two moves, one "political" and addressing human aggression and the other "economic" and addressing human acquisitiveness, boost the state into intellectual preeminence in relation to the production and distribution of political power, irrespective of their historical veracity.

In addition, I argue that personhood and statehood are not pregiven. Rather, they are both subjective identities established in the midst of the workings of power relationships. Starting with the flow of events and actions in social and political life, contingent identities as either persons or states are formed when social interaction and mutual recognition bring together various and sundry actors such as households, tribes, and dynasties. The identities as persons or states emerge to gain a footing or control in an uncertain world where goals or intentions are defined by presuming the intentions of others, errors in interpretation and judgment feed back into identity, and biographies or histories are told and written to clean up the identity and make it self-evident. This is the development of "personhood" as identified by sociologist Harrison White in his social theory of identity.[29] In this construction, personhood develops out of identity struggles for control in a mix of social networks in which putative persons are enveloped from childhood. White's main point in connection with the analysis of power relationships is that "stable identities [as persons] are difficult to build; they are achieved only in some social contexts; *they are not pre-given analytic foci*" (my emphasis).[30] Similarly, statehood is the outcome of struggles for control, not a preexisting basis upon which such struggles are built. A larger, geographically encompassing social world is required for a state's identity to develop. States become centers of power as identities are defined in networks of relationships that vary in their geographical density (from local to global) and the degree to which network links lead to mutual or asymmetric gains for actors. This is how a hierarchy of states from most to least powerful develops.

A state is defined and recognized as such only within a set of relationships that establishes rules for what is and what is not a "state." In other words, and to paraphrase political theorist Richard Ashley, a state is not ontologically prior to a set of interstate relations.[31] The power of states, therefore, is never the outcome of action at a single geographical scale, that of individual territorial states, but of social rules working at a broader geographical scale and "from below." Statehood results from mutual recognition among states.[32] It is not the result of "isolated states" achieving statehood separately and then engaging with one another as abstract individuals. The importance of the Peace of Westphalia of 1648, for example, lay in its legitimation among political elites of the emerging European territorial states as a set of neutral centers of public power imposing order on warring religious factions.[33] Statehood also acquires important popular legitimacy when associated regimes (institutional arrangements) and governments engender loyalty and support as the main source of political identity, heavily dependent as this usually is on a suitable cross-mapping of nation with state. Absent this crutch, interstate recognition is left vulnerable to "internal" challenge.

Lastly, power in networks of subjectivity emerges as a mix of quantitative capacity or conventional power over others *and* power in the sense of the ability to bind others into networks of assent. Terms such as "structural power" point to this power of assent. In this understanding, however, a single actor (such as a hegemonic state) cannot automatically create assent that is privileged; rather assent is seen as coming from *the strength of association between actors based on shared norms and values*. In other words, to quote the geographers Ash Amin and Nigel Thrift, power depends on

> the strength of associations between actors, which, in turn depends on the ability to use the network to enroll the force of others and speak for them.... Power is the action of others. If actors are successful they will be able to build, maintain and expand these networks so that they can act at considerable distances.[34]

This would include, but not be restricted to, the writing of agendas, the silencing of certain options, and other modes of "mobilization of bias." It necessarily covers, therefore, the "rules of the game" (or hegemony) among actors to which structural power draws attention. Historically, these rules among modern territorial states have emphasized "hard" or coercive power. Today, some commentators argue, they involve the much more pervasive use of "soft" or co-optational power in which assent has become more significant than coercion.[35] This reflects the emergence of a world in which diffuse economic transactions are increasingly more vital to the constitution of political power than are the means of military coercion. But, by definition, even coercion requires the application of commonly accepted and tacitly acknowledged rules of conduct.

The social networks in which quantitative and discursive power re-lationships are *embedded* have historically defined geographical settings. In nineteenth- and early twentieth-century Western industrial society, for example, networks were confined within rigidly bounded state-territorial, imperial, and world-regional settings. Jeremy Bentham's understanding of the power of the regulatory gaze exerted through state bureaucracies exemplifies the epoch, as Michel Foucault has fa-mously claimed. A core-periphery model ruled the spatiality of power. In Timothy Luke's terms, "relatively clear relational-spatial distinctions of social status, cultural preeminence, and political authority develop[ed] in line with a print-bound, panoptical space in traditional industrial societies or industrializing agricultural societies."[36]

In other words, raw material-manufacturing linkages within territo-rial empires, print-based communications, and centralized state appara-tuses produced a territorialized set of relationships between local nodes of networks with denser connectivity within state boundaries and more attenuated links across the globe.

In contemporary "informational society," however, the spatial-temporal character of power relationships is being transformed. As Luke expresses this trend:

> With the growing hegemony of transnational corporate capital, the means of information become the critical force in modern modes of production. A new politics of image, in which the authoritative allocation of values and sanctions turns on the coding and decoding widely circulating images by politicized issue groups, arises alongside and above the interest-group politics of industrial society. Contesting these mythologies can expose some of the contradictions and hidden dimensions of image-driven power. But, on the whole, the endless streams of mythological images in turn bring together the flow of elite control, mass acceptance, and individual consent in a new informational social formation—the "society of the spectacle."[37]

This is a deterritorialized network system in which nodes are widely scattered around the world, although more densely connected within and between Europe, North America, and East Asia, and still con-strained by the territorial structures of power inherited from the ear-lier epoch. The geographical embeddedness of power relationships to-day, therefore, is different from how it was in the past, in terms of the relative balance between territorial and geographical-network ele-ments and the geographical scope under which power relationships are produced.

U.S. Hegemony and the New Geography of Power

How did this new geography of power arise? Of course, technological and economic changes associated with shrinking or stretching the world (depending on how you think about it) have been important in making it possible. The growth of transnational corporations, global financial markets, and technological innovations, such as containerization, the fax, and the Internet, are primary. But the spread of these has only been possible because of profound changes in identities, values, and interests put into place while the United States had a major influence over world politics. For example, the economic history of the United States is largely that of the substitution of technological innovations for labor, such as containerization for manual dock labor, and the invention of the Internet came directly out of the Cold War conflict with the Soviet Union. In other words, the new geography of power to which I alluded earlier would never have happened without U.S. hegemony. This created a different global political environment by projecting political and economic practices and understandings developed previously in the United States into world politics.[38]

The U.S. influence has been particularly widespread and potent compared to previous epochs that might be identified with the "hegemony" of other states.[39] First, U.S. hegemony has been based on a rejection of territorial limits to its influence, as would necessarily come with empire. In this sense it has been a nonterritorial enterprise, notwithstanding periods when territorial strategies have been pursued, such as during the Spanish-American War. The United States is not just one on a long list of hegemons achieving global "power" and then all behaving the same way. In previous epochs, such as that of British hegemony in the nineteenth century, the influence exerted was much more geographically circumscribed. Indeed, Britain had little or no hegemony in Europe. Outside of Europe its empire was central to its enterprise, although there was considerable investment in and trade with the United States, Latin America, and elsewhere as well. The whole world has become America's oyster, so to speak, particularly since the end of the Cold War has brought even its erstwhile challengers such as Russia and China within its cultural-economic orbit.

Second, American hegemony has been a potent brew of cultural and political-economic doctrines and rules of conduct that are usually the outcome of assent and cooperation more than direct coercion. Except among certain groups of "anglophiles," the British never had close to the same influence around the world. More important, to see the resulting globalization as simply based on coercion is profoundly mistaken. It is the result of the self-mobilization of people around the world into practices, routines, and outlooks that they not only accept but think of as their own. This has been the "genius" of U.S. hegemony: to enroll others in its exercise. But this brew did not simply appear out of thin air once the United States came to use its power resources to make itself a global superpower. It was already brewing domestically in a cultural-political-economic context that has had any number of important historic similarities to the larger world: a history of serious and persistent social and geographical conflicts; a system of government founded on the institutional division of power; an industrial-capitalist system that evolved without much central direction or negative regulation; a population of multiethnic origins, weak political parties, and organized labor; and, from the 1890s onward, the first political economy devoted to turning production and consumption into a virtuous circle (eventually in the form of Fordism).

I now will turn to how U.S. hegemony connects to the new geography of power associated with globalization. A more empirically detailed interpretation of the "content" of American hegemony as it emerged in the nineteenth and early twentieth centuries is provided in Chapter 4. There are five logical elements to the argument of the link between American hegemony and the geography of power characteristic of contemporary globalization. First, of primary importance is that the United States has been a marketplace society more or less from the outset in which a social consensus about the rightness of market-based decisions, the "naturalness" of market transactions as determinant of life's course, has been widespread.[40] Market-exchange relationships, therefore, have tended to predominate over reciprocal (e.g., familial) or redistributive (e.g., state-mandated) relationships, to use Karl Polanyi's terminology, in most spheres of life. Although this was contested from the outset and from time to time thereafter (particularly in the New Deal era from the 1930s until the 1960s), the social conventions of the market concerning wages, costs, land prices, etc., have tended to be widely accepted as the right and proper way of organizing society (not just the "economy").[41] Thus, social status in the United States has been largely based on command over resources justified in terms of the outcome of market transactions rather than social inheritance, irrespective of whether this is, in fact, the case. The promise of American society, however, increasingly was expressed in terms of rising average incomes and the consumption that this made possible, more than the remote possibility of making it into the ranks of the rich and famous. If the "heroic phase" in American history ended in the 1890s as the settlement frontier of the pioneers came to a "close," it was replaced by one in which the factory and industrial production for mass consumption became the leitmotifs of the American "experiment."[42]

The market in marketplace society is not simply a mechanism or medium (as in classical Marxism or neoclassical economics); through its commodification of goods and people it provides the basis to the very culture of American capitalism.[43] But since the onset of capitalism, the market has always had to adjust to preexisting social institutions and to social activism directed against its economic depredations and redistribution of power. This was much less the case in the United States than in Europe or Japan, where from its founding as a European outpost in North America up to and after its independence from Britain, a thoroughly capitalist *society* came into existence in which the market was not grafted into existing social arrangements but provided the very fabric of everyday life for ever-increasing segments of the population in the interior as well as on the coast. In the words of historian Charles Sellers: "The American economy's takeoff was fueled by the unusually feverish enterprise of its market sector. Colonial Americans pursued wealth more freely than Europeans because they were not overshadowed and hemmed in by aristocrats and postfeudal institutions. And they pursued wealth more avidly because it made them the American equivalent of aristocrats."[44]

The term "Fordism" is usually applied to the programmatic transformation of an economy, as first experienced in the United States in the early twentieth century when Henry Ford and other big businessmen reorganized not only their factories but also their work forces. Increasing production (and hence profitability) was seen as increasingly dependent on increasing the purchasing power, and hence the consumption, of the workforce engaged in production. Through massive economies of scale, the products of American factories were made available to an army of American consumers who generated the incomes they needed to purchase those products by working in the factories. First applied to the American experience as explained in the 1920s by Antonio Gramsci in his *Prison Notebooks*, the term "Fordism" was revived in the 1970s to refer more generally to a mode of capitalist organization that had replaced the liberal capitalism studied by Karl Marx.[45] To Gramsci, however, Fordism had grown out of the concrete experience of American political-economic development; it was not born universal. As it spread elsewhere as a solution to the failings of liberal capitalism, he saw the emergence of an "Americanized epoch" based on a new balance between state and market that he termed "Americanism." He considered the power of the market relative to the state in the United States as the result, on one hand, of the weakness of rentier classes (outside the South), with their pressure on governments to keep up the value of land-based rents, and, on the other hand, of the "social simplicity" of the country compared to countries with large peasantries, aristocracies, and artisanal groups, whose population saw the emerging industrial model as the result of economic freedom and not of centralized imposition. As Fordism spread, so would Americanism, hollowing out strong states and creating greater social simplicity with respect to distinction and status along the way.

In Gramsci's view, Americanism "finds its political expression in a philosophy exactly the opposite of European-style Jacobinism" in which local government and private initiative are preferable to centralized government because they are seen as more efficient and responsive.[46] Ironically, of course, this marketplace society has produced monopoly capitalism. Because it has brought with it higher incomes, innovation, and consumption, it is popularly seen in a relatively benign light. Gramsci notes, however, that the marketplace itself is often insufficient to keep the industrial model in working order. Industrial capitalists must often impose behavioral norms upon their workers, and even the government steps in when some wider social "evil," such as alcoholism, is seen as requiring more concerted action, such as prohibition of the sale of alcohol. This is a sign that Fordism could not entirely depend on relations integral to the factory and the firm (such as the wage relation) but needed a rationalization of personal identities to create social consent that could only be provided by political mediation. Consent, then, is not freely chosen but constructed at the confluence between state and civil society where the market serves as the practical and ideological nexus between the two.[47]

Even as Fordism entered into crisis in the 1970s, however, the "magic of the marketplace" retained its appeal, suggesting that Americanism had always depended less on the factory and more on ideology and politics than Gramsci had perhaps thought. One of the main ironies of American society is that it is intensely religious even while it is extremely hedonistic. Religious justifications for market solutions to the dilemmas of life and the weakness of collective organizations that might question conventional wisdom, particularly labor unions that might move beyond the workplace in their conceptions of the "good society," undoubtedly account for some of the continuing appeal of the marketplace society. Religious belief is not simply an illusion that serious political analysis can push aside as epiphenomenal. In truth, America was "born Protestant," as the political philosopher Dick Howard puts it.[48] American views of liberty and equality thus have their source in "the stress on the equal validity of the (spiritual) experience of each person."[49] This leads away from an emphasis on securing material equality toward the goal of ensuring that each person has the possibility of self-perfection. Those who fail in this task—in their own and in other's eyes (and it is material success that is taken as the most visible indicator of success and failure)—are not just responsible for the result but are also condemned and merit neither compassion nor aid. This cultural outlook has two consequences. Socially, it suggests that stratification by class and status is primarily the result of individual effort and nothing much can be done about it without the moral hazard of rewarding the ill-deserving. Politically, it leads to an understanding of America as a "sort of living and lived ideology" that is chosen much like the church one chooses to join.[50] American Puritanism, therefore, could only be "called up" for duty to regulate social behavior under Fordism (in enforcing gender roles at home and work, in emphasizing work as central to life, etc.) because it already had a powerful and continuing cultural presence in American civil society.[51]

A related, if more secularized, national narrative of the "liberal self" has probably been of at least equal significance. Learned at home, at school, and through the popular media, the national narrative has been a "discourse on freedom" in which "the national culture has understood itself as a collective experiment in human liberty and as such a model and symbol for the aspirations of the world."[52] It is distinctive in its emphasis on the self as agent and thus on the absence of coercion relative to other societies. It was a propitious setting for the emergence of a hegemony heavily oriented to the marketplace, contradictory as the compulsion implied by hegemony and the voluntary action implied by marketplace would seem to suggest. Though questioned episodically in American history, and never so much as since the late 1960s, the national narrative has had a remarkable persistence, recycled in politicians' rhetoric and in public intellectuals' pronouncements. Its most vociferous proponents today are those neoconservatives and liberals critical of republican and multicultural re-readings of American society. In the past it had a largely unquestioned hold across large segments of the U.S. population. It rested finally on acceptance of unacknowledged authority, not of despotism or tyranny but of the power of "internalized limits" (largely from religious sources) and "institutional constraints" (from community, marketplace, and legal instruments) using "voluntarist incentives." Observers of antebellum America, like De Tocqueville, thought these incentives produced conformity in the face of rampant individualism.[53] American agency, therefore, is far from unconstrained individual freedom. It is, rather, the constrained pursuit by individuals of collective goals such as active membership in the American polity.[54]

The second link in the argument moves from the marketplace society and its mutation over time to the social and geographical consequences. The United States, because it was made up largely of immigrants who had abandoned strong local communities in their homelands because they were disaffected or excluded and went in search of better lives, became preeminently the land of "weak" social ties.[55] The market militated in favor of life as a perpetual deal-making activity while the intermixing of people from a wide range of national, religious, and ethnic backgrounds encouraged social networks in which a premium was placed on specialized rather than multipurpose relationships. Together, market and immigration disembed social networks from dense, multipurpose interactions into much more diffuse, special-purpose ones. Ease of internal migration and the creation of continent-wide national consumer markets after the Civil War combined to stimulate a network-based society in which flows of capital, people, goods, and ideas jumped between cities and across the country without the centralized control and state surveillance that characterized many European states. Territory was not seen as a major barrier to movement as it was in Europe, at least until the advent of the railway. It could be overcome by connecting widely scattered cities and outposts. The virtues and returns to *movement*, then, characterize the geography of American society more than commitment to territory and local, fixed assets.[56]

The third link in the chain is provided by the peculiar nature of American government. The functionally and geographically divided character of the U.S. government made American society particularly open to reliance on the market as both model and metaphor. In its seeming passivity relative to society, American government has usually served, except during special periods such as the New Deal in the 1930s, to make possible or give public blessing to private initiatives. The terms public and private have taken on meanings in the United States different from those they had in Europe in the eighteenth and nineteenth centuries. In particular, the scope of government action has been restricted to that of either constraining government itself or encouraging private enterprise, except crucially in relation to "national security." What has been called the "market revolution" of the late eighteenth and early nineteenth centuries produced a commercial boom that "made government promotion of economic growth the central dynamic of American politics. Entrepreneurial elites needed the state to guarantee property; to enforce contracts; to provide juridical, financial, and transport infrastructures; to mobilize society's resources as investment capital; and to load the legal dice for enterprise in countless ways."[57] This is anything but a simple pluralist state of mere tolerance or, as political theorists of the nineteenth century might have it, "a night watchman state." Rather, government has been an instrument of integration and equilibrium, smoothing the way for private initiatives and public priming of the national economic pump. In this sense, American government has served the "functions" for the wider society ascribed to it by American sociologists such as Talcott Parsons in the concept of "political system." This terminology precisely delimits the concrete historic difference between the institutions of political regulation in the United States and elsewhere, particularly France, whose "state" bears little or no comparison in either formation or functions to its equivalent "apparatus" across the Atlantic.[58] There is little surprise, therefore, that the U.S. government and U.S. businesses push a limited role for government in their lobbying efforts abroad and in the international institutions they dominate.

The fourth element in the argument is that as the United States became the world's wealthiest country in the early twentieth century and later translated this into political and military strength, it brought to bear its own historical experience on how to manage and develop its external relations. There was no mere "translation of empire" (or hegemony) in which the United States simply followed the ways and means of power previously exercised by the British or even the ancient Romans. The common cyclical view of the rise and fall of hegemonies draws attention to the roles of "key" states in the operation of world politics. But in focusing excessively on the identity of the hegemons, this view often misses the distinctive character of the hegemony that they exercise. In the American case this is a historic political economy whose motto "was, to paraphrase Robert Cooper, 'Thou shalt be free to make deals,' and a foreign policy that reconciled its belief in American exceptionalism with its belief in an American mission by acting on the principle 'We shall be free to act unilaterally.'"[59] Perhaps we project backwards onto previous hegemonies many of the features we have come to take for granted with that exercised in the twentieth century by the United States.

The United States only slowly and fitfully emerged as a global actor of preeminence, as I make clear in Chapters 4 and 6. Only after the 1890s did the United States emerge as one of the Great Powers, both economically and militarily. After his decisive intervention in the First World War, U.S. President Woodrow Wilson attempted to shape a world order based on a projection of American values and institutions. Though the Treaty of Versailles represented anything but what Wilson had wanted, he hoped that a future League of Nations might rectify its mistakes. This did not come to pass, mainly because Wilson was unwilling to compromise on some of its features and because many Americans were unwilling to venture into uncharted international waters. Wilson understood, however, as many at the time did not, that the world was on the verge of a historical crisis to which his version of capitalist internationalism would ultimately prove to be a solution.[60]

For present purposes, three points need emphasizing. The first is that President Woodrow Wilson's plan for world order after the First World War was in fact revived after the Second World War with a greater emphasis on creating a new international economic order. The response of the U.S. New Deal to the Depression of the 1930s suggested that markets require regulatory institutions to work adequately. The United Nations (UN), the World Bank, the International Monetary Fund (IMF), the General Agreement on Tariffs and Trade (GATT) (later the World Trade Organization [WTO]), and myriad other institutions have their origin in this period. The U.S. economic position at the end of the war suggested that only the United States was capable of enrolling other states in their operation.[61]

The second point is that without the challenge of the Soviet Union after the Second World War, American hegemony would have been without the major threat that gave impetus to the more formal programs and alliances (such as the Marshall Plan for Europe and the North Atlantic Treaty Organization [NATO]) that laid the political groundwork for bringing the world "to market." This ideological, military, and economic challenge had the effect of both bringing foreign political elites under the "umbrella" of American security and restimulating a military economy in the United States that had come to life during the Second World War.[62]

The third point is that, though paying lip service to "free trade" and freedom of capital, U.S. businesses and the U.S. government have been more oriented to incorporating the world into a single market than in ensuring that it works fairly. *Hegemony is by definition asymmetric.* But the incorporation of the world into an American-based marketplace society, initially in the "Free World" of the American sphere of influence during the Cold War but worldwide recently, has rested on the export of cultural-economic models, first that of Fordism but more recently that of flexible production with its own roots in the American experience.[63]

Parenthetically, and in this light, tracing globalization's ideological impetus (usually under the label "neoliberalism") to the market theorists who were popular during the Reagan presidency in the 1980s, such as von Hayek and Friedman, misses both the longer history of the American marketplace model and its practical as opposed to theoretical or academic origins. Reagan marketed himself as the quintessential American putting his faith in the "miracle of the marketplace." His widespread popularity reflected this identification more than commitment to certain market theorists.[64]

Beyond American shores, American hegemony has not been brought to bear in exactly the same way everywhere. There has been a definite geography to its operation. In some parts of the world and for many years, such as the former Soviet Union and China from 1947 until 1990, it was not operative at all except in terms of defining certain minimalist rules of interstate behavior. In relation to Western Europe and Japan, an emphasis on achieving a high degree of consensus has tended to prevail. Since the 1970s, however, the U.S. government has resorted to much greater coercion, especially through the use of monetary policies to benefit American interests, particularly export-oriented economic sectors. In coastal Southeast and East Asia, U.S. Cold War policies helped lay the groundwork for the establishment of export-based economies in the 1980s and 1990s. In much of the rest of the world, particularly in Latin America and the Middle East, the United States has adopted a much more coercive approach in overthrowing regimes and backing favored despots. Only since the 1980s, and largely through the offices of such institutions as the IMF and the World Bank, has American hegemony been extended, often coercively but also with foreign elite connivance, to the spread of the marketplace society all over the world.

The net outcome of this process has been an emphasis on extending power indirectly through private enrollment more than directly through coercion. Public threats may also be used, but if so, are usually aimed at much less powerful actors. It has been particularly since the 1970s, even as overall U.S. economic predominance has declined but its political-military position has been retained, that the U.S. government has had most recourse to precisely those market-oriented policies (often labeled collectively as neoliberalism or transnational liberalism) that combine co-optation and enrollment with background-coercive threats upon which domestic hegemony in the United States has long relied. Thus, it is no mere coincidence that the foundations for and the efflorescence of globalization have happened during the period of U.S. centrality to world politics. Its geography of power is one that follows logically from the networked power that has long been cultivated within American marketplace society. The revolution in information and communications beginning in the 1970s certainly accelerated its expansion. "But technology was not the cause, only the medium. The [immediate] source of globalization was the process of capitalist restructuring that sought to overcome the crisis of the mid-1970s."[65] And behind the "solution" to this crisis is the cultural-economic model of the United States and its hegemonic global position.[66]

The Contemporary Geographical Dynamics of Political Power

States never appear more "sovereign" in the conventional sense of singular entities endowed with power-monopolies over their territories as when they are associated with defining and enforcing rights of property ownership and citizenship. Both property and citizenship are areas that modern territorial states have strongly enforced. Much law in Western states and, by export, elsewhere has been devoted to establishing rights of ownership and access. Yet, at the same time, a home-territory provides a secure base from which to launch attempts at acquiring property assets elsewhere. Rules establishing the interstate transferability and liquidity of property have given impetus to the flow of capital investment in response to possibilities of greater profitability beyond state boundaries. People also move around in response to signals from labor markets and to escape political repression. As a result, citizenship rights are less easily restricted solely to those born within state boundaries. Pressures build to either admit immigrants to citizen status or, at least, to extend minimal social and economic rights to those officially recognized as immigrants. The circulation of assets and people beyond state boundaries, therefore, challenges the tight connection between sovereignty and territory that has underwritten the conceptual bonding of political power to statehood.

This process is not new. States have always had to fight to capture mobile assets and impose restrictions on rights of citizenship. What is new are the increased quantitative scale and the enlarged geographical scope of the mobile property and people now moving to and fro across the boundaries of the world's states. There is a decreased association between property rights and state territoriality. For example, a range of nonterritorial factors now determines the competitiveness of firms in many industries.[67] These include access to technology, marketing strategies, responsiveness to consumers, and flexible management techniques. With U.S. multinationals as the prototype, all of these are now primarily assets of firms, not territories. Firms grow and succeed by deploying their internal assets as efficiently as possible. States and lower-tier governments compete with one another to attract mobile property to their territories. The telecommunications revolution means that trade in many services (from banking to design and packaging), which have been hitherto more territorialized than trade in goods, can now be provided to global markets. The explosion of migration over the past thirty years owes something to the increased ease of international movement in the age of the jumbo jet, but it is also related to massive international income differences, labor demand in wealthy countries, and increased numbers of political refugees; this has put existing processes of citizenship under stress.[68] Not only are ethnic and birthplace definitions of citizenship called into question in destination states, but the concentration of immigrants in some cities and localities leads to de facto extension of some rights, which undermines the exclusivity of political membership as defined by state citizenship.

The contemporary geographical dynamics of political power can be illustrated by reference to several trends that together signify the disruption of state territoriality and stable political identity currently underway: the impact of population migration on citizenship, the changing geography of money, and the effect on states of new military technologies in a new global economy.

Migration and Citizenship

Modern citizenship is closely connected to the rise of the state. Conventional views of statehood see control over membership in its territory as a crucial requirement; exclusive loyalty to a specific state and political participation are seen as essential components of citizenship. Statehood has been conjoined to nationhood by means of citizenship. Struggles to extend and deepen political representation focused on democratic control of state institutions have served to give states one of their most important sources of legitimation. Consequently, most democratic theory and practice assumes a territorial political community, with citizenship as a means of delineating who does and who does not belong to the "people." Today, only states have the authority under international law to grant or deny the status of citizen. Thus, citizenship is strongly linked to the idea of political community, which, in turn, is seen as synonymous with the territorial exclusivity of the sovereign nation-state.[69]

But the historic tie between states and citizenship is under increasing pressure from immigration and multinational and global conventions governing human rights (such as those established by the European Union).[70] First of all, rights of residence as opposed to birthright are increasingly driving definitions of citizenship. In Europe and North America, a case can be made for a "paradigm (and scale) shift" in understandings of citizenship, a shift that relocates citizenship from nation-state sovereignty to the international human rights regime.[71] This reflects both pressure from the absolute numbers of immigrants and the fears of labor unions and other interests that, without some rights of political membership for immigrants, the rights of all will be undermined. Yet, at the same time, political rights that extend across borders from one state to others are also growing. Citizens of a country resident abroad now can have voting and pension rights hitherto restricted to those resident within the country in question. This is now the case, for example, with Mexican citizens resident in the United States. Within the European Union, the issue of dual or even multiple citizenship has been transcended by the possibility of a European citizenship that also allows for continuing allegiances at state and subnational scales of identity. Plural citizenship, therefore, is an emerging reality.[72]

Recent international migration is different than it was in the past in two ways that are particularly threatening to traditional conceptions of citizenship. One is in the long-term concentration of migrant communities in certain cities and localities that, rather than assimilating into a national "mainstream," maintain their cultural particularity.[73] This is a result of both greater cultural pluralism and tolerance in host countries and greater cultural differences between the new immigrants and their host societies. Many immigrants remain attached to their homelands and see themselves as temporary rather than permanent residents of the new society. Another distinctive feature of contemporary global migration is the ease of movement of people and ideas between source and destination areas.[74] With the new telecommunications technologies, it is relatively easy today to keep ties across state boundaries and to develop political and economic attachments without a final commitment to one state or the other.

As definitions of citizenship are disrupted by the novel character of contemporary global migration, there are countervailing pressures to reestablish "normalcy." "Invasion panics" based on exaggerated fears about the scope and impacts of immigration have afflicted such disparate destinations as California, France, and Italy over the past ten years.[75] Often these are cultural in inspiration, given the increase in flows of migrants who are more visibly different from native populations than previous generations of immigrants. But they also reflect economic concerns about job competition or burdens on public-sector spending for welfare or social security. Political parties play the "immigrant card" in certain areas and constituencies when they use the "threat" of immigration to mobilize native voters.[76] At a certain point in time, however, this strategy can backfire, as it has for the Republican Party in California, when sufficient numbers of immigrants acquire citizenship and demonstrate their electoral strength by voting en masse against those who demonize immigrants as the dominant source of local social and fiscal woes.

Citizenship is a core feature of state sovereignty. Whether democratic or not, states rely on a high degree of exclusivity of identity drawn by their citizens to maintain power within their jurisdictions. Historically, some civil and social rights have been granted to noncitizens. Increasingly, however, even political rights have become relatively mobile. Nonresident citizens, immigrant citizens, residents of encompassing jurisdictions such as the European Union, and multiple citizens are categories of people who experience citizenship in ways that violate the one-to-one correspondence of state and citizenship upon which state licensing of political power has long rested. One of the great advantages of states, to speak and act on behalf of nations, is undermined when the key link between the two, an affective and singular citizenship, is eroded by movements of people that transgress rather than reinforce the boundaries of states.

The Geography of Money

The control and maintenance of a territorially uniform and exclusive currency is often regarded as one of the other main attributes of state sovereignty. If a state cannot issue and control its own currency, then it is not much of a state. Benjamin J. Cohen offers a concise statement of this position:

> The creation of money is widely acknowledged as one of the fundamental attributes of political sovereignty. Virtually every state issues its own currency; within national frontiers, no currency but the local currency is generally accepted to serve the three traditional functions of money—medium of exchange, unit of account, and store of value.[77]

A currency has the further and vital role of symbolically underwriting statehood. The creditworthiness of the currency represents to a national population that "the ultimate object of their faith, the nation-state, is real, powerful and legitimate; it is the ultimate 'guarantor of value.' "[78]

Territorial currencies developed on a large scale only in the nineteenth century, long after the Westphalian system of states was in place.[79] Symbolically, however, currencies (including the symbols found on coinage and bank notes) were important elements in establishing state legitimacy long before the nineteenth century. As noted in connection with statehood and citizenship, modern statehood was not achieved without relation to nation-building, even though "state" and "nation" can be distinguished analytically and confused deliberately, the former referring to a set of institutions ruling over a discrete territory and the latter signifying a group of people who share a sense of common destiny and occupy a common space. That true territorial currencies are relatively recent should not detract from the persistence over many centuries of currency as an important representation of nation-statehood, however fuzzy in many respects the linkage between currency and state often was.

Increasingly, however, the notion that every state must have its own "territorial currency," homogeneous and exclusive within the boundaries of a given state, is under material challenge. Three developments have begun to delink currencies from states in the way they were once mutually defining. The first is the growing use of foreign currencies for a range of transactions within national currency territories. From the so-called eurodollar markets in London and elsewhere to the offshore financial centers of the Caribbean and the rapid-fire exchange of currencies between global financial centers, global financial integration is shattering the exclusivity of national currency spaces.[80] The second development is the spreading use of either supranational currencies (the Euro) or "hard currencies" (such as the U.S. dollar or Japanese Yen) as transnational currencies.[81] Much of world trade is denominated in dollars, Euros, or Japanese yen, regardless of its particular origins or destination. Economic reforms mandated by international organizations such as the IMF have also encouraged the use of currencies such as the dollar to stabilize flows of capital and prop up local currencies. Finally, strictly local currencies—forms of scrip or token money—have also shown signs of growth.[82] These do not substitute for national currencies, but they do provide alternatives to them in local communities. They are perhaps symptomatic of declining trust in territorial currencies, particularly in settings where high rates of inflation and currency instability push people out of the official money economy.

None of these trends signals the imminent demise of territorial currencies. The erosion of territorial currencies will continue only if the most powerful states allow it to. That there is now considerable advantage in this erosion for states, however, suggests that it will continue. As it deepens and spreads it could well gain a momentum of its own that will be difficult at that point to counteract, however powerful the state in question.

New Limits to Interstate Warfare

Political power beyond state boundaries has often been seen as the projection of force by one state against another. One way in which the sentiment is expressed is the idea of anarchy in the space beyond the confines of one's ordered and domestic space that can only be managed by vigilant preparation for warfare. Without a substantial war machine prepared to strike at adversaries, a state is vulnerable to conquest and subjugation. A second way is the commonly held view that states are in perpetual competition and go to war with one another for scarce resources.

Beginning with the Cold War, however, the most militarily powerful states began showing reservations about using force against one another and, to a lesser extent, against weaker states. It is reasonable to assume that this is because the orthodox assumptions no longer hold up.[83] Parenthetically, it is important to note that this trend does not necessarily portend a decline in total political violence. Indeed, there is a contemporaneous trend toward an increase in the prevalence of internal wars as state authority collapses in multinational states.[84] This rather makes the point that state monopoly over the use of force is as increasingly problematic within state boundaries as it is beyond them.

What is at the root of the apparent declining utility of military force by states against one another? The impact of nuclear weapons is among the most critical changes in military technology.[85] These weapons have had the effect of not only introducing mutual deterrence but also of imprinting on potential combatants the likely escalation of all organized interstate violence into nuclear exchange. The unprecedented destructiveness of nuclear weapons and their likely negative impact (through delayed radiation) on victors as well as the vanquished mean that their possessors paradoxically limit their military options by possessing them. They discipline allies and adversaries alike by introducing the prospect of rapid escalation. Nuclear weapons also seem to favor defensive more than aggrandizing military actions by raising the stakes for potential aggressors.[86]

Even before the advent of nuclear weapons, however, a second feature of modern warfare had begun to erode the rational basis for its use. The economic and political costs of war between reasonably well-matched adversaries now exceed any conceivable collective benefit national populations can derive from it.[87] There are, of course, domestic interests that are still served by war and preparation for it (weapons makers, military officers, etc.), but war now requires very costly investments that do not guarantee favorable results. The civil wars involving the intervention of the United States in Vietnam and the former Soviet Union in Afghanistan are reminders that even in apparently asymmetric conflicts the best-armed may not prevail.

Third, with respect to military factors, there is increasing revulsion among the world's most affluent populations over the human costs of war and the seemingly feeble benefits it generates. The use of military force faces a legitimation crisis. The loss of even a single pilot or soldier, particularly if a conscript or from an influential group, now often causes a total rethinking of American force commitments. This is perhaps a reflection of the increased visibility of the conduct of warfare in a visual age. Though televised war often takes a spectacular or entertainment form, it also introduces an immediate sense of the deadliness of war that civilians in previous epochs never experienced. At the same time there is disillusionment with the "fruits" of war. Gains often seem incommensurate with sacrifices. The political inconclusiveness of many recent wars (such as that against Iraq in the Gulf in 1991, the NATO "intervention" in Kosovo in 1999, the "overthrow" of the Taliban in Afghanistan in 2002, and the U.S. occupation of Iraq in 2003–2004) adds to skepticism. The democratization of foreign policy making in many countries has probably added to the questioning. Once reserved for small elites, foreign policy is now increasingly subject to public challenge and debate (not least from those with nonsingular citizenship) in ways unheard of thirty years ago.[88]

Paralleling these military-related trends are two developments related to the world economy. First, interstate competition is now largely about capturing the benefits of global economic growth for one's territory more than about conquering another state's territory to capture its resources.[89] Insertion into global corporate and financial networks now seems crucial to the course of national economic development. Exceptions help to show what is now largely the rule. Iraq's invasion of Kuwait in 1989–1990 was designed to capture that country's assets. What it revealed was the extent to which Kuwait's assets, other than its oil reserves, were mobile beyond the boundaries of the state. Indeed, the Kuwaiti government in exile contributed handsomely to Kuwait's liberation from Iraqi occupation by a UN-sanctioned force through its continuing access to a large number of significant foreign investments.[90]

Second, technological change has opened the possibility of escaping from the dilemma of competitive states going to war with one another because of chasing the same resources. In the present era of informational capitalism, the most productive and profitable activities are no longer resource-intensive ones, such as heavy industries and extensive agriculture, but technologically intensive manufacturing, such as electronics and biotechnology, and service industries, such as tourism, finance, and personal services. These are best achieved by either generating external economies in local clusters of firms (as in California's Silicon Valley) or by tapping into global networks of specialized labor and customized production.[91] This is no longer a world in which territorially bigger is automatically economically or politically better. Hence, it is a world in which military force to achieve such rational goals as increased resources or to cope with the anarchy threatened by other states no longer makes much sense.[92] In a world of rapid economic circulation, the rational link between states and military force has become frayed, if not yet cut.

Conclusion

In this chapter I have challenged three crucial conventions about political power and statehood in mainstream understandings of world politics: (1) the trap of a historically constant spatiality, that of state-territoriality in a field of forces model of political power; (2) the dyadic conception of power as involving persons or states as ontologically preexisting units in bilateral relations at a single geographical scale; and (3) the state as a unitary and singular actor having a moral status equivalent to that of the individual person in Western thought. I have done so by providing four perspectives on how to go about assessing the workings of political power outside of a singularly state-centric framework. The first perspective is explicitly *historicist*, using ideal-type models of the spatiality of power to trace a historical survey of the relative grip of different geographies of power, particularly historical changes in the relative significance of territory as a means of organizing political power. The second is *geosociological*, critically questioning the ontological and moral grounds upon which dominant understandings of political power rest, in particular their atomistic conceptions of the identities of persons and states.

In place of such conceptions, I propose in a third perspective a *geographical* focus on how U.S. hegemony has altered the basis to world politics and that it has done so because of the projection beyond U.S. borders of the practices of a marketplace society initially developed "at home."

The final perspective is more *contemporaneous* and global in orientation. It points to recent empirical trends in the movement of people and money and the problematic rationality of interstate war in the light of changes in military technology and the workings of the world economy to suggest that political power now circulates in ways that are not best captured by the theoretical equation of fixed state-territoriality, pregiven political identities, and limited movement of goods, investment, and people. U.S. hegemony is given a directing role in explaining how world politics has moved increasingly in recent years toward a networked geography of power.

During periods of seeming political-economic stability such as that of the Cold War (at least within the economically developed countries of the West), "geography," in the form of assumptions about territoriality, identity, and movement, hid the history of power. The mainstream international relations theories developed in the United States and Western

Europe to help understand and manage conflict between Great Powers must now be made to confront their geographical representations in light of new realities. The end of the Cold War and the emergence of a more globalized world economy have increased awareness of their limitations. As a result, established state boundaries are losing their ability to monopolize the representation of political power. But theoretically, we have not caught up. One way to do so is to address the workings of political power through mapping its attributes of territoriality, identity, and movement. The geography of political power is a function of historical change in combinations of material and representational processes. Political power does indeed have a history, but it is one that can be best understood through its changing geography and how that geography has come about. Most recently, this has been under the aegis and in the shape of American hegemony.

4 Placing American Hegemony

The twentieth century was by many accounts the American century. The twenty-first century, however, is not likely to be. Between these two sentences lies the history of American hegemony. In this chapter I show how American hegemony started. It began at home. Only later did it extend outward, and it was the U.S. interventions in the two world wars of the twentieth century that made this possible. After the Second World War in particular, the United States formed NATO and other alliances to contain the former Soviet Union and its allies. This required significant military and political commitments beyond the boundaries of North America, changing previous intermittent involvement in world affairs into a permanent and decisive presence. At first glance, this turned out seemingly positively for the United States, with the decay and finally the collapse of the Soviet Union from 1989 to 1992. The longer-term prognosis, however, is far from clear. The globalizing world that the United States has done so much to realize is an emerging geographical structure that seems likely to pose serious challenges to a continuation of American hegemony in the form that it previously has taken both at home and abroad. I will go into further detail on this in later chapters. In this chapter I will spell out the origins and course of American hegemony in its home territory.

The story of American hegemony is not that of the simple rise of yet another hegemonic state in succession to previous ones. Rather, it is the creation of a global economy under American auspices, reflecting the content of a hegemony arising from the development of the United States, and the feedback of this system on the behavior of the U.S. government. In this chapter I show why the later hegemonic strategies of the U.S. government in world politics that favor the "soft" power of assent, cooperation, co-optation, and consensus (even if invariably self-interested and backed up by coercion) grew out of the particularities of American historical experience, especially the divided political institutions and marketplace society that made it distinctive from other states. This does not involve endorsing the exceptionalist claim that the United States is not just different from but simply better than other places. Rather, it replaces the narrative of hegemony as essentially one Great Power indistinguishable from others substituting for another now in decline, a mechanical model of hegemonic succession, with a narrative that gives hegemony distinctive content depending on which society exercises it. Globalization is the outcome of the geographical projection of American marketplace society allied to technical advances in communication and transportation.

In pursuit of these objectives, the chapter is broken into two sections. The first section gives a description of the hegemony that emerged from the founding of the United States and how it evolved from providing a propitious context for a national "marketplace society" to one that stimulated the beginnings of what we now know as "globalization" as early as the 1890s. The second section identifies the critical causal factors of *why* this hegemony emerged in the United States rather then elsewhere. Therefore, the roots of the U.S. hegemony exercised later around the world can be found in the history of the United States. To reiterate, this is not an argument for the superiority of the United States, as those who confuse arguments about the specificity of the American experience with American "exceptionalism" tend to claim. It is, rather, that world history has its roots in specific places, not everywhere at once or in behavioral imperatives that emanate from some global totality such as "capital." This is not, therefore, an argument for either an overarching *telos* (such as capital accumulation, technological change, or liberalism) or a single cause that lies "behind" everything else. I emphasize, rather, the collective and acquired experiences of the American population and the stories told about these experiences by leaders and later generations, particularly in relation to critical junctures such as the late nineteenth century, and the cumulative effect of these on popular practices and attitudes. In this connection I am reminded of a passage from a letter written by Karl Marx in 1877: "Events strikingly similar but occurring in a different historical milieu lead to completely different results. . . . By studying each of these evolutions separately and then comparing them it is easier to find the key to understanding of this phenomenon; but it is never possible to arrive at this understanding by using the passe-partout of some universal historical-philosophical theory whose great virtue is to stand above history."[1]

From Marketplace Society to Globalization

The making of a global economy under American auspices reflects the working out globally of the hegemony based in the historical experience of the United States. Understanding how U.S. hegemony has given rise to globalization and not to some other political-economic form such as empire, therefore, requires understanding how this hegemony developed first in the United States. After providing a narrative of the nineteenth-century development of American marketplace society and its inherent expansionism beyond fixed territorial boundaries, I identify the crucial causal factors in why the United States has been the seedbed for a hegemony based on market-oriented social relations.

It is commonplace now to see the genius of the American Constitution of 1787, as expressed most eloquently and persuasively in the writings of James Madison, as tying freedom to "empire." But this was not empire in the sense the founders associated with the British and the French. They had experienced the limits (and abuses) of imperial power before and during the War of Independence.[2] Madison maintained that in place of the British colonial system, the best solution for the American rebels would be the creation of a powerful central government that would provide the locus of security for the survival of republican government. The central government would oversee geographical expansion into the continent, which would guarantee an outlet for a growing population that would otherwise invade the rights and property of other citizens. In this way, republican government was tied to an ever-expanding system. Madison had brilliantly reversed the traditional thinking about the relationship between size and freedom. Small was no longer beautiful. Of course, Thomas Jefferson and others less connected to the fortunes of land acquisition and growing markets initially opposed the logic of expansionism. But eventually they too came around. Indeed, when he became president, Jefferson justified the acquisition of Louisiana and the prospective addition of Canada and Cuba by claiming the extension of an "empire for liberty."[3]

Although couched in the language of political rights and citizenship, the association of freedom with geographical expansion reflected two important political-economic principles. The first was that geographical expansion of the marketplace is necessary for political and social well-being. The conception of frontier that evolved in the United States was not one of limits or boundaries but rather one of an ever-expanding zone. This differs profoundly from European understandings that equate frontiers with boundaries and borderlands. Geographical expansion, initially into the continental interior but later in all sorts of directions including into outer space (the "final frontier" of *Star Trek*), was to release economic and political passions that might otherwise challenge the social status quo upon which the founding of the United States was based. The second principle was that economic liberty is by definition the foundation for freedom per se. Freedom for Americans was to be the freedom "to truck and barter," as Adam Smith would have it. Other freedoms were seen as flowing from or secondary to economic liberty, the freedom to own property and do with it as you pleased, rather than co-extensive with it. From the start, therefore, the United States was a profoundly economistic society, reflecting the values and interests of the merchants, bankers, and plantation owners who were the architects of its political institutions. Thus, the totally new political system after independence was designed to combine these two principles: (1) the central government guaranteeing the capacity for expansion into the continental interior and into foreign markets and (2) lower-tier government (the states) and the division of powers between the branches of central government restricting the power of government to regulate and limit economic liberty.

The American Constitution and early judicial interpretations of it combined these two principles to create a uniquely American version of democratic capitalism. On the one hand, the federal government underwrote expansion into the continental interior and stimulated interest in foreign markets for American products; on the other hand, the federal subunits (the states) and the division of power between the branches of the federal government (the Congress, the presidency, and the Supreme Court) limited the power of government to regulate private economic activity. Max Edling has recently noted that the successful Federalists (as opposed to those who wished to have a looser confederation) developed "a conceptual framework that made it possible to accommodate the creation of a powerful national government to the strong anti-statist current in the American political tradition."[4] They did so by designing a federalism that would be both "a blueprint for a state that would be powerful yet respectful of the people's aversion to government."[5] Notwithstanding the genius of the founders, however, the qualities of "powerful" but "light and inconspicuous" government have not always sat easily together.[6]

Each of the political-economic principles can be seen at work in stories about American "national character" and the model of citizenship offered by the vision of American exceptionalism. Although Americans celebrate some historic occasions, such as Independence Day (the Fourth of July), and founding documents, such as the Declaration of Independence and the Constitution, they have not had much history by which to define themselves. America has been defined not so much by a common history, as most imagined nationhood communities seem to have.[7] Rather, Americans have defined themselves through a shared geography expressed in the future-facing expansion of the frontier by individual pioneers. Founding Father Thomas Jefferson said he liked "the dreams of the future better than the history of the past."

The founders of the United States could find ready justification for their institutional creation in the timely publication of Adam Smith's *Inquiry into the Nature and Causes of the Wealth of Nations* in 1776. Smith stood in relation to the founding as Keynes did to the political economy of the New Deal in the 1930s: a systematizer of an emerging "common sense" for the times. The Constitution is open to contrary interpretations on the relative powers of both federal branches and tiers of government.[8] Through the years, however, the federal level has expanded its powers much more than any of the founders, including its greatest advocate Alexander Hamilton, could have foreseen. At the federal level, and reflecting the essential ambiguity of the Constitution, the Supreme Court has also come to exert great power through its capacity for interpreting the meaning of the founding document.[9] But the spirit behind the exercise has remained the institutionalization of commercial society, as the Scottish philosophers who wrote about progress in such terms earlier in the eighteenth century would have been pleased to see.[10]

As the dominant social group numerically at the time of independence and for many years thereafter, American farmers rapidly came to see themselves as intimately involved in marketplace relations. Apart from those farmers wresting from the forest a subsistence agriculture:

> a market revolution was surmounting the overland transportation barrier [by 1815]. While dissolving deeply rooted patterns of behavior and belief for competitive effort, it mobilized collective resources through government to fuel growth in countless ways, not least by providing the essential legal, financial, and transport infrastructures. Establishing capitalist hegemony over economy, politics, and culture, the market revolution created ourselves and most of the world we know.[11]

The "culture of the market" thus directly challenged and quickly overwhelmed that of "the land" and opened up localities to long-distance movement. The market revolution of the early nineteenth century, however, had older roots. The commercial outlook of many farmers had its origins in the spatial division of labor organized under British mercantilism, in which they came to serve distant markets rather than engage in subsistence agriculture. Much of the basis for American independence lay in the struggle to expand the boundaries for individual economic liberty within a system that was more oriented to a sense of an organic whole: the British Empire. American "marketplace society," therefore, was not a pure intellectual production or entirely postindependence in genesis, but arose out of an evolving material context in which it served the emerging identity and interests of a dominant social group of capitalist farmers.[12] As the industrial bourgeoisie rose to prominence in the nineteenth century, they inherited the hegemony of marketplace society already in place but expanded it both geographically, into every nook and cranny of the expanding country, and functionally, into every part of everyday life.

The common sense of American society, therefore, is a profoundly marketized one in which everything and everyone has their price.[13] But this does not mean that there has ever been total agreement about how far to push this, or whether government is solely its instrument or can be its restrainer. Certainly, the excesses of the marketplace have never been without resistance or challenge from the Age of Jackson in the late 1820s and early 1830s to the present. Indeed, within the broad parameters of marketplace society, American politics has always oscillated between attempts at policing and disciplining the marketplace in the interests of various groups through the use of governmental power and letting market forces loose from tighter institutional moorings.[14] Generally, it has been during times of economic distress or in response to perceived political threats (internal, as with the Civil War, or external, as with the world wars) that the balance has shifted toward restraint. The two ramshackle political parties that since the Civil War have tied American society to its political institutions, however, both accept the marketplace model but have had shifting attitudes toward managing it. With the exception of the Democratic Party during the 1930s, however, which profoundly increased the federal role in the U.S. economy and society, both parties have tended to shy away from interfering much with the political dominance of private economic interests.

Early U.S. history, from 1775 to the end of the War of 1812, suffered from periodic warfare, chronic threat of warfare, and profound disagreements about the roles of such institutions as the Supreme Court and the powers of the states in relation to the federal government. Different interests and identities tended to coalesce around the two major political factions that emerged in the 1790s: the Federalists and the Republican-Democrats. If the Federalists, such as Alexander Hamilton and John Adams, desired to concentrate power at the center, the Republicans (with Jefferson in the lead) wanted to shrink it. The Constitution gave the South, where the Republican-Democrats predominated, a built-in electoral advantage. The so-called three-fifths clause stated that each slave would count for three-fifths of a person in determining the number of people in each state and congressional district and hence the numbers of both the congressional representatives and electoral votes for the presidency each state could claim. Though the population balance between North and South changed once immigrants in larger numbers settled in northern manufacturing areas, until the Civil War the South dominated national politics in large part because of the three-fifths rule.[15]

With a populace increasingly divided along North-South lines over the issues of the extension of slavery into the continental interior and the role of the federal government in sponsoring infrastructural development and economic growth, Thomas Jefferson's conception of the federal union as a compact among sovereign states provided no solution to such emerging problems.[16] Even if allies such as James Madison remained confident that the American "model" had lessons for others, toward the end of his life Jefferson was not so sure that the "extended republic" might itself long survive the tensions implicit in the system inaugurated in 1787.[17] A set of important place differences in the nature and level of economic development, as well as in outlooks on the balance between federal and state levels of government and conceptions of the public good, took root during the process of settlement and development of a national economy to challenge the idea of an idealized, abstract American space.[18]

The widely shared view among the Founding Fathers that they were creating a potentially continental "empire" did not extend to the question of means. The central figure in early American diplomacy was undoubtedly Thomas Jefferson, and he objected to the old European-style "reason of state." Though he pursued ambitious goals, above all territorial expansion and commercial reform, he was determined to dispense, as far as was possible, with the armies, navies, and diplomatic establishments that had badly compromised the prospects for political liberty and economic prosperity abroad and would do so at home if ever they became firmly entrenched.[19]

To "conquer without war"—to pursue the objectives of American policy by economic and other peaceable means of coercion and consent—was Jefferson's main bequest to the United States.

When composing the Declaration of Independence, Jefferson had included in the second paragraph the phrase "that all men are created equal, and Endowed by their Creator with certain inalienable rights." This was to become the clarion call in the mid-nineteenth century for those, particularly Abraham Lincoln, who regarded the Declaration of Independence (more than the Constitution) as the moral basis for the American Revolution.[20] In this reading, the ideals of the nation trumped the interests of particular factions, states, or groups over slavery and other issues (such as a national bank or industrial development). This wholehearted emphasis on the sentiment of the Declaration of Independence regarding human equality and national purpose was to become the basis for fighting the Civil War. It was also the basis, because of the triumph of the Union over the southern Confederacy, for the creation of a more politically centralized and economically integrated United States. Slavery was an abomination to Lincoln not on simple moral grounds, such as the argument of some abolitionists that all people had to own their personhood to own their soul, but because it undermined equal access to the marketplace for free labor by pricing people without paying them. It was slavery's extension into the western territories that Lincoln most feared. Essentially, the expansion of slavery discriminated against achieving a national free labor market. Only a free market in labor could realize the promise of the Declaration of Independence. Of course, sectionalism, specifically that between North and South, continued to divide the country after the Civil War and distinctive attitudes to domestic and foreign policies followed these lines. Until the 1890s, however, the integration into a national marketplace society of the territories acquired through the Louisiana Purchase of 1803 and the Mexican War of 1847–1849 took priority over anything else.

The American two-party system after the Civil War helped to further underpin marketplace society. If the modern Republican Party has had a common theme since its founding in 1854, it has been to represent itself as the party of an American nation, of patriotism, and of the national economy. The Democratic Party (the Jacksonian transformation of the Republican-Democrats), with its powerful southern base until recent times, became the party of moderation and compromise across sections. All progressive movements for change—the labor movement, civil rights, the women's movement, etc.—have had to come from outside the Democratic Party even as they have tried to influence it. In contrast, the Republicans have been the party of uncompromising, frequently draconian solutions to perceived national problems premised on an identity between national purpose and business enterprise. Particularly after the Civil War, the Republicans did the most to foster marketplace society. From this perspective, the U.S. Civil War and Reconstruction era can be understood best as a period of liberal revolution.[21] Though republican in name, the Republican Party was in fact the Trojan horse for full-blooded liberalism. This was how the contradiction of the founding between its republican and liberal tendencies was resolved. Following Lincoln's death, private interests completely trumped public virtue.

The expansion of the United States into the interior of North America in the nineteenth century created a land mass and resource base unmatched by other territorial empires save that of Russia. Initially geared toward agricultural development, the national policy of conquest, settlement, and exploitation gave way after the Civil War (1860–1865) to the establishment of an integrated manufacturing economy. The Civil War was a struggle over the economic trajectory of the country as a whole as well as a conflict over the morality of slavery.[22] The victory of the industrial North over the agrarian-slave South ensured the shift of the American economy from an agrarian to a manufacturing base. The South and the West became resource peripheries for the growing manufacturing Belt of the Northeast, providing food and raw materials to the factories of the then dominant northern industrialists and their banker allies.[23]

Federation was itself a patchwork solution to the problem of keeping together a set of regional societies with divergent cultural and economic characteristics. At the same time, an emerging "geographical morphology" worked to undermine both economic equality and a common national identity. *The tension between market and place was resolved by incorporating them within a national marketplace.* Donald Meinig has proposed a heuristic model to illustrate the main elements of this morphology in the early United States, around 1800 (Figure 4.1).[24] But this morphology has had a persisting influence through the years both in terms of the geographical structure of the U.S. economy and its influence on national politics and policy (e.g., attitudes toward trade

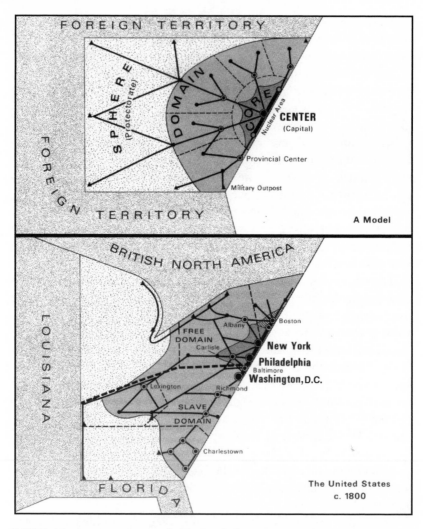

FIGURE 4.1. American Geographical Morphology, circa 1800
Source: D. Meinig, *The Shaping of America. Volume I: Atlantic America, 1492–1800* (New Haven, CT: Yale University Press, 1986), 402. Copyright Yale University Press.

restrictions, foreign military interventions, etc.). Particularly important has been the grip on national development exerted by the city-regions of the Northeast. New York and Philadelphia quickly became national rather than state or regional centers. They thrived on interaction with provincial centers and internal hinterlands. They also served as the primary points of intersection with the Atlantic economy. As nodes in a transatlantic network of trade, capital, and labor flows, they mediated between the continental interior and the world beyond.

In Meinig's terms, a *nuclear area* including New York and Philadelphia rapidly gave way to a *core region* with such important regional centers as Baltimore and Boston. Beyond this was a *domain* of areas linked directly (in the North) and indirectly (in the South) into the national road, and later, canal and railroad networks. Finally, at the greatest distance from the core was the frontier region, or *sphere*, exerting a powerful imaginative pull but until later in the nineteenth century only weakly incorporated into the economic-communication structure of the nation. Relative power, or capacity to affect political and economic decisions, tended to parallel the basic geographical morphology.

The regional balance achieved by the 1830s rested on a series of key economic specializations. The cotton-exporting South tied the United States directly into the world economy through exports largely to Britain. The South imported increasing amounts of foodstuffs from the West (the present day Midwest), and with the income received the West bought manufactured goods from the Northeast. Thus, a regional specialization with between-region links was established and created three distinctive regional economies within it. Slowly the balance came apart. Industrial growth in the Northeast accelerated to the point where the region was a manufacturing economy generating its own internal demand. This in turn stimulated a demand for agricultural products from the West. As new railroads increasingly integrated the Northeast and the West, the South was increasingly isolated as an agricultural export economy based on a system of plantation slavery that did not fit with either the emerging northern industrial economy or the tenets of marketplace society. The fundamental question the Civil War was fought over concerned which economy would be favored by the federal government.[25] Neither could coexist any longer in the same national space with the other. If the South had won, it is doubtful anyone would be writing books about American hegemony.

The emerging national economy of the late nineteenth century was based in large part on the growth of the first capitalist consumer economy. American businesses pioneered in advertising and salesmanship as ways of bringing the population into mass markets for manufactured goods and processed foodstuffs. Relative to the rest of the world, American growth in manufacturing output was incredible. Much of this growth depended upon expanding markets for products as well as accessing the vast raw material resources of the American interior

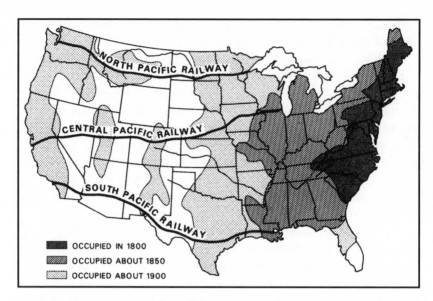

FIGURE 4.2. The Continental Expansion of American Settlement.

(Figure 4.2). Growth depended on four factors: the expansion of the railroads, the removal of legal barriers to interstate commerce, the development of large businesses or trusts exploiting economies of scale to capture national markets, and the explosion of marketing, salesmanship, and advertising to drum up demand.[26] Alan Trachtenberg well captures the creation of a truly national and incipient international market this combination entailed:

> Following the lead of the railroads, commercial and industrial businesses conceived of themselves as having the entire national space at their disposal: from raw materials for processing to goods for marketing. The process of making themselves national entailed a changed relation of corporations to agriculture, an assimilation of agricultural enterprise within productive and marketing structures.... Agricultural products entered the commodities market and became part of an international system of buying, selling, and shipping.[27]

The entire economic edifice was underwritten by a rapid expansion of consumption based on the growth of a "sales culture" in which purchasing goods was established as a means to achieve personal satisfaction and happiness. Though other factors—such as the railroads, big business, and the removal of barriers to national business operations—undoubtedly had great significance in creating a national market, they

have perhaps received undue attention. Indeed, they can be seen as enabling more than as fundamental to the *type* of economy that emerged by
the early 1900s. American businesses pioneered both in advertising and
salesmanship as ways of incorporating the population into mass markets
for the goods pouring out of their factories. The ethos of mass production for mass consumption was an American invention. The promise of
the marketplace—the things it could provide and the status that possession of them entailed—served to socially and geographically integrate
the population of a vast territory otherwise divided by class, race, ethnicity, religion, and sectional economic interests. This was heralded by
popular commentators and politicians as the pursuit of the "American
Dream." Eventually, however, the limits set to consumption by the size
of the national market, gigantic as it might seem, could only be overcome by expansion over the horizon. Feeding the dream could not be
confined territorially. Its geographical scope had to be expanded.

The rise of American consumer culture in the late nineteenth and
early twentieth centuries can be seen in several different ways. From
one viewpoint, it represented a "democratization of desire" or the conversion of what had been luxuries consumed by elites into commodities
sold to the masses. This not only depoliticized "freedom of choice"
from republican ideals of self-governance to choosing among different products, but it also provided solutions to the economic problem
of expanding opportunities for capital accumulation and the political
problem of tying wage-labor into capitalist production by means other
than the wage relation. A vision of the "good life" based on material consumption, and available potentially to everyone, increasingly marginalized other visions in late nineteenth-century America.[28] The idea of
being middle class became the self-defined status of many of those who
senso strictu remained workers. Being middle class meant liking and living for things. In other words, "The promise of democracy was that of
plenitude."[29]

From another viewpoint, the rise in American consumer culture represented a fundamental shift in the nature of the bourgeois ethic associated with early capitalism and its theorists such as Adam Smith and Karl
Marx. In the United States, as elsewhere, this ethic "had enjoined perpetual work, compulsive saving, civic responsibility, and a rigid morality
of self-denial. By the early twentieth century that outlook had begun to
give way to a new set of values sanctioning periodic leisure, compulsive
spending, apolitical passivity, and an apparently permissive (but subtly coercive) morality of individual fulfillment."[30] This transformation

took place slowly but inexorably. On one side, businesses increasingly appealed to status anxieties as a means of expanding consumption that could only be resolved (advertising claimed) by owning some product. Consumption is driven primarily by what other people are consuming.[31] On the other side, status anxieties emerged in the population because of increasing social mobility, the arrival of immigrant groups with distinctive customs and status-markers that needed some lowest common denominator to coexist socially, increasing demands from women for recognition as social equals, and the shift within mainstream American culture from a Protestant morality of self-denial to a therapeutic ethos emphasizing personal self-realization.

Institutional changes pointing to a more fully integrated marketplace society prefigured the psychological and religious shifts. However, it is important not to see the latter simply as functional to or following automatically from the former. They happened in concordance, not in priority of one to the other. A series of legislative acts from the Civil War years set the scene for the creation of a truly national marketplace. The most important of these was the National Bank Act of 1863. This brought a modicum of homogeneity to bank note circulation throughout the United States. Previously, the costs of doing business across the national territory had been raised substantially by the existence of thousands of different bank notes circulating locally, many of which were counterfeit. The Bank Act not only helped define a circulation space for U.S. currency (complete with national symbols), but it also marked the beginning of a process whereby control over money would become a major lever for federal government regulation of the national economy.[32]

Also vital to development of the overall enterprise was the special legal status given to business in the years after the Civil War.[33] If the Civil War enriched businesses that made war material and the railroads that transported it, the emergence of a nationwide market in its aftermath also encouraged the growth of large firms to capture the economies of scale needed to prosper in it. These firms aggressively maneuvered through the federal courts to gain the same status for themselves as legal agents that the U.S. Constitution had hitherto restricted to individual persons: corporate personhood. In an 1886 Supreme Court case, *Santa Clara County v. Southern Pacific*, a corporation was recognized as equivalent to a person with respect to constitutional rights under the Fourteenth Amendment, the 1868 measure whose aim was to guarantee full personhood to freed slaves. Subsequently, businesses have managed

to gain First Amendment guarantees of political speech (including political campaign contributions), Fourth Amendment safeguards against
warrantless regulatory searches, Fifth Amendment double-jeopardy
protection, and Sixth Amendment rights to trial by jury. Arguably, businesses have acquired greater rights than individual persons, particularly when the capacity of corporations to protect their legal interests
is so much greater than that of the average individual. The net effect
of these protections was to free businesses from government oversight
and to limit judicial regulation of business conduct. In no other country
do businesses have such constitutional protection without government
direction.

Consumer capitalism received a major fillip from the concentration
of business in the hands of ever-larger firms. From the 1870s, American
economic growth was increasingly managed by large industrial firms
and investment banks such as J.P. Morgan. The first phase of industrial
concentration coincided with the beginning of the long economic depression in 1873. Many firms had overexpanded during the post–Civil
War years to meet the demands of the expanding national market. After realizing that excess capacity was forcing prices below the cost of
production, small businesses engaged in a flurry of pooling and merg-
ing. The result was a massive consolidation and centralization in a wide
range of industries, especially those in consumer goods. The most famous firm produced by this wave of consolidation was the Standard Oil
Company (kerosene production) of John D. Rockefeller. Though many
of the firms that engaged in takeovers and acquisitions began as family businesses, ownership and management quickly became separated in
the United States, unlike in many other countries where family control remained central to firm operations. Not only did this stimulate the
growth of a class of business "experts," complete with their own credentials (particularly the MBA), but it also led to an emphasis on spreading
ownership through the sale of shares to raise capital for investment and
to limit the control exercised by family interests.

The severe downturn of 1893–1896 brought a temporary halt to business concentration. But the question of the "trusts" had already become
a key issue in American national politics, dividing the country between
the northeastern "core," where concentration was favored or accepted,
and the rest of the country (the "periphery"), where concentration was
widely seen as an instrument of domination by northeastern capital.[34]
Antitrust legislation such as the Sherman Act of 1890 continued to give
the impression of a country committed to small-scale capitalism, but

this was not the case. The economic recovery of the period 1896–1905 marked the largest spate of mergers and acquisitions in U.S. history, larger in real terms than those in 1925–1929, the late 1960s, and the 1980s. The firms created included General Electric, Eastman Kodak, International Harvester, and U.S. Steel. The original shareholders were often "robber barons," such as Cornelius Vanderbilt, John D. Rockefeller, and Andrew Carnegie. Many of the negotiations over the buy-outs were negotiated by J.P. Morgan, the investment bank that dominated American finance throughout this period.[35] The close relationship between investment banks and businesses signified the rapid shift that had taken place in the American economy from family ownership to stock-market listings and managerial capitalism. Other countries lagged behind.[36]

By 1905 roughly two-fifths of U.S. manufacturing capital was controlled by 300 corporations, with an aggregate capitalization of $9 billion (at 2002 prices). Various stimuli caused the consolidations. One was the cost of mass production and the consequent need to exploit economies of scale that required large capital investments. Another, important in the early mergers, was the desire to eliminate competition and set monopoly prices. A third, and major, stimulus came from the desire to expand abroad. Bigger firms could better handle the initial costs and political difficulties involved in foreign direct investment. More important, once big through domestic expansion, firms could achieve greater profits, market share, and market dominance only through foreign expansion.[37] By 1914, a minimum of forty-one U.S. companies, mainly in the machinery and food processing industries, had constructed two or more factories abroad. That the greatest number after Canada was built in Britain—a country committed to free trade—shows that transport costs and meeting the demands of local foreign markets were more important goals in American foreign direct investment than simply avoiding tariff barriers.[38]

The creation of an integrated national economy, however, did not mean that the major sections or regions of United States agreed on the direction that American expansion beyond continental borders should take. Indeed, American political disputes over trade, investment, banking, and military policies have always taken a sectional cast given the different needs and expectations of the populations associated with the major sections of the country.[39] For example, the dominance of manufacturing in the Northeast from the Civil War to the 1950s encouraged a more positive attitude in that region toward tariffs on the import of manufactured goods than did the resource-based economy of the South, where such tariffs were seen as raising the costs of manufactured goods in the region without commensurate compensation to the needs of the regional economy. What is not at issue, however, is that such disputes have always taken place within a dominant discourse that has privileged the presumed benefits of continuing economic growth and the need to expand economically beyond current territorial boundaries to realize that objective. In other words, interregional disputes over foreign policy have been waged principally over means more than ends.

Certainly by the 1890s, the United States had, in the eyes of influential commentators and political leaders from all over the country, fulfilled its "continental destiny." The time was propitious, they believed, to launch the United States as a truly world power. One source of this tendency was a concern for internal social order. Not only did the late nineteenth century witness the growth of domestic labor and socialist movements that challenged the preeminence of business within American society, but it also saw a major period of depression and stagnation—the so-called Long Depression from the 1870s to 1896—in which profit rates declined and unemployment increased. This combination was seen as a volatile cocktail, ready to explode at any moment. Commercial expansion abroad was viewed as a way of both building markets and resolving the profits squeeze. Unemployment would decline, popular consumption would increase, and the appeal of subversive politics would decrease. Another source was more immediately ideological. U.S. history had been one of expansion: why should the continent set limits to the "march of freedom"? To Frederick Jackson Turner, the historian who had claimed the internal "frontier" as the source of America's difference from other societies, the United States could only be "itself" (for which one reserved the term "America," even though it applied to the entire continent, not just the part occupied by the United States) if it continued to expand. An invigorated American foreign policy and investment beyond continental shores were the necessary corollaries:

> For nearly three hundred years the dominant fact in American life has been expansion. With the settlement of the Pacific Coast and the occupation of the free lands (sic), this movement has come to a check. That these energies of expansion will no longer operate would be a rash prediction; and the demands for a vigorous foreign policy, for an interoceanic canal, for a revival of our power upon the seas, and for the extension of American influence to outlying islands and adjoining countries, are indications that the movement will continue.[40]

The outburst of European colonialism in the late nineteenth century was also important in stimulating American designs for expansion beyond continental limits. Home markets were no longer enough for large segments of American manufacturing industry, particularly the emerging monopolies such as Standard Oil and the Singer Sewing Machine Co. It was feared that if they didn't emulate the Europeans, American firms would be cut out of overseas markets that exercised an increasing spell over the American national imagination, such as China and Southeast Asia. The difference between the Americans and most of the Europeans, however, was that American business expansion did not necessarily entail territorial expansion. Guaranteed access was what they craved. Indeed, colonialism in the European tradition was generally seen as neither necessary nor desirable. Aside from being expensive for governments, in many cases it also involved making cultural compromises and deferring to local despots of one sort or another, costs many Americans were not anxious to bear. There was also the difficulty of squaring empire with a national identity that had long had a considerable anti-imperial component.[41]

It took some time for the United States to react to the outburst of European imperialism beginning in the 1870s. Indeed, not until the 1890s did the United States embark on an explicit imperialist project, as the post–Civil War integration of the U.S. economy concluded and the industrial and agricultural sectors entered recession. Undoubtedly for a time, and as a result of both economic imperatives and the desire to avoid lagging behind the Europeans (and Japanese) in "imperial prestige," the U.S. government did pursue territorial possessions. From around 1910 until the 1940s, however, a reaction against this set in (at least as far as territories outside Latin America are concerned), with a return to suspicion of territorial expansion. After the Second World War, security and stability considerations in the Cold War with the Soviet Union tended to trump anti-imperialism but in the context not so much of pursuing American territorial empire as in restricting the development of regimes seen as sympathetic to the Soviet Union: from Iran and Guatemala in the 1950s, to Cuba, Chile, Nicaragua, Angola, South Vietnam, and myriad other countries later on.

From the 1890s, the American approach to economic expansion tended to favor direct investment rather than portfolio investment and conventional trade. Advantages hitherto specific to the United States in terms of economic concentration and mass markets—the cost-effectiveness of large plants, economies of process, product and market integration—were exportable by large firms as they invested in overseas subsidiaries. For much of the nineteenth century, capital exports and trade were what drove the world economy. By 1910, however, a largely new type of expatriate investment was increasingly dominant: the setting up of foreign branches in other industrial countries by firms operating from a home base. U.S. firms were overwhelmingly the most important agents of this new trend. They were laying the groundwork for the globalization of production that has slowly emerged, with the 1930s and 1940s as the unique period of retraction.[42] The globalization of production through direct investment and strategic alliances and an allied loosening of financial markets from national-state control constitute the most significant driving forces behind contemporary globalization. The globalization of production has its roots in the American experience of foreign direct investment from the 1890s onward.

But American expansionism after 1896 was never simply economic. As with hegemony at home, it was always political and cultural. There was a "mission" to spread American values and the American ethos as well as to rescue American business from its economic impasse. These were invariably related to one another by American politicians and commentators as parts of a virtuous circle. Spreading American "values" led to the consumption of American products, American mass culture broke down barriers of class and ethnicity, and undermining these barriers encouraged the further consumption of products made by American businesses. American foreign policy largely followed this course thereafter, with different emphases reflecting the balance of power between different domestic interests and general global conditions: making the world safe for expanding markets and growing investment beyond the borders of the United States. America itself was sold as an idea. The field of public relations was a quintessential American art form from the start:

> American traders would bring better products to greater numbers of people; American investors would assist in the development of native potentialities; American reformers—missionaries and philanthropists—would eradicate barbarous cultures and generate international understanding; American mass culture, bringing entertainment and information to the masses, would homogenize tasks and break down class and geographical barriers. A world open to the benevolence of American influence seemed a world on the path of progress. The three pillars—unrestricted trade and investment, free enterprise, and free flow of cultural exchange—became the intellectual rationale for American expansion.[43]

The movement from a territorialized marketplace society to globalization was based on the prior existence of the "open borders" that characterized the American experiment. Though there were periodic political pressures to close the national territory to foreign products, people, and capital that emerged into prominence during times of declining firm profitability, rising unemployment, and social upheaval, the general trajectory of American politics from 1890 onward was toward opening up the national economy in relation to the rest of the world.

This reflected the origins of the United States as a set of settler colonies in which space was open to expansion rather than enclosed in defense from outsiders. Spatial orientations are of particular importance to understanding America, therefore, whether this is with respect to foreign policy or to national identity. It could be argued that a geographical imagination is central to all national political cultures. Imagining a coherent territorial entity containing a group of people with a common attachment to that territory has been crucial in the making of all national states. However, if all nations are imagined communities, then America is the imagined community par excellence.[44] The space of "America" was already created in the imaginations of the first European settlers en route to the "New World" as a space of openness and possibility.[45] It was not constructed and corrupted by centuries of history and power struggles as was Europe. Even now, America is a country that is easily seen as both "nowhere" and "pastless," constructed as totally modern and democratic against a European (or some other) country mired in a despotic history and stratified by the tyranny of aristocracy. The ideology of the American Dream, an ideology that stresses that anyone can be successful in acquiring capital and goods given hard work, luck, and unobtrusive government, marks the American historical experience as unique or exceptional. The dominance of this liberal ideology has meant that America has never had the revolutionary or reactionary traditions so prevalent in modern Europe. In narrowing the political field, the American liberal tradition protects the goals of the individual against the state and social collectivities.[46] Narratives of the history of America as a country of migrants successfully seeking a better way of life provide practical evidence for this imagination. The enslaved Africans and conquered Indians who made constructing the New World possible are largely absent from this vision, except as incidental characters or as barriers to be overcome.

The mindset of limitless possibility was reinforced by the myth of the frontier experience of individual social mobility and of the energy of a youthful country in contrast to the social stagnation and economic inequality of "old" Europe. Americans were free to settle in the vast expanse of "empty" land available on the frontier, discounting the presence of natives whose self-evident technological and religious "backward-ness" justified the expropriation of their land. All settlers were equal on the frontier (so the myth goes), and those who succeeded did so because of their own hard work, not through any advantage of birth. Clearly there are historiographic problems with this national myth, not the least the violent erasure of other people and their pasts that occurred as part of this geographical movement.[47] However, the myth has long remained a powerful aspect of American culture. The initial presumption was that as long as the frontier continued to expand, America would flourish. This mindset remained influential beyond the physical expansion of the United States across the continent, as "the frontier" was reconfigured around the necessity to expand the "American way" and "American good" beyond American shores. This was especially so in the years following the end of the Second World War when another power (the Soviet Union) offered a competing utopian rendering of political economy. The frontier story is not simply an elite construction told to the population at large, but is one retold and recycled through a variety of cultural forms: through mass education as well as through the media and in popular culture.[48]

The "frontier" character of the American economy—expanding markets for goods and opportunities for individuals beyond previous limits—figures strongly in the American stimulus to contemporary economic globalization. As I have argued, this is itself tied to a particular cultural image: the ethos of the consumer-citizen.[49] The American position in the Cold War of defending and promulgating this model ran up against the competing Soviet model of the worker-state. The resultant geopolitical order was thus intimately tied to the expression of American identity. This was spread through ideas of "development," drawing clearly on American experiences, first in such acts as the Marshall Plan to aid the reconstruction of Europe immediately after the Second World War, and then in the modernization of the "Third World" following the elements of a model of American society pushed most strongly during the short presidency of John Kennedy (1961–1962). The Age of High Mass Consumption that Kennedy (and Johnson) advisor Walt Rostow proclaimed as the end of history (and the goal of worldwide development efforts) was a reflection in the mirror that America held up to the world.[50]

This selective historical narrative points to how the foundations for globalization and the new geography of power associated with it were laid out initially in the United States in the late nineteenth century. But an alternative way of examining this process is to highlight analytically *why* the United States provided this grounding. A number of social, economic, and political features of American society have been responsible for underwriting the development of a vigorous "marketplace society," its widespread acceptance across social classes, and openness to expansion into the world at large. These have distinct echoes with elements of the argument about the construction of American hegemony in Chapter 3 but are raised here to reinforce the idea that American hegemony beyond U.S. national boundaries reflects the earlier achievement of the hegemony of marketplace society within the country itself. Capitalism has developed in different ways in different places. The fact that contemporary global capitalism reflects much more the characteristics of American marketplace society than it does other varieties of capitalism suggests the power exercised by this particular projection.

The Hegemony of Marketplace Society

The first feature is one identified by Karl Marx in the very last chapter of his book, *Capital* (Volume I). Marx contrasts the labor markets in Old World capitalism with that of the New World, noting at some length the lack of what he calls the "social dependence" of the laborer on the capitalist. In particular he suggests a corollary to this: because labor in the New World is in relative short supply and can always move into self-employment (as a farmer or artisan) "the degree of exploitation of labor of wage laborers remains indecently low. The wage laborer loses into the bargain, along with the relation of dependence, also *the sentiment of dependence on the abstemious capital*."[51] Marx never went into this difference in any depth. Perhaps he should have done so because, as Desai notes, the profitability of American capitalism based on high wage/high productivity/high profitability "foretold the new phase of capitalism."[52] Crucially, therefore, American experience of capitalism was totally different from that of Europe, with fateful consequences for predictions about the future acceptability of capitalism on the part of American wage laborers and the future trajectory of capitalism elsewhere when it came under American influence. Relative to Europe, greater economic freedom (ability to change jobs, move into independent employment, etc.) combined with greater political rights (at least for white males, whose status then became the standard to which all other groups [African Americans, women, etc.] aspired) produced greater acceptance of America as a "marketplace society":

A lack of feudal aristocracy meant that as westward expansion took place, land was not monopolized and parceled into latifundia in the USA, as it was in South America. This made the labor market tight. But there were also higher levels of literacy in the USA compared to Europe. To become a citizen, an immigrant had to demonstrate the ability to read, and some knowledge of the American Constitution. The higher literacy in America is thus a part of the concept of citizenship as a right, not as a gift.[53]

One corollary of the shortage of labor, particularly skilled labor, was an early emphasis on substituting capital (in the form of technology) for labor. From the 1820s onward, but with increased vigor after the Civil War, U.S. businesses pioneered new products and new process technologies. Making more efficient use of labor with assembly lines and Taylorist time-and-motion studies became the norm in U.S. industry much earlier than elsewhere. The structure of American business, increasingly in large vertically integrated firms with professional management, spurred rationalization of production through market segmentation and cost reduction. The U.S. system of patent protection encouraged invention by granting inventors a monopoly on the profits from their inventions for long periods of time when this was rare elsewhere: fourteen years in 1790 and seventeen years after 1861. It also restricted diffusion of inventions to other countries. Implicitly, it protected domestic producers, if more subtly than the relatively high U.S. tariffs on industrial products. Foreigners could license patents but, particularly with new industrial products, the patent system encouraged U.S. businesses to expand their operations abroad. They could bring novel products to new markets without fear of local competition. From the 1890s onward they were laying the groundwork for the explosion of globalized production in the 1980s and 1990s that by then included businesses with all manner of national origins. An initial disadvantage, in the sense of relatively expensive skilled labor, became an incredible advantage in the ease with which technologies were brought to market and accepted as natural improvements in workplace settings and in everyday life in general. Novelty and fashion in consumer products were thus built-in features of a capitalism that thrives on the duality of innovation and obsolescence.

The divisions between skilled and unskilled labor in social/ethnic backgrounds and wages splintered the world of labor, making it difficult for workers to unite in the way that laborers tended to in Europe, where the struggle for more stable and better working conditions combined with the struggle to extend the franchise. At least for white male workers in the United States, the franchise was already available by the late nineteenth century. Indeed, citizenship rights and worker-status served to divide the population of manufacturing workers rather than to unite them. This made it difficult to articulate a widely appealing vision at odds with that of marketplace society, even if the socialist and populist movements of the time had been able to go beyond short-term and workplace-related concerns. Mike Davis provides a brief summary of what had transpired:

> The premonitory signs of a political break in the middle [nineteen] eighties turned out to be spurious, as renewed ethnic and racial divisions undermined the embryonic unification of Eastern industrial workers. Fledgling "labor parties" collapsed, as workers were successfully reabsorbed into a capitalist two-party system that brilliantly manipulated and accentuated cultural schisms in the working class. The six per cent of the presidential vote that Gene Debs won in 1912—internationally acclaimed as the beginning of the Socialist Party's ascent to majority representation of the American proletariat—turned out to be its high-water mark, followed by bitter conflict and fragmentation. The socialist fratricide was, in turn, a manifestation and symptom of the profound antagonisms within the early twentieth-century labor movement between organized "native" craftsmen and unorganized masses of immigrant laborers.[54]

The sheer size of the American economy once the Civil War had settled the basis on which it would be built—the free industrial labor of the North versus the slavery of the agrarian South—also encouraged the growth of large nationally oriented companies. This was further stimulated by the latitude of the federal government toward monopoly ownership. The Republican federal administrations of the post–Civil War years saw themselves as facilitators of a national territorial economy irrespective of the concentration of economic power this entailed. The obstacles to exploiting the enormous but geographically diffuse resource base of the continental United States, the challenge of constructing railroads over long distances, and the difficulty of raising capital to finance such enterprises all conspired to encourage the growth of large-scale industrial enterprises. As these enterprises faced declining rates of profits by the turn of the twentieth century, they turned to expanding markets at home through the Fordist model and to expansion abroad through direct investment. In each respect they were avatars of post–Second World War globalization: large firms searching for markets and lower production costs by stimulating domestic consumption and relocating operations abroad.

The notion of the frontier as a moving line of settlement captures another important feature of the American "marketplace society." This was the ease with which people moved from place to place, putting down few roots and accepting the need to relocate when thrown out of work or when greater opportunities beckoned from somewhere else. To this day, Americans migrate much more readily than do people in other capitalist societies. The origins of the country as a settler colony, the availability of land on the frontier, the rapacious character of the resource economy, and the association between upward social mobility and geographical movement all contribute to the widespread acceptance of social change through mobility. The early establishment and spread of country-spanning information technologies, from the postal system to the telegraph and the telephone, also made movement relatively easier even as they stitched together a national marketplace. It could be said that Americans entered the "information highway" in colonial times and slowly stimulated technologies that expanded the spread of information across a continent and into the world at large.[55] The American unconscious has long been a technological one.

The American predisposition is to what can be called "exit" rather than "voice" or "loyalty" strategies of personal adjustment to social and economic change.[56] This makes Americans much more accepting of market-based decisions (such as plant closings, housing market fluctuations, pension fund crises, etc.) because of the possibility of salvation through movement—the grass might just be greener somewhere else. At the same time, the heterogeneous origins of the population put a premium on finding means of establishing status distinctions and political solidarities that are readily replicable wherever one moves and that are communicable across ethnic and social barriers. Social distinction is near impossible in the United States except by showing off your material possessions. The calculus of political action, therefore, tends to favor exit over voice. Why stay here to fight or engage in political action with others in similar situations in what may well be a losing battle if you can simply move on? The heroes of so many American movies (especially Westerns) are invariably drifters who never hang around town long enough to put down roots or run for office.

This tendency to personal flight rather than to political fight reflects another feature of "America" that has long and continues to set it apart from Europe: the strangely individualist and nationalist-populist character of much religion in America. The French traveler De Tocqueville commented most eloquently on this in *Democracy in America* (Volume II,

Part 3, Chapter 24). From the outset of settlement in Puritan New England, America was widely seen as a "new Israel" or "Promised Land," with Europe in the role of "Egypt." As religious refugees, the early New England settlers were particularly given to a visionary and crusading interpretation of their endeavors. They identified themselves with Good and elsewhere (and their opponents) as Evil. The frequent recourse to this religious language in American political rhetoric (not the least during the Cold War and in relation to the current "War on Terrorism") shows how an individualist American religious passion is readily made into a sort of populist political morality distant from its particular theological roots. What made this possible was that, "America was the first Protestant nation.... In effect, 'America' represents a unique and unified experiential system of belief, a sort of living and lived ideology that *one chooses in the same way that one chooses to enter into a denominational sect.*"[57] Though analogous to a purchase in the marketplace because this choice is between good and evil, there is no in-between. Thus, "everything that falls into the domain of the uncertain, the ambiguous, or the undetermined has to be rejected. The paradoxical result is that the populist and democratic individualism that was expressed in the plurality of sects becomes messianic: rigid, exclusive, and doctrinaire."[58]

In this "American religion of the nation" is found one of the major anchors of both marketplace society and openness to globalization: that individual choice is a sacred and not simply a profane imperative. This is not to say that religious criticism of consumerism has been absent in the United States. It is more that such critique was in conflict by the late nineteenth century with the increasingly popular idea in mainstream Protestantism that the profusion of goods was "God's gift to mankind."[59] In this way, the language of the marketplace was totally collapsed into that of religion. The emergence of self-realization through consumption can indeed be seen as a material manifestation of salvation, in which the marketplace substitutes for the hand of God in marking out the successful from the losers. This is religion as a form of "cargo cult," something that the appearance of Americans (and all their "stuff") frequently induced in the Pacific islands. The feeling was, "We will get all this stuff too, if only we worship their god or them." Ironically, however, even as they help justify marketplace society, religious belief and practice also provide a haven from its excesses by offering ideals of shared experience and collective action, if only of a localized variety, that point beyond it. Perhaps it is no coincidence, therefore, that the most vigorous challenges to the excesses of marketplace society in the United States often come from less fundamentalist religious groups, such as Quakers, Unitarians, and socially conscious Catholics.

A major boost to marketplace society has also come from popular American distrust of government. Unlike the Russians, French, or Chinese, who look to national government for solutions to their problems, Americans have tended always to look to spontaneous action. A widespread antigovernmentalism pre-dated the founding of the United States itself, particularly among those groups disadvantaged within marketplace society. Rather than attempting to control the national government as a means of offsetting their problems, Americans have a tendency to belittle it. This plays right into the hands of those who for more self-interested reasons wish to limit governmental powers to tax and redistribute wealth as much as possible. These people believe that the best government is that which governs least. Though obviously challenged by material realities that have led to expansion of central governmental powers (such as the Depression of the 1930s and the militarization of the Second World War, the Cold War, and now the "War on Terrorism") and by groups that favored a more powerful national government (from the Civil War Republicans to civil rights campaigners in the 1960s), there have been recurring periods in American history when governmental authority has been openly vilified and challenged.

Since the 1960s, the federal government as an agent of imposed values has been a persisting motif of American national politics. Initially the target of civil rights and antiwar movements, the federal government was vilified for its betrayal of the American political promise. Then, the social and cultural changes of the 1960s associated with the "sexual revolution," the challenge to racial hierarchies, and the questioning of consumerism by hippies and others provoked a "backlash populism," in which an American "silent majority" was recruited by a revitalized Republican Party to a culture war that denigrated the social "dependency" and political "nihilism" spawned by an overactive federal government. From this viewpoint, the federal government was occupied by ideological aliens at war with the "true" values of America. That many of the revolutionaries of the 1960s themselves became captives of the self-same commercial values that they had previously criticized (from selling Che Guevara tee-shirts to selling out in the job market), even as they turned off from regular politics, only compounds the terrible irony.[60] On both sides, therefore, markets came to be seen as more truly democratic than the elected government. This is what Thomas Frank has memorably named "market populism."[61]

The period since the 1970s has seen the deepening of strongly antigovernmental attitudes. In 1998, for example, President Clinton's pollster, Mark Penn, reported that in the twenty-five years after 1973, the percentage of American voters agreeing with the statement "The best government is the government that governs the least" went from 32 to 56 percent. Only 16 percent in 1998 agreed with the statement "Government should spend on social programs where necessary, because America is not about leaving everyone to fend for himself" [sic]. Just 12 percent of the Americans polled agreed with the statement "Government should solve problems and protect people from adversity." Of course, this consensus is one of voters, not the population in general. Other polls suggest that many who do not vote, particularly Latinos and African Americans, have more positive attitudes toward government.[62]

The negative American attitude toward government has always included two elements. One is a general anti-authoritarianism displayed in such phenomena as suspecting the Constitution of militating against local power, preference for states' rights over the federal government, the individualism of American political theory, and the fervent cult of gun ownership. The other is the belief that government not only is but in fact *should be* inefficient. Such phenomena as recall elections, term limits for representatives, initiative ballots, two-thirds majorities in legislatures for tax increases, and short terms of office are all designed to maintain a pervasive amateurism in politics and to frustrate the concentration of public power that might then be arrayed against particular groups. The net effect is to diminish the role of government and popular participation in its workings. Indeed, deliberately trying to undermine or bankrupt state and federal governments could be viewed as one of the strategies the administration of George W. Bush has used to rein in "runaway" (i.e., redistributive) government. The Reagan administration in the 1980s claimed that one of the side benefits of high federal budget deficits was that they discouraged attempts at using the federal government to regulate the private economy by encouraging demand-stimulus (Keynesian) measures. These would all violate the workings of the "magic of the marketplace." Ironically, it is a tradition that

> belittles America, that asks us to love our country by hating our government, that turns our founding fathers into unfounders, that glamorizes frontier settlers in order to demean what they settled, that obliges us to despise the very people we vote for.[63]

Yet, the growth of marketplace society in the United States has always depended to a large degree upon the policies of successive governments. It is a laissez-faire myth that marketplace society was itself entirely the fruit of the hidden hand of the market. Left to their own devices, people could be intensely suspicious of the logic of marketplace competition; they have often desired to undermine it or subvert it by challenging the claims made for particular products or the investment decisions made by particular firms.[64] But government often barred the way. If the beginnings of the national hegemony of marketplace society lie in the favorable judicial and legislative treatment of business in the late nineteenth century, its hold deepened with the adoption of demand-management economic policies in the aftermath of the Depression of the 1930s. The biggest strides in expanding the mass consumer economy came with the "Consumer's Republic" that emerged after the Second World War but that had its roots in the New Deal policies of the 1930s.[65] This was partly about using consumption to stimulate the national economy, but it was also about spreading the possibilities of consumption to segments of the population hitherto largely excluded from it. Questions of consumer protection from shoddy and dangerous products were not so central to government policy. Rather, it was increasing the aggregate purchasing power of consumers that was emphasized through such programs as insured housing loans and tax subsidies for various products. Reviving American capitalism depended on stimulating spending, not on encouraging personal saving. As a result, "Citizen consumers were made from the top down as well as the bottom up."[66]

Finally, the late nineteenth century, when American marketplace society had first taken its recognizably modern shape, was a time of significant disruption in the lives of American elites as well as the mass of ordinary people. The period from 1870 to 1900 saw more social and economic change in everyday lives in the United States than either before or since: vastly expanded foreign immigration, the growing economic role and political independence of women, extended agricultural crises, land and other speculative bubbles, disputes over monetary and trade regulation, the concentration of industrial ownership, and the growth of urban populations at the expense of the rural. This was a crucial period in the development of a truly national culture. It was a culture of consumption. Of particular importance, a new managerial-professional class emerged with the new businesses and was caught between older values relating to work and leisure and new imperatives associated with expanding markets and increasing profits. This new class, devoted to efficiency in production and to stimulating consumption, molded a new morality that converted salvation into self-fulfillment and the virtue of labor into the reward of gratification. "This late-nineteenth-century link between individual hedonism and bureaucratic organization—a link that has been strengthened in the twentieth century—marks the point of departure for modern American consumer culture."[67] This is not to say that this involved a simple elite conspiracy to dupe people as might be portrayed in a made-for-TV movie. That view of culture simply does not wash, because people are not that passive or uniformly stupid. Rather, consumption became a hegemonic "way of seeing," as advertising, conversation and social interaction, and devotion to status symbols converged to create a new cultural climate. This cultural brew has long since cast its spell over parts of the world where it certainly could never have been initiated.

"Americanism," the peculiar character of the American society and economy and the glue of consumer culture that increasingly bonded them together, therefore, has a number of distinctive roots in the American historical experience. But they came together to define a particular national culture that was more or less in place by the 1890s and early 1900s. This was fatefully reinforced by the "Consumer's Republic" of the 1950s and its recruitment into the ideological geopolitics of the Cold War.[68] It has been the projection of this hegemony from home, so to speak, out into the world at large that has set the political basis for the globalization of the world economy over the past thirty or so years.

The various elements of what brought about and reinforced marketplace society in the United States were not present elsewhere, at least not in their particular "mix." That mix is what set the United States apart. But under American influence, many of its consequences for social, economic, and political organization have become the global "common sense," ruling popular debates and restricting policy options around the world. This is the essence of hegemony beyond national boundaries: to project what you take for granted is the "best" way of doing things, and to cajole, co-opt, collaborate, and enroll others into not simply doing what you want but making them think that this is actually what they want. I continue with this story in Chapter 6. First, in Chapter 5, I address the connections between American political constitutionalism and globalization, both with respect to the alleged mimesis of the latter with the former and to the difficulties that the U.S. form of government entails for either the construction of empire or the future sustenance of American hegemony at home and abroad.

Conclusion

The U.S. commitment to external expansion to manage conflicts at home and serve the commercial ethos of dominant social groups underpins the character of U.S. hegemony. Moving from a peripheral to a central position within world politics, the United States brought to that position an ethos established in its history as a peculiar national state with a relatively weak and divided government. Its absolute economic predominance and a number of key institutional changes produced in the critical years during and after the Second World War allowed the successful projection of the American hegemony beyond its shores (see Chapter 6). This hegemony rested on the geographical spread of American marketplace society as manifested in globalization. For a long period of time, expansion seemed to produce not only economic but also political returns for the American system. A later chapter (Chapter 8) questions whether this is any longer the case. The fragmentation and increasing entropy of the American governmental system that produced U.S. hegemony strongly suggest, however, that achieving centralized control and direction to reinstate American power beyond American shores (or even within them) will be no easy task (see Chapter 5). This is particularly the case when, as I suggest in Chapter 6, the world that U.S. hegemony has made is less and less subject to any singular central direction, from wherever it might come.

5   U.S. Constitutionalism or Marketplace Society?

The uniqueness of the United States is often attributed to the structure of its political organization rather than to its political economy. As the first fully modern polity built from scratch, with reference to classical and early modern political theories of republicanism and liberalism, the United States has often been presented as a constitutional model for the world at large. The strand of American political thought associated most closely with President Woodrow Wilson—arguably the founder of modern American political science and the prophet of American global institutionalism—lends itself to world politics not only as a model for emulation but also as a representation of the threefold division of political powers—executive, legislative, and judicial—irrespective of their institutionalization in the specific form taken in the United States (see Chapter 4). From this viewpoint, American hegemony rests on the projection of its mode of political organization onto a world scale.

Because the U.S. government is the most significant political force in world politics, especially since the collapse of the Soviet Union, the idea of the United States bringing to bear its "constitutional order" on world affairs has a certain plausibility. Certainly, there is logic to the separation of executive, legislative, and judicial functions of government that can be seen as recapitulated in the seemingly inchoate practices of world politics beyond American shores. From a certain point of view, there is a global constitutional order that provides the political-juridical foundation for globalization by, for example, making available mechanisms for resolving trade disputes (judicial), negotiating investment rules (legislative), and enforcing order (executive).

The analogy to a division of powers is so generic, however, without any necessary connection to a specifically American hegemony, that it is difficult to see why this feature of the American experience, rather than the achievement of marketplace society, is sometimes singled out as the defining trait and modus operandi of American hegemony. Even Philip

Bobbitt, who sees the end of "epochal wars" as the moments when new "constitutional orders" for world politics are imposed by the victorious states, draws back from pushing the analogy too far.[1] In the aftermath of the "Long War" from 1914 to 1990, he sees the United States as imposing its vision of a "market-state" on the rest of the world, but with allowance for institutional variation among states as long as the overall goal of "opportunity" is maintained. If he does not account for why it is a "market-state" that the U.S. government now sponsors, neither does he insist that there is a direct analogy between the U.S. domestic constitutional order and the new global one. Indeed, at one point he suggests the limitations of such an analogy specifically in relation to the failure of Woodrow Wilson (and his strategist, Colonel House) after the Treaty of Versailles, when he writes: "Wilson and House had attempted to reform the deep structure of state sovereignty. Ironically, it was precisely the American system of limited sovereignty that crushed their plans, for it was the U.S. Senate's refusal to consent to the treaty that prevented ratification of the Versailles agreement and then thwarted U.S. participation in the League of Nations."[2]

I take up the claim to an emerging identity between the structure of U.S. political organization and global "constitutional order" here with reference to the actual workings of American constitutionalism. That American political arrangements can be seen as implicit in the political-juridical order of globalization (if it has such an order) is deeply problematic. To say that an analogy can be drawn between the divided and decentralized system of rule that is characteristic of the United States and that of contemporary globalization, as if the latter somehow were entailed by the former, is appealing but mistaken. I also move on from this account to point out some of the serious problems of the contemporary American system of government. This is important with respect both to questioning the exaggerated portraits of the effectiveness of U.S. governmental power in much contemporary writing—in which it takes on God-like or, more frequently and more effectively, Satan-like qualities—and the difficulties confronting the U.S. government in regaining control over the very processes of globalization and the associated new geography of power that it previously helped unleash. In sum, the American form of government is neither correctly seen as the constitutional form underpinning recent globalization nor as a political system responsive to the tensions between a globalizing world economy on the one hand and the U.S. territorial economy and population on the other.

American Federalism

The American political scientist Samuel Huntington once referred to the United States as a "Tudor polity."[3] By this he meant that the U.S. Constitution was not so much a product of the eighteenth-century America in which it was written as a formal restatement of principles of national government that had arisen during the reign of the Tudors in sixteenth-century England. Unlike France, where power was concentrated in the hands of the absolutist monarch, in Tudor England power was dispersed across a wide range of institutions: the monarchy, the two houses of Parliament, the Church of England, and a host of lesser bodies such as the municipal corporations and the Inns of Court. A web of customs and traditions held the whole fabric in place; it was called the Ancient Constitution, although it was neither old nor formally written down in a single document. Likewise in the United States under the Constitution, power was dispersed and decentralized, only now it was formalized in a written constitution. As in Tudor England, but without the decisive role of the monarch, power in America was divided both horizontally between the branches of central government and vertically between the constituent units, in this case the states, which, in coming together following American independence, had created the larger (nation-) state itself.

American Constitutionalism

James Madison, the main architect of the codification of the system of divided public power, saw particular virtue in the tension between the executive branch and the legislature. He represented that ideology within the Anglo-American world of the eighteenth century which saw politics eternally poised between law and public virtue on the one hand and tyranny on the other, with the advantage in recent years clearly going to the latter. The question of sovereignty was central to this world-view. Rather than resting with the monarch or with the population through representative institutions, it was seen as resting *in* the law. This was the basis to constitutionalism, the idea that the basic law had to be codified and placed more or less beyond the reach of the institutions it brought into existence. "Madisonian" federalism, therefore, starts with a formal constitution in which the distribution of powers between branches and levels of government is formally codified and with little possibility, except through judicial review and a cumbersome process of amendment, of adapting the Constitution in response to political and economic change. Its basis in law leads to textual exegesis as a permanent part of the political process. In other words, politics in considerable part is reduced to disputes over the meaning and scope of the various sections of the Constitution and the Amendments to it (including the Bill of Rights).[4]

American "centralizing federalism," to use Riker's phrase, came into existence in the historical context of a colonial war of independence and was a compromise between "nationalists" and "provincials" once the war was underway.[5] The former stood for a powerful central government, whereas the latter represented the view that more powers should be vested in the states than at the center. Only the pressure to aggregate resources and coordinate rebellion led to the adoption of the U.S. Constitution. In the absence of something as equally compelling as a colonial rebellion, Riker sees little incentive for existing territorial units, such as nation-states, to throw in their lot with a federal supranational authority. Many of the federal schemes invented and imposed around the world over the past century without some local or world-regional military pressure to counteract disorder and dissatisfaction have either not lasted or been wracked by instability. New Zealand, Yugoslavia, the West Indies, Czechoslovakia, and Nigeria are a few examples of this.

Federal constitutionalism, however, has had a number of advantages for a geographically large, culturally diverse, and conflict-ridden polity such as the United States. First, it provided a political means of overcoming fundamental economic differences, particularly those over slavery, by imposing a "pure" territorialism in which each state, irrespective of area or population size, had equal representation in the Senate, and representatives to the House were drawn from single-member districts whose territorial interests they were to represent at the federal level. This provided a second advantage: different governmental functions could be allocated at different levels—federal, state, and municipal— depending on the match between the spatial scope (or necessary size of territory) of a given function and the level of government that seemed most appropriate to it. Vesting directional authority at the federal level was a particularly important feature of the Constitution in contradistinction to the weak central government of the Confederation it replaced in 1789, and notwithstanding the popular contemporary American folklore that the Founders saw the federal government as only a "necessary evil."[6]

Third, territorial representation served to entrench the idea of individual representation as the basis for representative democracy. The legal focus on the aggregation of individual voters into single-member districts that elect *local* representatives obscured the possibility of group rights and ideological politics.[7] In this way, the American conception of the "collective" has been defined territorially in terms of the formal aggregation of individual votes, rather than socially with respect to distinctive group identities and interests.

Fourth, constitutionalism institutionalized a mechanical balance of powers between the various branches of government. Indeed, deadlock between the executive (President) and legislative (Congress) branches was written into the system. American constitutionalism, therefore, is more about limited and limiting government than about balancing the concentration of power and personal liberty.[8] It has become popular to criticize the "deadlock" in Washington,[9] but this was in fact part of what Madison had in mind. He feared concentrated public power and its threat to private property from the propertyless more than he feared deadlock within the federal government.[10] That this was at odds with the republican belief in the need to withstand the corrupting influence of private interests, particularly as articulated in the essentially Christian view of the Founders in the possibility of a "perpetual republic" that could resist corruption and decline from public virtue, was perhaps the main contradiction within American constitutionalism from the start.[11] Unlike Europe, however, where constitutional regimes have come and gone with a certain rapidity, the American regime has remained in place since the late eighteenth century. In this context it is the United States and not Europe that appears as the idealistic "old" system.[12]

Fifth, and finally, the focus on a founding document encourages a scripturelike attitude toward it. This is a very important part of socialization into American citizenship. The U.S. Constitution is a key element in the "Americanism" or civic nationalism by means of which diverse peoples have been inducted into a common identity as "Americans." Along with the flag and the national anthem, discovered as powerful symbols in the 1890s, the Constitution embodies a firm datum for "naturalizing" people into belonging to a national enterprise that is thought of as having sacred, more than secular, roots. It also provides the foundation for a national political consensus within narrow ideological limits that De Tocqueville contrasted to the vibrant oppositionalism that characterized the European politics of his day.[13] Americanism based on constitutionalism begets the "Un-Americanism" around which so much American politics has been organized in this century. Every political position outside of the "mainstream" is thereby made potentially sub-versive of the Constitution itself.[14]

U.S. Hegemony and American Constitutionalism

The possibility of attributing the basis to American hegemony to this po-litical model as opposed to the model of marketplace society has always been problematic, yet some commentators interpret U.S. hegemony and its effects largely in such terms. Most important, of recent commentators on the relationship between the United States and globalization, Hardt and Negri argue that contemporary globalization directly reflects the singular American constitutional motivation that there is no role for the "transcendence of power."[15] This fits neatly with their poststructuralist imperative to avoid transcendence, even while, as Marxists, they try to rescue universalism.[16] It necessarily leads to seeing globalization as the projection of American constitutional order onto the world as a whole. Of course, there is more to their intellectual apparatus than solely this emphasis on *Empire* as a scaled-up version of American constitutional-ism. To them, *Empire* is a new paradigm that issues from modernity's transfiguration into postmodernity. It leaves in its wake both sovereign states and imperialism. It has no "center." So, it "is not American," even if the United States provides the political inspiration for its division of powers. But like the United States' constitutional system, it is a "sys-temic totality" in which "power has no actual and localizable terrain or center. Imperial power is distributed in networks through mobilized and articulated mechanisms of control." A world market provides the necessary context for the dawn of *Empire*, a new "*decentered* and *deter-ritorializing* apparatus of rule that progressively incorporates the entire global realm within its open expanding frontier."[17] What could be more American than that?

Rather than turning to the specifics of political economy to explain how the world is becoming a "smooth space" across which capital, peo-ple, goods, and ideas move freely—albeit with barriers of class, race, and ethnicity that by and large do not follow the boundaries of modern states—Hardt and Negri invoke a universal conflict between capital and labor. *Empire* is a response to labor struggles evoked by exploitation, but the structural form it takes is modeled on the U.S. Constitution. From this viewpoint, U.S. sovereignty was always postmodern in never ac-cepting territorial limits. *Empire* follows where it led. To Hardt and Negri, therefore, it is the U.S. Constitution that is the defining essence of the influence of the United States on the world at large. *Empire* is the world made in an American constitutional image. Specifically, the U.S. doctrine of the separation of powers, they claim, originated in a republican reading of the ancient Roman principle of balancing monarchic, aristocratic, and democratic power by assigning such roles, respectively, to the executive, judicial, and legislative branches. Under contemporary globalization, an analogous "mixed constitution" has gained a de facto hold over world politics presumably because of the previous power of the United States. This mixed constitution consists of a

> monarchic unity of power and its global monopoly of force; aristocratic articulations through transnational corporations and nation-states; democratic-representational *comitia*, presented again in the form of nation-states along with various kinds of NGOs, media organizations and other 'popular' organisms.[18]

Within this domain the restless pursuit of investment opportunities by capital and resistance from labor (the "multitude") leads to a continuous fragmenting and recombination of social identities. Although this is how a specifically "postmodern" world of *Empire* differs in appearance from the "modern" world of settled identities (particularly national ones) that came before, it is the political-juridical framework that defines the foundation of the new regime of accumulation associated with globalization.

But how fruitful is the constitutional analogy between the contemporary globalizing world and the United States in explaining globalization if U.S. constitutional arrangements are in fact very different from the ideal that Hardt and Negri allege is actually empirical, and if the spread of such arrangements is precluded by their very particularity, specifically their inherent territoriality in a globalizing world that defies bounded spaces? If their model of American constitutionalism is mistaken, then its analogous forms in *Empire* will be also.

In fact, the American constitutional model is entropic and deterritorialized precisely because it is based on a radical striation and territorial layering of institutional power designed to balance regional interests, political identities, and cultural practices. Thus, a direct analogy to the American system at a global scale would involve a similarly radical geographical division rather than the smooth placelessness that Hardt and Negri insist defines the nature of *Empire*. Geographical variation is philosophically entrenched in American constitutionalism. Consequently, seeing the American division of powers as analogous or homologous to the division of powers within a centerless *Empire* misses exactly what is characteristic of the "actually-existing" postmodern polity they invoke as its inspiration.

Though the League of Nations and the United Nations both incorporated American ideas about the division of powers within them, both bodies' failure to have a major impact on world politics, absolute in the first case and relative in the second, suggests how limited the effect of American constitutionalism has been beyond national boundaries. The spread and acceptance of American hegemony have been uneven and subject to frequent challenge. Nevertheless, despite the ups and downs of the Cold War and U.S. involvement in it, the American model of liberal capitalism and the federal system of governance associated with it have emerged as the dominant ideological elements in the hegemony that now governs the world after the Cold War. This is not to say that the Wilsonian model of a world order built on the American example has been realized. Indeed, in practice, American foreign policy has tended to favor the defense and extension of liberal capitalism over the spread of any sort of democratic ethos.[19] In other words, it has encouraged economic globalization over Madisonian federalism, notwithstanding the rhetorical support given to the latter. There are good reasons why this has been so.

There are a number of major problems with the U.S. model of federalism that deserve wider discussion. The first is the inflexibility of the division of powers and the difficulty of revising it within a rigid constitutionalism. The second is its reliance on consensus more than oppositional politics. The third is its hierarchical territorialism. The fourth is its reliance on folk beliefs about historical chosenness. In combination, these are very serious limitations to Madisonian federalism as either a model or an image of constitutional order for the world beyond American shores.

Inflexibility. The United States is in many ways a "frozen republic" in which political change is held hostage to a system designed in the late eighteenth century to bind together in a limited way a set of distinctive and often hostile subunits, the states.[20] The vaunted "checks and balances" system between the branches and levels of government serves to frustrate collective adjustment to changing times. Unlike, for example, the more flexible British system of government that slowly emerged in the eighteenth and nineteenth centuries in response to changing material conditions, the American system was designed to restrain institutional change in the face of new conditions of life.

Inflexibility has several problematic consequences today. One is that the system is only partially democratic. Though open to public gaze, institutions such as the U.S. Senate, the Electoral College, and the judiciary are essentially elite-based, the result of attempts at democratizing predemocratic institutions but still largely based on appointment and privilege. The Senate represents the equality of the states, not the equality of citizens. Election to it requires resources that tend to restrict membership to wealthy individuals capable of financing statewide campaigns. The Electoral College, notorious after the 2000 presidential election, filters direct election of the president through a system that weights states with smaller populations more than larger ones. It was invented to give the South greater representation in presidential contests than it deserved on the basis of its white population alone. That it still functions is testimony to the essential conservatism of American political institutions. The appointed federal judiciary has powers of legislative review that involve constant reference to the founding document and subsequent amendments. It is a fundamentally conservative institution. Amending the Constitution is also next to impossible without a very large nationwide majority of support. It requires a two-thirds vote of both houses of Congress and three-quarters of the state legislatures by simple majority.

Finally, and more controversially, incomplete power, such as is built into the U.S. separation of powers, can potentially reduce both public accountability and the possibility of coordinated policy making. De Tocqueville, often quoted to justify the separation of powers and a high degree of decentralization as universal norms, in fact thought of American federalism as suitable only in social conditions such as those he saw on his American travels.[21] He also was a powerful advocate of a strong national government with "its own fiscal basis and capacity to act upon individual citizens directly (by force if necessary) independent of its member-states."[22] Using a *Titanic* analogy, however, Lazare makes the point both colorfully and with a degree of exaggeration that De Tocqueville's expectation has not been realized: "Rather than placing the navigator in one part of the ship, the captain in a second, the helmsman in a third and seeing to it that they all worked at cross-purposes, modern democratic theory [from the nineteenth and twentieth centuries] called for them to be placed in a single room so they could coordinate their actions in case an iceberg loomed suddenly ahead."[23] Some sort of "constrained parliamentarianism" may provide a better model for the separation of powers than the U.S. one, with the law-making powers of a parliament "constrained by other institutions of democratic self-government, including popular referenda on the national level and the representation of provincial governments in federal systems."[24]

In actuality, the separation of powers is hardly as immobilizing as Lazare contends.[25] There is considerable cooperation between the various branches. If anything, U.S. history suggests that the system—contrary to Woodrow Wilson's opinion as founder of American political science rather than as president of the United States—has been to the net benefit of the presidency and to central direction, particularly from the Depression of the 1930s until the end of the Cold War.[26] It is the control of the two different branches by different political parties that has tended to produce the greater immobility of the federal government in recent years. Be that as it may, many commentators and reformers see the U.S. separation of powers in a largely negative light: as frustrating decisive government and protecting vested interests.

Consensus Politics. De Tocqueville, in his writings on American democracy and the impact of the French Revolution, plausibly claimed that the blessing of the United States and the misfortune of Europe lay in the "living intellectual unity" of the United States.[27] This gave American politics a set of shared presuppositions that was—and if commentators such as Larry Siedentop are correct, is still—lacking, for example, in Europe.[28] Above all, however, Americans shared an intellectual constraint, furnished, De Tocqueville thought, by a widely shared faith in the divine, which limited that questioning of institutions he associated with the excesses of the French revolution. Yet, one critical test of modern democracy is the extent to which opposition is not only allowed but also nurtured within institutions. If the century after De Tocqueville established anything at all, therefore,

> it is that we must reverse Tocqueville's terms and take as essential traits of democracy what he imputed to the consequences of the revolutionary accident—whether with regard to internal discord concerning the forms of government or to debates over the fundamental issues. Since the day in which Tocqueville wrote, neither intellectual unity nor constraints on intelligence have appeared as irreducibly original contributions to the democratic universe. To hold men [*sic*] together by means of their opposition, to engage in endless appraisal of the signification uniting them in society: in the final analysis, these are the crucial properties of democracy in the Old World. . . . Contrary to Tocqueville's earliest American vision, democracy is not the profound agreement of minds; it is the merciless dissolution of meaning and antagonism of ideas.[29]

The historic basis of the American model in widespread social consensus over values, even though today that consensus has long since receded, nevertheless sets limits to the export of a constitutional model that requires identification with a set of beliefs associated with a particular set of institutions. At a global scale, an oppositional model of democracy in which everything is in question, including the institutions themselves, seems more appropriate. Within the European Union, for example, an argument could be made that what is required to reduce the current "democratic deficit" is not a formal federal structure so much as openings for systematic access to and opposition within existing institutions, in order to work toward a common good through contest and critique.[30]

Hierarchical Territorialism. Madisonian federalism rests on a fervent commitment to territoriality as a spatial organizing principle, notwithstanding Hardt and Negri's vision of it as essentially without geography. Two tiers of government, one (the states) nested within the other (the federation), are designed to provide the public goods and services demanded by a citizenry in conformity with the most efficient mode of administration. Historically, as demands on government changed, the balance shifted from the states to the federal government, although recent attacks on the power of the federal government have led toward some devolution of power to the states. In a globalizing world, however, the pattern of private *and* governmental externalities is less territorial than before. Transnational forces create communities of interest and defense that are not well accounted for within a territorial conception of the public realm. In this setting, the possibility of neatly allocating different regulatory, distributory, and allocative functions to different sizes of territorial units is much reduced. As the span of control governing various economic and cultural activities conforms more to webs of interconnection between regional nodes widely scattered in space, the territorial structure of American federalism offers less and less purchase on the "real world" to which it must adjust. Finally, beyond the American context, construction of a federal model of transnational democracy would require centralized action, and the danger is that it would create an even greater "top-down" flow of privately organized power than that which characterizes the American system today.

Historical Chosenness. The term "manifest destiny" was coined in the 1840s to refer to the civilizing/constitutionalizing mission inherent in the progressive expansion of the United States from its eastern origins to the Pacific Ocean. This reflected an older sense of providential mission that inspired early European settlers and their descendants, the Founding Fathers. But it also had its origins in the defence of colonialism offered by seventeenth-century political theorist John Locke to the effect that those who used land productively (i.e., in systematic agriculture) were those who had the right to own it. Settlers could thus claim land if the natives were defined as *un*engaged in its productive agrarian use.[31] Manifest destiny had two contradictory impulses. One was to point to the uniqueness of America and, in particular, its Constitution; the other was to suggest its own universal appeal. Either way, U.S. federalism has always had a set of cultural loadings that differentiate it from a merely technical or instrumental "solution" to the "problem" of governance. These came out of the American historical experience.

First, balance between the states (and, thus, within the system) depended historically on the expansion of the whole. Madison believed that expansion by addition of new states was the secret to preventing any one region, faction, or interest from dominating and subverting the whole. In practice, this is not how it worked, because the conditions for inclusion of new states—particularly whether slavery would be allowed or not—provided a major impetus for the crisis that gave rise to the Civil War and the subsequent enlargement of the powers of the federal government relative to the states. Second, the Constitution quickly established itself as the key to American identity. This was a political identity that rested on belief in and subscription to the Constitution. Third, there was a racial element in the continuities that were drawn between American expansion and the civilizing proclivities of America's English forebears. Anders Stephanson nicely captures the mutual dependence of American constitutionalism and American colonial expansion into the interior of North America:

> There was a huge and empty land here to be transformed. The new nation was a condensation of all that was good in the hitherto most advanced and westward of civilizations, namely the British.... A set of simple symbols was required that would distill the past and at the same time proclaim the future. The extraordinary rapidity with which the Revolution was *monumentalized* actually showed the urgency: the revolutionary avant-garde turned into the Founding Fathers, biblical patriarchs, Washington presiding as a near-deity, all evoked with ritual solemnity every July 4.[32]

Finally, the U.S. model of federalism has relied on a fusion of two distinctive understandings of a political community that is neither readily transferable elsewhere nor expresses a coherent definition of political community suitable for global adoption. On the one hand, the division of national space into purely territorial units rests on a Cartesian rendering of terrestrial space as an abstract surface upon which political representation can be inscribed. On the other hand, this division is justified on Aristotelian grounds as a world of particular places in which different modes of political attachment and contrasting ideals of justice, equality, and liberty can be pursued within the broad confines of a wider constitutional framework.[33] The tension between these two conceptions of political space has long riven American political life, from conflict over slavery to contemporary disputes over state-level boycotts of trade with and investment in specific foreign countries. Yet, the "pure" territorialism of the U.S. model relies for political justification in large part not so much on its aggregation of individual voices as on an appeal to different political traditions associated with different places (regions and localities).

In any number of respects, therefore, U.S. federalism is not easily disentangled from its particular roots. Its projection by analogy into the structure of globalization is anything but enlightening. Indeed, it is positively misleading in directing attention away from sustained analysis of the *lack* of adoption of established institutional forms under globalization and missing the marketplace-society basis to the decentering and diffusion of power that is a noted feature of globalization. In interpreting globalization as an extension of American constitutionalism, authors such as Hardt and Negri are giving it a territorial solidity and stability that their own claims about the diffuse and fragmented nature of power under globalization explicitly contradict.

Madisonian Entropy and the Political Limits to American Hegemony

The American system of government, as set up under the influence of the ideas and compromises of the Founders, has always been in tension with the centralized conduct of world politics. Not only has such a vast country in population and area had distinct regional economies with different identities and interests that had somehow to be managed collectively, but the episodic yet undeniable trend toward an increasingly powerful central government has had to cope with a constitutional framework designed to frustrate the achievement of concentrated public power. It may well be that "the United States is too big to be governed."[34]

But the federal division of powers between the states and the central government and the separation of powers at the center between the legislative, executive, and judicial branches also pose a major challenge to the creation of any coherent response to the dilemmas facing the United States in a globalizing world. A governmental system set up to facilitate the expansion of private economic interests yet restrict the exercise of collective political power has built-in disadvantages for dealing with adjustments to a new world economy in which it is no longer the singular center. Those approaches to understanding world politics that presume all states to be close kin to a Jacobin French state are thus dangerously deficient when they consider the United States in that light.[35]

Philip Cerny has provocatively referred to the particular architecture of the U.S. state as giving rise to the problem of what he calls "Madisonian entropy" in the face of external challenges to American economic well-being.[36] By this he means that the "US system of government . . . is characterized by a great deal of energy which is absorbed or dissipated through the internal workings of the structure, and which is unavailable for the policy tasks which modern states must perform."[37] In physics, entropy refers to the measure of energy unavailable for work within a system. Madisonian entropy signifies the dominant influence of James Madison on the final form taken by U.S. institutions at the time of ratification of the U.S. Constitution.

In Cerny's view the U.S. geopolitical position during the Cold War was based on three institutional developments within the U.S. government that went around the blockages built into the system. Absent these developments, however, the institutional fragmentation characteristic of U.S. government will return to frustrate the capacity to rescue the country from internal conflicts through external expansion, the leitmotif of American foreign policy from the late eighteenth century to the present but achieving realization only after the Second World War. The first was the development of the "imperial presidency" in which the president emerged as a monarchlike figure short-circuiting the other branches of government because of the imminent threat of nuclear war and the need to plan rapid responses to foreign crises.[38] The second was the long-term maintenance of a cross-party consensus about most major foreign-policy issues with congressional deference to presidential authority over foreign affairs. Third, was the superior capacity of the federal executive branch to manage trade and monetary issues without interference from the legislative branch or the states.

Each of these has been undermined. The Vietnam War began the erosion of both the imperial presidency and bipartisan consensus between the Democratic and Republican parties over the conduct of foreign affairs. The Watergate scandal in the 1970s and the Iran-Contra scandal in the 1980s further undermined presidential authority to carry out foreign policy initiatives unimpeded by Congress. The attempted impeachment of President Clinton in the late 1990s, though over his sexual proclivities rather than anything related to policy implications, has further weakened the office. The intervention of the Supreme Court to declare George W. Bush the winner of the 2000 presidential election, even though he had fewer popular votes than Al Gore, has probably further undermined presidential (and judicial) legitimacy, at least in the eyes of those whose votes were discounted.[39] Weakened political parties, in which politicians increasingly represent geographical and sectoral or single-issue constituencies, have retreated from the consensus that marked U.S. foreign policy in the 1950s and 1960s. The outcomes of elections are now largely determined by incumbency and the ability to raise funds from private means or from lobbyists.[40] Influence can be openly bought through block voting by ethnic and immigrant groups or campaign contributions from business interests to impede policies that might be in the "national interest" but that would damage random foreign countries or business investments. Classic examples would be how current policies on Cuba, Taiwan, and Israel are directly responsive to electoral vetoes and campaign contributions by interested parties such as Cuban immigrants, Taiwanese business interests, and Jewish voters.

More directly economic in nature, though the U.S. dollar has retained considerable importance in the post–Bretton Woods system of floating exchange rates, its liberation from a system of fixed exchange rates by the U.S. government in 1971 removed the central plank from the international stage upon which the domestic financial power of the federal executive branch rested. Markets have replaced central-governmental power in this critical area, notwithstanding the emergence of a Washington–Wall Street nexus during a Clinton Administration intent on *trying* to use the U.S. dollar as a weapon for national economic growth.[41] In the judicial realm, since the 1980s the Supreme Court has shifted the balance of power in interpreting the Constitution away from the federal government toward the states and to the court itself.[42] For example, using the common law doctrine of sovereign immunity, the Supreme Court under Chief Justice William Rehnquist shielded the states from damages for age discrimination, disability discrimination, and the violation of patents, copyrights, trademarks, and fair labor standards. Emboldened, the various states are also striking out on their own to attract external investment, pursue industrial and trade policies, and place limits (for example, with respect to immigration controls) in areas traditionally reserved to the federal government. The state of California, for example, which on its own constitutes the world's seventh largest economy, has ten trade representative offices around the world, from Mexico City to Tokyo. It has tried to create its own immigration policy, operates its own welfare and healthcare systems for the poor, and passes laws restricting investments by the state in other countries and protesting U.S. policies on human rights abroad.[43] With states asserting their powers, and given the balance of regional interests in Congress, the achievement of a national industrial policy or coherent national-level response to the globalization of labor markets seems next to impossible. As Cerny concludes:

> The United States may not be a 'stalemate society,' to borrow Stanley Hoffman's well-known description of France under the Third Republic. Indeed, American society is, as always, energetic and creative on many levels. What absorbs and dissipates that energy, however, is the complexity, duplication and cross-purposes which were not only built into the Madisonian system, but which have also been increasing faster than the problem-solving capacity of the system, especially where international interdependence is concerned. The US suffers from a kind of dynamic immobilism, creative stagnation or stalemated superstructure, which I have called Madisonian entropy.[44]

Conclusion

In this chapter I have shown that because of its design and devolopment, the American form of government is not best seen as either a constitutional form underpinning recent globalization or as adaptive to the friction between a globalizing world economy on the one hand and the U.S. national territory on the other. The analogy that can be drawn between the divided and decentralized system of rule characteristic of the United States and that of contemporary globalization, as if the former somehow entailed the latter, is attractive but fallacious. Not only are the nature of globalization and the geography of power it occasions hardly mimetic of the territorial form central to American constitutionalism, they are also alien to its very qualities. Moreover, rather than a diffuse but efficient organization of power (such as that of Hardt and Negri's *Empire*), it is a system with serious inefficiencies, built-in redundancies, and bias toward uncoordinated action. Indeed, it was designed as such to favor the creation of what became the first marketplace society.

American government, dynamic, deadlocked, contradictory, and immobilized as it may be, also still has a definite if ever-changing geography of power. As a corollary, this suggests that the United States has never been well-prepared to pursue a strategy such as empire in world politics. The irony is that in helping to give birth to marketplace society and sponsor it around the world, the U.S. government now suffers the consequences of what have been, from the viewpoint of American hegemony, its very strengths. Unable now to respond adequately to the various global challenges that confront it, its dynamic immobilism has become the epitaph for the ultimate triumph, at least for now, of a globalizing marketplace society. This sets the scene for the possible development of a globalizing world in which, with the fading of U.S. governmental authority, the hegemony established under American auspices can continue to exist without a central directing hegemon. Marketplace society will then have truly come home to roost.

6 Globalizing American Hegemony

"Globalization" is one of the premier buzz words of the early twenty-first century. In its most general usage it refers to the idea of a world increasingly stretched, shrunk, connected, interwoven, integrated, interdependent, or less territorially divided economically and culturally among national states. It is most frequently seen as an economic-technological process of time-space compression, as a social modernization of increased cultural homogeneity previously national in character scaled up to the world as a whole, or as shorthand for the practices of economic liberalism spontaneously adopted by governments the world over.[1] I do not want to deny the truth in each of these perspectives. Rather, in rethinking globalization as geopolitical, I will attempt to put it in the historical context of the growth of a world economy that has only recently become more globalized under largely American auspices.

As a new "master concept," globalization is often seen as replacing geopolitics.[2] From this viewpoint, if globalization is all about a world that knows no boundaries, geopolitics was all about Great Powers and empires dividing up the world and imposing territorial control over it. But this draws too bold a line between a world that is and a world that was. Globalization as we know it today has definite geopolitical roots and biases. I begin the chapter, therefore, by examining the geopolitical origins of globalization in American policies and practices during the Cold War but that have older roots in American history, particularly the experience and ideology of the "frontier" (as explained in Chapter 4). This will then politicize the topic in direct opposition to the tendency to naturalize it in much recent writing, as if it were an entirely technological, sociological, or ideological phenomenon. This is important because it suggests that the form that recent globalization has taken is the result of political choices that can be reversed or redirected. A theme common in much writing on globalization is that it represents a stark break with the geopolitics of the Cold War (and previous epochs). I argue that this is anything but the case. Indeed, the "free world" economy that was an invention of the U.S. side in the Cold War is still the mantra of the "new" globalizing economy. To understand contemporary globalization requires examining the practices and ideas that laid its foundations in the period from the 1940s to the 1970s. In the first part of the chapter, I identify those features of the "embedded liberalism" of the postwar period that helped lay the foundations for the post-1970s acceleration of globalization.

The second section describes how this system began to erode in the 1960s. During the Nixon administration it was replaced by the beginnings of a new "market-access regime," in which the roles of such international organizations as the International Monetary Fund (IMF), the World Bank, and the General Agreement on Tariffs and Trade (GATT) (later the World Trade Organization [WTO]) were revolutionized by devoting them to the enforcement of a much more radical economic liberalism that seemed to serve American economic interests, at least in the short run. It is in this context that a new global economic geography emerged in which there is tension between continued state regulation of economic activities, on one hand, and a world economy increasingly organized by flows of capital and goods between sites in widely scattered locations, on the other. Although large parts of the world are increasingly left out of global economic development, this is in a context where the scale of uneven development is increasingly shifting from a national to a local and regional level.

This recent transformation introduces the question of the meaning of the "geographical" in relation to the globalization of the world economy and the long-term tension between *territorial* and *interactional* (flow-based) modes for organizing global capitalism (see also Chapter 4). Is the hegemony of a single state, however relatively powerful it may be, compatible politically and economically with a globalizing world economy? A third section provides a broad outline of the geographical dynamics of the emerging globalized economy. Particular attention is given to the dual process of globalization and fragmentation in which financial and production processes increasingly militate against seeing the world economy as simply an international or interstate one.

Making the Free World Economy

In the late nineteenth century, the United States, like most industrializing countries, sheltered its industries behind high-tariff barriers; however, it also remained attached to the Gold Standard, even in the face of tremendous domestic opposition, and thus subordinated itself to an international economy underwritten at that time by Britain. This "system" remained largely in place until the 1920s. The mobilization of national economies for war between 1914 and 1918, the economic drain on Britain from the First World War, Britain's failure to invest in new technologies to update its industries, and the rise of antiliberal ideologies such as Bolshevism and Fascism across a range of countries conspired to doom the further expansion of the international economy. It was beginning to close in on itself even before the economic cataclysm of 1929 to 1938. The U.S. government in the 1920s refused to step forward to rescue the international economy by replacing Britain as its lender of last resort and official conductor. This partly reflected the relative unimportance of international transactions to the U.S. economy, at least compared to Britain's, but also, and more important, it reflected the regulatory and ideological weakness of the federal government. The government was not capable of stepping up. President Calvin Coolidge posed the position of those in the seats of power very clearly: "If the Federal Government should go out of existence, the common run of people would not detect the difference in the affairs of their daily lives for a considerable length of time."[3]

Under the banner of the New Deal, the economic reforms that followed the onset of the Depression massively expanded the powers of the federal government to intervene in and direct the national economy. Yet, stimulating economic growth in the sense of manipulating fiscal and monetary policies to achieve sustained growth in output and incomes was not the central goal. Attempting more forceful regulation of business, managing industrial relations, and supporting aggregate demand through stimulating housing construction were much higher priorities. Such structural reforms were designed to encourage private-sector solutions to the problem of economic recovery. Only after 1938 did a more "Keynesian" national economic policy oriented to demand-side economic stimulus start to emerge into prominence. What is undeniable, however, is that the New Deal policies of the Roosevelt administrations in the 1930s and into the Second World War led to a profound empowerment of the federal government.

Initially, this assertion of central power was not matched by a more directed and outward-looking foreign policy. Indeed, beginning in 1930 the United States became more assertively protectionist and isolationist. The Hawley-Smoot Tariff of 1930 had raised import duties to their highest levels in American history. After his election, Roosevelt first promised and then recanted on efforts at exchange-rate stabilization and a return to the Gold Standard. In 1933 he dismissed the World Economic Conference by announcing that he had national, not international, priorities. Since these were inflationary by design, there was little alternative but to avoid international coordination. "Old fetishes of so-called international bankers," Roosevelt said, "are being replaced by efforts to plan national currencies."[4] In the 1930s the major industrial countries all "slid further down the ugly helix of economic isolationism and military rearmament toward the ultimate catastrophe of global war. Roosevelt had shown no more vision than the other desperately self-protective nationalists in 1933, perhaps even somewhat less. Having bled a while, America laid down its international commitments. Who could say if it would rise to fight again? Falsely thinking themselves safe behind their ocean moats, Americans prepared to take up arms against the Depression."[5]

Yet, early in his first term Roosevelt also sent a very different message in his support for the Reciprocal Trade Agreements Act (RTAA) of 1934, as well as in his follow-up efforts to negotiate bilateral treaties based on the trade-favoring "most-favored-nation" principle. He also recognized the Soviet Union and in 1936 negotiated an exchange stabilization agreement with Britain and France. The historian David Kennedy astutely notes, however, that "[F]or a long season, Roosevelt seemed more committed to a kind of abstract, prospective internationalism than to anything concrete in the here and now. As a Wilsonian, he no doubt hoped that a world of liberalized trade and international cooperation would one day emerge from the sorry mess that war and depression had inflected on the planet."[6] The time was not ripe for either liberalized trade or international cooperation. But the RTAA in particular proved fateful, to the extent that some see it as the foundation of post–Second World War U.S. hegemony beyond American shores.[7] What was important was that the RTAA represented the coming of age of an activist federal government in foreign affairs. It transferred tariff-making authority from Congress to the executive branch, thus allowing the U.S. government to make credible commitments to use the market power of the U.S. economy to liberalize international trade. This one piece of legislation pointed forward beyond the New Deal to an entirely different global situation. At the time, however, the United States was constrained to act within a system of inter-imperial rivalry that could only be overcome once its main agents—Germany, Italy, and Japan— had been defeated.

In 1945, the completeness of the American-Anglo-Soviet victory over Nazi Germany and Imperial Japan and their allies had two immediate consequences. First, Soviet influence extended across Eastern Europe and into Germany. When the war ended Soviet armies were as far west as the River Elbe. This encouraged both a continuing American military presence in Europe and a direct confrontation with the Soviet Union as a military competitor and sponsor of an alternative image of world order. This was quickly to find its clearest expression in the geopolitical doctrine of "containment," whereby through alliances and military presence the U.S. government committed itself to maintaining the political status quo established in 1945. The American development of nuclear weapons and a demonstrated willingness to use them meant that the security of the United States itself was beyond doubt.[8] Indeed, the relative geographical isolation of the United States from most of its historic adversaries has always been an American advantage, if one discounts threats from nuclear-armed terrorists or states that reject the "norms" of interstate behavior. What was in doubt was the allegiance of other countries to the United States and its political-economic model.

Second, in economic and political terms the United States was without any serious competition in imposing its vision of world order on both its vanquished foes and most of its recent allies. Unlike after the First World War, when the United States turned its back on expanding its hegemony, this time there seemed to be no alternative. Europe and Japan were devastated. The reading of the origins of the Great Depression and the Second World War that predominated in the Roosevelt and Truman administrations suggested that the continued health of the American economy and the stability of its internal politics depended on increasing rather than decreasing international trade and investment.[9] Europe and Japan had to be restored economically, both to deny them to the Soviet Union and to further American prosperity. Robert Morgenthau's early 1940s plan for the "ruralization" of Germany was quickly dismissed in 1945.

This is not to say that there was no opposition to the "internationalist" position. Indeed, the Republican majorities in the U.S. Congress in the immediate postwar years were generally as skeptical of the projection of the U.S. New Deal experience of government economic intervention overseas as they were of its application at home. U.S. forces demobilized rapidly after 1945. Only after 1947, with the growing fear of the Soviet Union as both foreign enemy and domestic subversive, did an internationalist consensus begin to emerge. The Soviet acquisition of the atomic bomb and the victory of the Chinese communists in the Chinese civil war were particularly important in creating a foreign policy consensus in the United States that enveloped both the Democratic and Republican Parties by 1950. But recurrent problems in reviving the world economy also served a role. Japan and Western Europe had been laid to waste during the Second World War. Civil wars and political independence effectively removed Japanese markets throughout Asia. The slow growth in the reestablishment of primary production, largely because of the disruptions caused by decolonization in India and Indonesia, limited the reestablishment of markets for European manufacturers. Import substitution policies in Latin America and elsewhere and the shortage of dollars in Europe to buy capital goods in the United States limited global growth. These problems all militated in favor of an activist role for the United States in both containing the Soviet Union and its allies and finding ways to stimulate global economic recovery. Even the most isolationist of American politicians came to see that American economic growth and prosperity depended on jump-starting the world economy.

The period from 1945 to 1970 was one in which this consensus—at home and abroad—played itself out. After an initial attempt at returning to business as usual (defined as the 1920s before the Depression and its aftermath) between 1945 and 1947, the U.S. government set out after 1947 to sponsor an international order in which its military expenditures would provide a protective apparatus for increased trade (and, if less so, investment) across international boundaries. These would, in turn, rebound to domestic American advantage. The logic behind this lay in the presumed transcendental identity between the American and world economies. The expansion of one was seen as good for the other. Achieving this involved projecting at a global scale those institutions and practices that had already developed in the United States, such as Fordist mass production/consumption industrial organization, electoral democracy, limited state welfare policies, and government economic policies directed toward stimulating private economic activities.[10] John Ruggie calls the normative content of these policies "embedded liberalism" because they were institutionalized in the Bretton Woods Agreement of 1944 and such "Bretton Woods institutions" as the IMF, the World Bank, and the GATT (WTO after 1994).[11]

Yet, the national economy was still seen as the basic building block of the world economy. The idea of markets completely replacing state-based institutions as the basis for international relations was widely seen as a relic of nineteenth-century thinking. A fully liberal agenda—free market, free trade, laissez-faire—was never adopted. As the enemies and allies of the Second World War in Western Europe and Japan recovered from the devastation of war, the United States was there encouraging, chiding, and coercing them into following certain courses of action that allowed for considerable institutional and policy variation across countries. Unlike after the First World War, "This time the United States abandoned its isolation and became actively engaged in fashioning postwar Europe [and Japan]."[12] It is a popular view that this commitment helped usher in what became from 1947 to 1970, at least in retrospect, the Golden Age of National Capitalism.

Several features of the American economy were particularly important in underpinning the internationalism of American policy in the immediate postwar period through the 1960s. One was economic concentration. Continuing an intermittent trend from the 1880s, in almost every American industry control over the market came to be exercised by ever fewer firms. Expanding concentration was accompanied and encouraged by the growth of government, especially at the federal level. Much of this was related to military expenditures designed to meet the long-term threat from the Soviet Union. These trends were reinforced by what became the main challenge to the perpetuation of the model within the United States: the direct investment of U.S. corporations overseas. Much of this was in other industrialized countries. The axis of capital accumulation now ran through the core rather than between the core and periphery. In the short run the repatriated profits benefited the American economy. Beginning in the late 1960s, however, as domestic technology and management followed capital abroad, traditional exports were replaced by foreign production of U.S. affiliates, to the detriment of employment in the United States. American mass consumption was no longer fully supported by the relatively high wages of its workers in mass production, and this is what defines the crisis or impasse facing the American model in the United States.[13] What Giovanni Arrighi calls a Free Enterprise System—"free, that is, from . . . vassalage to state power"—had now come into existence to challenge the interstate system as the singular locus of power in an increasingly global economy.[14]

Hegemony does not just happen; it is made. A base of economic and military power is necessary for any hegemony, but that is not sufficient in itself, as so many of the structural accounts of American hegemony seem to allege. A vision and a will to pursue hegemony are vital ingredients.[15] In the aftermath of the Second World War, the U.S. government had both: the vision came from the successful New Deal experience allied to economic internationalism, and the will came from an elite of businessmen, labor leaders, and politicians closely associated with the last Roosevelt administration. The Marshall Plan of massive U.S. financial aid to Europe actively managed by Europeans is their most enduring monument.[16] The logic of this approach was to stimulate demand through mass consumption. Mass consumption, therefore, became the leitmotif of the world political economy.

The spread, acceptance, and institutionalization of the American approach was by no means a preordained or easy process. In the United States itself, approaches to regulating American interaction with the world economy and coordinating economic policies with other countries have shifted over time. In particular, the balance between market and institutional mechanisms in managing international transactions (such as trade, exchange rates, and capital flows) has fluctuated over time rather than being set in a single mold. Some of these shifts, such as that of the first Reagan administration, can be seen as ideologically inspired—a strange mixture of monetarist and supply-side economics, with the latter in the ascendancy premised on the superiority of markets—or in the later Nixon years as the result of the demands of nationalist or protectionist forces within American national politics. The increased volatility in shifts in the operationalization of hegemony since the final breakdown of the Bretton Woods monetary system in 1971 is indicative of the rising economic power of other countries, particularly Germany and Japan, and the increasingly globalized world financial system. But there is also an interesting coincidence between confusion and disarray in U.S. foreign economic policy, especially in the early postwar years and during 1967 to 1980, and the relative prevalence of left-of-center governments in other industrialized countries.[17] This suggests, perhaps, the importance of at least a degree of elite solidarity across countries in the successful operation of American hegemony.

The key institutions and practices spread rapidly in the late 1940s and early 1950s. They were eventually accepted in all of the major industrialized countries either through processes of "external inducement" (e.g., Marshall Aid) and coercion (e.g., the British loan of 1946), or through direct intervention and reconstruction (as in West Germany and Japan). In all cases, however, there was considerable compromise with local elites over the relative balance of growth and welfare elements in public policy.[18] This process also applied to approaches to military security, where it often extended beyond elites to include mass publics. In Japan, for example, the so-called Yoshida doctrine, integrating Japan into American hegemony while concentrating on national economic development, signaled a massive shift away from the previously dominant imperial identity. Though the subject of contentious public debate, the Yoshida doctrine became the centerpiece of Japanese foreign policy with a wide degree of public acceptance. This cultural transformation resulted from both external events, such as the disastrous war that Japan had just fought, and the choice of centrist politicians to propagate the doctrine as a reasonable solution to Japan's postwar situation.[19]

Acceptance of key norms and practices was crucial to the socialization of elites (and mass publics) into U.S. hegemony. That these remained largely predictable until the 1960s was one of the main reasons for their acceptability. The key elements to U.S. hegemony under the Bretton Woods system were: (1) stimulating economic growth *indirectly* through fiscal and monetary policies; (2) commitment to a unitary global market based on producing the greatest volume of goods most inexpensively for sale in the widest possible market by means of a global division of labor; (3) accepting the United States as the home of the world's major reserve-currency and monetary overseer of the world economy (the Bretton Woods system, 1944–1971; dollar-based floating exchange rate system, 1971–present); (4) unremitting hostility to "communism" or any political-economic ideology that could be associated with the Soviet Union; and (5) the assumption of the burden of intervening militarily whenever changes in government or insurgencies could be construed as threatening to the political status quo established in 1945 (the Truman Doctrine).

Not only international relations, therefore, but also the domestic social order of other states was at issue in constituting the geopolitical order of the Cold War period. All states ideally were international ones, open to the free flow of investment and trade and the establishment of marketplace society.[20] What mattered to the Americans who formulated the Marshall Plan and other mechanisms of U.S. hegemony was the role of domestic policy performance in creating a "shared political community" that reflected debate and voluntary choice across countries to facilitate international balance and incremental openness.[21] Quite how the debate and choices turned out in fact varied considerably, suggesting that early American hegemony had discrete limits once conformity to certain global norms of international and domestic behavior was indicated. For example, commercial banks retained a role in the management of industrial companies in Germany and Japan that was frowned upon in the United States, Japan imposed content and product liability criteria on imported industrial and agricultural products, and central banks had varying degrees of independence from political management. More important, what the economist Meghnad Desai calls "socialism within capitalism," involving business nationalization, government-run health services, and expansive welfare states, was looked upon with dismay in many quarters in the United States but was nevertheless tolerated without a collapse of basic institutions, from military alliances such as the North Atlantic Treaty Organization (NATO) to the various Bretton Woods institutions.[22]

It is little exaggeration to claim that in the two decades after 1947 American dominion was at the center of a remarkable explosion in "interactional" capitalism. Based initially on the expansion of mass consumption within the most industrialized countries, it only later involved the reorganization of the world economy around a massive increase in trade in manufactured goods and foreign direct investment. But this was not a recapitulation of the previous world economy. Having abandoned territorial imperialism, "Western capitalism [under U.S. auspices] . . . resolved the old problem of overproduction, thus removing what Lenin believed was the major incentive for imperialism and war."[23] The major driving force behind this was the growth of mass consumption in North America, Western Europe, and Japan. *The promise of ever-increasing consumption for increased segments of national populations became both the driving force behind economic growth and its self-evident justification.* The United States provided the prototype consumer society, but beyond the broadest parameters it took on different characteristics in different countries. Manufacturing production everywhere, however, depended on stimulating demand. The products of such industries as real estate, household and electrical goods, automobiles, food processing, and mass entertainment were all consumed within (and, progressively, between) the producing countries. The "Keynesian" welfare state helped sustain demand through the redistribution of incomes and purchasing power. The old "cross-over" trading system of the colonial era was no longer needed. If before the Second World War the prosperity of industrial countries depended on favorable terms of trade with the underdeveloped world, now demand was stimulated at home. Moreover, until the 1970s the income terms of trade of most raw materials and foodstuffs tended to decline. This trend had negative effects on the economies of the Third World as a whole and of certain regions, such as Sub-Saharan Africa, even more so. It also, however, stimulated some countries to engage in new models of industrialization, particularly in East Asia and Latin America, which later paid off as these countries found lucrative export markets for their manufactured goods. The globalization of production through the growth of these newly industrializing countries (NICs) (also aided by U.S. Cold War military expenditures in the case of countries such as South Korea and Taiwan) and the increased flow of trade and foreign direct investment between already industrialized countries finally undermined the geographical production/consumption nexus (often referred to as "central Fordism") that was the leitmotif of the early postwar decades. Manufacturing production and consumption could now be in widely separated places.

A vital element in allowing the United States to have such a dominant presence within the world economy was the persisting political-military conflict with the Soviet Union. This served both to tie Germany and Japan firmly into alliance with the United States and to define two geographical spheres of influence at a global scale. For a long time this imposed an overall stability on world politics, since the United States and the Soviet Union were the two major nuclear powers, even though it also promoted numerous "limited wars" in the Third World of former colonies where each of the "superpowers" armed surrogates or intervened to prevent the other from achieving a successful "conversion."[24] The marketplace ethos, with its culture of managerial-consumerism that spread relatively successfully in Western Europe, in Japan, and in pockets elsewhere after 1950, was largely ineffectual in most postcolonial settings: "Here the representative American nostrums of evolutionary reform, necessarily based on a middle class that was fragile if it existed at all, were repeatedly challenged and sometimes trumped by ardent nationalists or radical revolutionaries inspired by such iconic figures like Lenin, Mao, and Castro. Their resistance led to a long series of American interventions, often in league with badly compromised local despots, and sometimes in remote areas where there was no obvious national interest."[25] Coercion in the Third World proved much less successful than did the quieter overtures of hegemony in the First.

For all their weakness, however, Third World and other small countries could not be treated as passive objects of imperialist competition during the Cold War. They had to be wooed, and often they resisted. This limited the ability of the superpowers to extend their influence. Unlike in the nineteenth century, the world map was no longer a "vacuum" waiting to be filled by a small number of Great Powers. But the boundaries and integrity of existing states were protected by the military impasse between the superpowers. Any disturbance of the status quo threatened the hegemony of each within its respective sphere of influence. When this happened, as, for example, in Cuba in 1962, in the Middle East in 1956, 1967, and 1973, and in Central America in the 1980s, the Cold War always threatened to heat up.

The years 1956–1967 were epochal in establishing the main features of American hegemony. In the Suez crisis the American attempt to manipulate the Egyptian President Nasser into abandoning "nonalignment" in return for financing the Aswan Dam failed. The outcome of the crisis, however, with U.S. pressure forcing Britain and France to withdraw their troops after their intervention against Nasser's nationalization of the Suez Canal, showed who was in change of "western" policy and suggested the importance of using aid more straightforwardly and in more fruitful places than Egypt. One major consequence was the search for "moderate" regimes, rather than "nationalistic" ones such as Nasser's, to serve as regional allies and stabilizers all over the world.

But 1956 was also a turning point in the creation of the international economic order that was the centerpiece of American hegemony. GATT, founded in 1948 but hitherto moribund, came to life as an instrument for negotiating multilateral reductions in tariffs and enrolling all of the main capitalist industrialized countries into a regime favoring free trade and free exchange under U.S. auspices. Full convertibility between the U.S. dollar and the major European currencies finally came about in 1958. The European Economic Community (EEC) came into existence as a means for lowering barriers to trade and capital flows between its member states, even as its members were tied politically to the United States through the NATO alliance dating from 1949. Finally, the dollar gap closed for both Japan and Western Europe, signaling the ultimate success of U.S. efforts to stimulate the world economy through maintaining U.S. balance-of-payments deficits.

These successes proved more fragile than they seemed at the time. First, without Britain (which had not decided whether it was part of Europe), the European Community was potentially a vehicle for French ambitions to create a European bloc between the United States and the Soviet Union. Moreover, the EEC was potentially an economic threat to the United States, particularly if it restricted U.S. multinational businesses and raised tariffs against American goods and services. Second, the stationing of large U.S. military forces in Western Europe and Japan, one of the main ways in which the United States transferred dollars abroad, was increasingly costly to the United States. By the late 1950s, the U.S. balance-of-payments deficit was threatening the ability of the United States to meet its obligations under the Bretton Woods Agreement of 1944—to keep a steady relationship between the dollar, the price of gold, and the values of other currencies—as the economies associated with these other currencies began to experience higher rates of growth in productivity and profitability than the United States. At home, military spending was also out of control with limited spin-off into the general economy and increasingly funded by the mid-1960s through expansion of the money supply rather than through increases in revenues. Finally, the financial support for so-called moderate regimes in the decolonizing world not only embroiled the United States in increasingly expensive military adventures, most infamously in South Vietnam, but also imposed a stress on the U.S. economy as the U.S. federal government expanded its social security and welfare expenditures in the late 1960s without raising taxes.[26]

Despite the drag of military expenditures, the U.S. economy grew phenomenally between 1961 and 1967: in excess of 6 percent annually. But in 1967 and 1968, unemployment and inflation went up together. A period of "stagflation" set in that lasted until the early 1980s. The early 1970s were marked by large trade deficits, to be exceeded only by those of the 1980s and early 2000s, which, in combination with currency speculation, brought about the final demise of the Bretton Woods system of international monetary regulation. That system, however, was already badly out of step with the reemergence of global finance, quietly sponsored by the U.S. and British governments, through the mechanism of the so-called Euromarket "created in the late 1950s and based primarily in London in the 1960s, [that] allowed international financial operations to be conducted relatively freely; transactions could be made in nonlocal currencies, especially dollars, completely free of state regulations."[27] Real median American household incomes peaked in 1974, never to come close thereafter. In the same year world oil prices were forced up at a rapid rate by the Organization of Petroleum Exporting Countries (OPEC), producing a major transfer of wealth within the world economy from the industrialized world to the oil producers. Unable to handle the infusion of dollars, the oil producers recycled them through international banks who lent them out in high-risk ventures in Latin America, Africa, and Asia, given the lack of attractiveness of investment in the United States and other industrial countries at the time. There was no longer a clear identity between the U.S. territorial economy and the working of the world economy. What had gone wrong?

Under the political economy that had prevailed in the late 1950s and 1960s, economic concentration had paid off in the United States through expanding business profitability and providing higher median incomes that in turn stimulated demand for consumer goods. But big firms, protected from price competition by oligopolistic practices, failed to engage in the type of research and development that would fuel innovation in the civilian economy. Spin-off from military research was no longer stimulative of the general economy. Productivity began a long slide compared to foreign producers, particularly in Germany and Japan. Built-in wage increases for workers in large firms cut into profits. Corporate control over pricing prevented prices from falling quickly enough to mirror new economic conditions. This increased inflation.

The massive growth of government spending was also a major culprit in the inflationary spiral. The huge sums required to prosecute the failing war in Vietnam, to maintain the vast U.S. military presence around the world, and to pay for the social policies enacted in the late 1960s to meet the demands of the social groups not sharing in the current prosperity gave rise to the bureaucratic state that the United States had managed to avoid previously. Because tax increases to pay for this were unpopular given the hostility of different organized groups to various types of government spending, stimulation of the economy was possible only through increasing the supply of dollars and encouraging private indebtedness. The net effects were a tremendous boost to inflation, over and above that from within the corporate sector, massive public-sector borrowing in the bond market, and a dramatic increase in the instability of financial markets. Between 1968 and 1971, the U.S. economy came close to meltdown.

At first a consequence and then the cause of the economic slowdown in the United States, American multinational companies found overseas direct and portfolio investment more profitable than investment at home. This not only increased unemployment, especially in the high-wage manufacturing sector, but it also reduced the availability of capital for retooling factories and investing in product innovation in the United States.[28] The troubles of the economy and dissent over the Vietnam War effectively ended the "Cold War consensus" that had prevailed in national politics over the previous two decades. The increased exposure of industries in the U.S. manufacturing belt to competition in domestic markets from foreign producers (including the subsidiaries of U.S.-based companies) led to an increase in calls for protection on the part of political representatives from the most affected regions. The economic and moral costs of policing the world were increasingly brought home and could be seen on the nightly news and in local communities.

The effects of the crisis beginning in the early 1970s were not only economic. This period has been named the "end of victory culture" by one commentator because of a crisis of confidence by many Americans in the seemingly inevitable—and necessary—expansion of American influence and the American way.[29] American failure to win the war in Vietnam—for the global hegemon to have met its match in a seemingly insignificant Third World country—had a particularly profound effect on the national psyche. For some people, the right of America's manifest destiny to serve as global role model had been challenged by reports of the brutality of American soldiers toward Vietnamese soldiers and civilians alike. "We" were not supposed to behave like that. Winning somehow was supposed to take place effortlessly and with a minimum of violence. Reports from Vietnam led to a reexamination of earlier wars, such as the Indian Wars of the 1800s and the U.S. occupation of the Philippines in 1900, suggesting a somewhat less noble application of force by U.S. troops to just about everyone, not just military combatants. This coincided with the growing power and effectiveness of the civil rights movement in the 1960s and its forceful reminder of the ugly violence of American domestic history, from Indian massacres to lynching of blacks in the South in the aftermath of the Civil War. For others the issue was simply that the nation's might had been successfully challenged. Some interpretations have suggested that weak (and feminized) politicians were not sufficiently committed to the war (or to the American soldiers fighting it). The *Rambo* films illustrate this most clearly, with supine leaders refusing to support their men, instead looking to compromise and negotiate with the enemy.[30] The personal identities of many American men were particularly affected. The long-running American celebration of successful war (from Native Americans to the Nazis and Japanese) and returning warriors had come to an ignominious end in the jungles of Vietnam. Whatever the particular effect supposed, the depth of feeling is clear: the Vietnam War has been fought over and over again on American cinema and television screens, demonstrating an agonized contemplation of an American self-image that the war cast into doubt. The strange American fixation with gun ownership and the celebration of redemption, both religious and political, through violence are important indications of the continuing, if increasingly challenged, mythology of a nation nurtured on individuals taking the law into their own hands.

The response of the Nixon administration to the problems it faced was fourfold. First, through cajoling and coercion, it made Japan and Western Europe revalue and later float their currencies against the dollar. In the short run this made American exports more competitive and imports less so. Its long-term effects, however, were the demise of a system of stable gold-exchange rates and a major boost to a global financial system largely exempt from direct government control as it had been, to a high degree, under the Bretton Woods system.[31]

Second, with respect to the Soviet Union, Nixon and his foreign-policy guru, Henry Kissinger, recognized military parity, particularly in terms of strategic nuclear weapons. During the Brezhnev years, as the rest of the Soviet economy stagnated, a major emphasis was placed on achieving parity with the United States in strategic weapons systems. This did not increase Soviet security, nor did it improve the generally low quality of Soviet forces as a whole.[32] What it did was increase U.S. perceptions of the Soviet Union as a serious adversary. At the same time, however, the split between the Soviet Union and China made it possible for the United States both to accept the Soviet Union as a military equal and to use China as a potential counterweight if Soviet demands proved excessive. This realist reading was the essence of the Nixon policy of détente with the Soviet Union and the opening to China. But it also carried potential economic benefits in terms of U.S. trade and investment if the entire Second World could be opened up.

Third, as a consequence of the disastrous involvement in Vietnam, the Nixon administration substituted arming and support of "regional surrogates," such as the Shah's Iran, for direct American military intervention (the Nixon Doctrine). This brought the advantage of increased exports of military goods and the promise of "no more Vietnams" in which Americans would be the victims of America's wars. As a corollary, it also led to renewed emphasis on subverting regimes, such as that of President Allende in Chile in 1973, that even if elected to office (and hence democratic by most measures), represented a challenge to the global spread of marketplace society signified by the inviolability of private property, middle-class consumerism, and open access to foreign capital.[33]

Fourth, the Nixon years saw an attempt at paring back the expansion of the federal government through such devices as sharing revenue with the states, reorganizing bureaucracies, and cutting military spending. Paralleling contemporary calls for the "limits to growth," President Nixon was preoccupied, at least until the Watergate scandal, with urging a sense of limits on Americans who had come to expect ever-expanding paychecks and escalating consumption. Unlike the Republicans who came after him, Nixon was not primarily a proponent of big-business interests, presuming that releasing corporate America from taxes and other obligations would set everything right. Indeed, more like a Democrat, Nixon believed in benevolent government (at least for the silent majority of whites) and was "desperate to stop the economy from wrecking his presidency."[34]

Nixon was aware that the United States could no longer simply assume a dominant international position. As a result, historian Robert Collins has portrayed Nixon as a tragically prophetic figure rather than as the dark, criminally inclined consummate political opportunist that most accounts have made of him:

> Nixon presented his foreign and domestic initiatives as preparation for the new global economic competition. The struggle would be fierce, the outcome was not guaranteed, but the goal was continued American preeminence. The United States needed, in Nixon's words, "to run this race economically and run it effectively and maintain the position of world leadership." Détente and the Nixon Doctrine would contribute by lessening the likelihood of catastrophic, Vietnam-style embroilments abroad. But the prospect of global economic competition also dictated that "America now cannot be satisfied domestically."[35]

Nixon was prescient, therefore, in noting that the period 1967–1974 marked a watershed in America's relations with the rest of the world. An administration that spoke openly of geopolitics as a form of calculation among Great Powers was the first one since the Second World War so constrained—domestically, by dissent and conspiratorial reactions to it (as in the Watergate affair), and internationally, by an increasingly hostile economic environment—that it could not effectively practice it.[36] Rather, *the United States had itself succumbed to the logic of the very marketplace—now scaled up from the national to the global scale—its government and society had been imposing on the country since the nineteenth century and imposing on the world since 1947.* The shifting understanding of American hegemony in the early 1970s can be attributed particularly to the emergence of foreign competition against American business within the United States; the relative decline of American-based manufacturing industry; the collapse of an American-operated international monetary system; the perception of strategic parity between the United

States and the Soviet Union; and domestic division of opinion over America's global policing and the virtue of an increasingly open world economy.

In the end, the Cold War world came undone with the collapse of the Soviet Union in the late 1980s because it failed to deliver both "guns and butter," to innovate technologically, and to make state bureaucracy answerable to an increasingly restive population. But this was only the final sign of an old order in demise; the free world economy was also in disarray in the 1970s, as mounting stagflation, indebtedness, and balance-of-payments disequilibria clearly and successively indicated. Indeed, the stability of U.S. hegemony had been in trouble since around 1960, when the London gold crisis showed the potential weakness of the gold-dollar exchange mechanism at the heart of the Bretton Woods system.[37] Financing the Vietnam War without raising taxes and vastly expanding the expenditures of the federal government to provide welfare benefits, housing subsidies, and healthcare programs (Medicare for the elderly and Medicaid for the poor) created massive fiscal pressure in the latter part of the 1960s. By 1971, when the Nixon administration abrogated the Bretton Woods Agreement, the United States faced a rapidly declining rate of economic growth and needed recourse to a competitive devaluation of the dollar. In other words, the domestic economic needs of the United States were seen by the Nixon administration as more important than maintaining the U.S.-centered Bretton Woods monetary regime. President Nixon was not "forced" into abrogation. The consensus within his administration was that "survival of the postwar international monetary regime [was] a distant third in the priorities of the United States, lagging far behind the goals of maintaining a prosperous domestic economy and ensuring the achievement of U.S. security objectives."[38] Thus, and ironically, the explosion of globalization that followed this fateful decision is based on what was an explicit pursuit of U.S. national economic interest without much by way of either negotiation or agreement with other states. In point of fact, the U.S. government, since 1971, has tended to be increasingly nationalist and unilateral, combining an economic focus on using the global role of the dollar to export the costs of U.S. fiscal policies (in particular, the twin balance of payments and federal deficits) and a political focus on coercing recalcitrant states that are seen as threatening to either or both globalization and U.S. hegemony.

In other words, the market-based globalization that was long the inherent goal of American hegemony has been increasingly challenged by a U.S. neoimperialism, with the U.S. government disciplining others fiscally and monetarily even when profligate themselves and threatening military intervention in pursuit of security threats to the United States and its economy. More internationalist phases, such as from the second Reagan administration through the Clinton years, which drew the United States toward more multilateral and less militarily oriented foreign policies, suggest how much American politics is now centered around weighing the costs and benefits for the territorial United States of continuing American hegemony as opposed to either realist retreat or imperial ambition. Whether the genie of marketplace society unleashed on the world can be put back into its territorial bottle, however, is open to serious doubt. Whether the consequences of the genie for Americans and others are singularly beneficial is another thing entirely.

Building the "Market-Access" Regime

By the mid-1970s, the Nixon nationalist approach to resolving America's difficulties in the world economy was increasingly in question. Its heavy emphasis on U.S. diplomatic relations and unilateral economic action led to considerable unease among the most internationalized sectors of American business.[39] How to turn this unease into national policy was another issue. During the Ford interregnum of 1974–1976, little or anything was done. In his first two years in office, President Carter tried policies that would make the United States less dependent on foreign sources of oil, would stabilize arms competition with the Soviet Union, and would encourage a greater respect for human rights among regimes allied to the United States. These policies quickly foundered, however, because of three trends. One was the increased influence of groups and individuals who saw the Nixon policy of détente as nothing short of appeasement of the Soviet Union. Out of fiscal necessity, U.S. military spending had declined since 1970, but now, it was claimed, the United States was being "overtaken" by the more relentlessly militaristic Soviet Union. Unsurprisingly, many of the advocates of increased defense spending had close ties to the military-industrial complex President Eisenhower had warned about in his final address.

A second trend was that the recycling of so-called petrodollars produced by the OPEC price increases into loans to the industrializing countries of the Third World through American and other banks had by 1978 created the beginning of what became the global debt crisis. Servicing loans became difficult when U.S. interest rates went up to keep attracting foreign capital to pay for domestic consumption and government deficits. It became near impossible once oil prices went up again in 1979–1980 and the demand for the basic commodities that many of the heavily indebted countries exported declined in the face of global recession. The United States encountered the specter of major bank failures if several of the largest debtors (such as Mexico and Brazil) were to default simultaneously.

A third trend was the erosion of the Nixon Doctrine with the disintegration of the Shah's regime in Iran and the instability and unreliability of surrogate regimes in the Horn of Africa and Latin America. The Soviet Union faced a similar problem in Afghanistan. Altogether, therefore, superpower competition could no longer be sublimated through the use of surrogates. President Carter lost the 1980 election in large part because of the fall of the Shah and the embarrassment of the hostage taking by the replacement regime.

In the absence of a viable strategy for a national industrial policy (such as that later advocated in the first Clinton administration by Robert Reich) allied to capital-export controls and a decline in military spending, the only tried and true solution to the multiple dilemmas facing the country was a revival of militarization (or "military Keynesianism" as it is sometimes called). Both the later Carter administration and the Reagan administrations of the 1980s chose this course. The logic was that increased military spending would stimulate investment and spending at home, at least in those places where defense industries were located, and increased military commitments abroad would demonstrate American resolve to reassert its centrality to the "free world" it had created. For President Reagan, by 1984, "It was morning again in America."

The first Reagan administration carried through the remilitarization strategy begun under Carter to a level not seen since the Second World War. Major emphasis was placed on developing new weapon systems rather than upgrading existing forces. This provided a major economic stimulus that upgrading would not. The political purpose was to remind Western Europe and Japan that they relied on an American military commitment that underwrote their economic development, to counter the Soviet attempt at military equality with the United States, and to encourage regimes friendly to American economic interests in the Third World. With his "Star Wars" proposal of a missile defense "shield" for the United States, President Reagan also attempted to use a military initiative to both appeal to popular fears and feed the urge to constantly expand military programs.[40]

Alongside massive military spending, the Reagan administration attempted to reverse America's competitive slide in the world economy and get control of inflation in four ways: recession, tax cuts, deregulation, and new-style international coordination. To bring down inflation, cut wage rates, and reduce the number of inefficient producers and thus make U.S. industries more competitive at home and abroad, the first order of business was a tightened monetary policy.[41] This was done so drastically through increased interest rates and limiting the money supply that in 1981, the United States experienced its most severe economic downturn since 1937. Attention then switched to the "real economy." Under the guise of "supply-side economics," income taxes, especially for those with high incomes, were cut dramatically on the theory that the extra money put into circulation would end up as productive investment. Supposedly, loss of revenue in the short term would be made up by the expansion of the economy, producing a long-term uptake in revenue. Deregulation was also pushed hard to allow the "market" to choose between candidates for growth and for bankruptcy. The main path was to encourage mergers, acquisitions, and strategic alliances. But associated policies included reduction in environmental and safety regulations, assaults on unions, and the elimination of many rules governing the conduct of financial institutions. Finally, the U.S. government engaged in attempts at coordinated action with other major industrialized countries to respond to the debt crisis, realign currencies (particularly after 1985), and restructure the world economy along more liberal, market-oriented lines.[42]

The stagflation of the 1970s had largely discredited conventional demand-side intervention by governments (associated with Keynesian economics), in which the rate of unemployment supposedly correlated inversely with the rate of inflation. This provided an ideal opportunity for a reassertion of liberal economic ideas that had been marginalized within the economics profession and in policy circles during the Bretton Woods era.[43] Particularly in the United States and Britain, the governments of President Reagan and Prime Minister Thatcher embarked on economic policies designed to decrease the power of labor unions and assert the centrality of markets in both domestic and international transactions. Although frequently paired together, Thatcher's approach was much more ideologically coherent than Reagan's. With the Thatcher government, there was none of the hostility to governmental power or belief in the magic of relieving the tax burden of the rich as the key to economic growth that marked the Reagan version of liberalism. Thatcher had a clearer focus on privatizing state assets, freeing labor markets, and enforcing tight monetary policy. Indeed, the letters between Thatcher and Reagan, deposited in the Reagan presidential library, suggest that the relationship between them was less close personally and ideologically than contemporary propaganda and scholarly studies suggested.[44]

In the short run Reagan's policies seemed a stunning success, particularly in reducing inflation. They ensured his reelection in 1984 and encouraged widespread imitation abroad. The American political economy's peculiar qualities compared to other industrialized countries— lower public spending on services, low levels of worker unionization— became global standards of excellence in economic performance.[45] The long-term effects were much more problematic, at home and abroad. The tax cuts largely failed to stimulate capital investment in the United States. The money went into consumption, often of foreign-made goods, which thus increased the trade deficit; into a frenzy of mergers and acquisitions among large firms; and, in a world economy with minimal capital controls since the late 1970s, into overseas investment.[46] The federal budget deficit exploded from $59.6 billion in 1980 to $202.8 billion in 1985. In lieu of the taxes foregone after 1981, the massive increases in military spending (along with a failure to cut domestic spending) had to be financed by borrowing. Because the U.S. savings rate was so low, most of the borrowing had to be done abroad.[47] Added to the trade deficit stimulated by the tax cuts, the U.S. current-account deficit ballooned. The U.S. economy was increasingly dependent on foreign financing and thus subject to external shocks from which it had hitherto remained largely sheltered. Within the United States there was a massive redistribution of income to those groups and regions that benefited from "Reaganomics." Military spending pumped huge sums into southern California, New England, and Washington state. Other regions, such as the Midwest, received little. The wealthy everywhere benefited at the expense of the poor, who saw their taxes decline little as their services from government declined. The size of the middle class shrank as well-paying manufacturing jobs disappeared and were replaced by lower-paying, insecure jobs in the service sector.[48]

A strange mix of military Keynesianism, monetarism, and supply-side economics had certainly turned the economic corner from the "limits" of the 1970s. It also played a role in the Soviet collapse of 1989–1992 by out-spending the not-so-great adversary into decline, spread neoliberalism (deregulation, privatization, and free-market ideology) through imitation by governments around the world, and laid the groundwork for an entirely new spurt of globalization in the 1990s.[49] The Bush Senior and Clinton administrations inherited this mantle. The former foundered on the promise to continue the Reagan obsession with tax cuts only to have to reverse this stance in 1990; the latter opted for deficit reduction as the influence of the Federal Reserve and advocates of the bond market trumped proponents of a national economic policy.[50] In both cases, however, the discipline of markets set severe limits to independent government action. The Clinton administration's mix of tax increases and spending cuts (in defense, welfare spending, and infrastructure) along with the explosion of speculative investment in real estate and the high technology sector certainly did produce dramatic reduction in the federal debt. But the balance of payments never came under control. The United States was just too strongly tied to production and financing from abroad. Like Gulliver tied down by small fry, the huge American economy was now dependent on how relations with the larger and faster-growing world economy could be managed. How had this occurred?

Wide acknowledgment that the world economy has undergone a fundamental reorganization since the 1970s has not meant that there is agreement as to how and why this has happened. Agreement is confined only to the sense that the world economy has entered a phase of flexible production and accumulation in which business operations around the world are increasingly taking the form of core firms (often transnational in scope) connected by formal and informal alliances to networks of other organizations, firms, governments, and communities (also sometimes known as disorganized capitalism).[51] The paradox of this trend, and hence why it has generated intense debate, is that while networking allows for an increased spanning of political boundaries by *concentrated* business organizations, it also opens up the possibility of more *decentralized* production to sites with competitive advantages. At the same time, networks take on different forms with in different sectors and in different places.[52]

One account of the source of this shift in the world economy from big, vertically integrated firms organized largely with reference to national economies to globe-spanning networks of production and finance emphasizes the declining rates of productivity and profits of major corporations in the years between 1965 and 1980.[53] Profit rates, averaged across the seven largest national industrial economies and defined as net operating surplus divided by net capital stock at current prices, declined

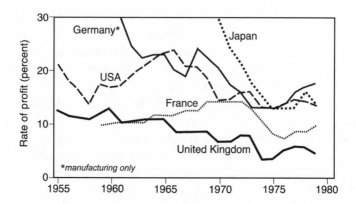

FIGURE 6.1. Declining Rates of Profit for Various Industrial
Countries, 1955–80
Source: U.K. Department of Trade and Industry, *British Business,*
1981, 17.

in these years in the manufacturing sector from 25 percent to 12 percent. Across all sectors, the average rate of profit fell from 17 percent to
11 percent.[54] There was considerable variability in rates of profit in the
1950s and 1960s, however, so the story of a long boom (or "golden age")
shared by all industrialized countries followed by a sudden collapse is
open to question.[55] What appears to have happened is that the period
from 1960 to the early 1970s was one of generally rising profit rates.
Thereafter, rates of profit began to decline, but at different rates and
following different trajectories (Figure 6.1). These seem tied more to
declining rates of productivity (efficiency in the use of equipment and
resources) than to increasing labor costs. Although there has been a
recovery of rates of profit in some economies (such as the United States)
since the mid-1980s, this seems fueled in part by suppressing wages and
other labor benefits more than by returns to new technologies (such as
computers) or new investment.[56] It also reflects the results of the "global
turn" taken most aggressively by large (and other) American firms since
the 1970s. Individual cases, such as General Motors or Ford, suggest
as much. Each has come to depend increasingly on the profitability of
its worldwide ventures to compensate for the loss of market share and
profitability in the United States. The George W. Bush administration,
while adopting many of the features of the Reagan strategy (although
in inheriting a federal budget surplus and then rapidly turning it into a
massive deficit, monetary tightness was not required), has favored treat-
ing U.S. multinational firms' profits at home and abroad as equivalent

for tax purposes.[57] Allied to massive corporate tax cutting, a greater fiscal stimulus to rapid movements of foreign direct investment cannot be imagined.

Globalization is partly about firms attempting to cash in on the comparative advantage enjoyed in production by other countries and localities and gain unimpeded access to their consumer markets. But it is also about governments wanting to attract capital and expertise from beyond their boundaries so as to increase employment, learn from foreign partners, and generally improve the global competitive position of "their" firms. The combination of the two has given rise to a "market-access" regime of world trade and investment.[58] This has eroded the free-trade regime that had increasingly predominated in trade between the main industrial capitalist countries in the post–Second World War period. In its place is a regime in which acceptable rules governing trade and investment have spread from the relatively narrow realm of trade to cover a wide range of areas of firm organization and performance.

The flexible monetary regime that replaced the Bretton Woods system after the American abrogation in the early 1970s provided encouragement to this shift, although the trend toward increased foreign-direct investment by U.S. and European multinational firms was already under way as one solution to their declining rates of profit. Not only did it encourage increased capital flows between currencies because of the ability to take advantage of exchange-rate differentials, but it also stimulated businesses to concern themselves with the relative macroeconomic condition (exchange rates, interest rates, inflation rates, etc.) of the countries in which they invested, and thus to concern themselves with the enhanced profitability that could result from locating investment in various countries rather than leaving it put. Perhaps of equal significance were the negotiated declines in average tariff levels on trade in manufactured goods between industrial countries, beginning with the so-called Kennedy Round of the GATT in the mid-1960s; the growing strength of the European Union (or Community, as it then was) in reducing barriers to trade and capital mobility between member countries; pressures on the Japanese government from the U.S. government to admit more imports and "voluntarily" restrain exports which, in turn, encouraged Japanese companies to locate production facilities abroad; and the combination of lower productivity/higher wages in the 1970s produced by either or both increased labor union leverage and decreased investment in technology. By the late 1970s the challenge in manufacturing prices, particularly in sectors such as clothing, electronics, and shipbuilding, from producers in the NICs and more recently

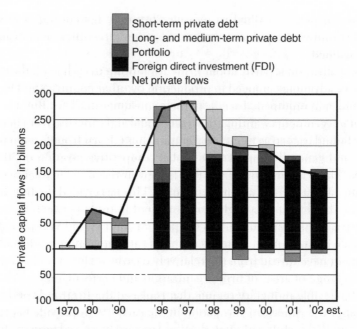

FIGURE 6.2. The Changing Composition of Foreign Investment in
Developing Countries, 1970–2002
Source: World Bank, *World Development Report* (New York: Oxford
University Press, 2003).

from China, also encouraged a search by American firms for more profitable sites in which to locate production facilities. Many of these sites
are also in developing countries—such as China and the other NICs—
where, as a consequence, foreign direct investment by U.S. and other
multinational firms has increasingly replaced other forms of external
investment (Figure 6.2).

At the same time, however, markets for consumer goods have also
changed. The American paradigm of mass production/mass consumption (Fordism) associated with both postwar U.S. economic growth and
the Marshall Plan began to unravel in the 1970s. Although many goods
are still made in a mass-produced manner, they are now often produced
somewhere else and by different people than those who consume them.
This is a major change from the Fordist system in which production
and consumption were geographically parallel. Classic Fordism was by
definition territorial in nature, relying on a high geographical correlation between production and consumption regulated by active territorial
states. But many goods are also increasingly made according to an older

but revitalized "craft paradigm," mainly because this approach responds more rapidly to changes in consumer demand (and, hence, can exploit sudden shifts in fashion), allows for rapid technological innovation, and relies on nonunionized labor forces that are less demanding of wage and benefit improvements. Overall, the customized goods produced by this older model of industrial organization have increasingly challenged the mass-produced commodities that hitherto tended to drive economic growth in the United States and elsewhere. This is partly a response to higher disposable incomes on the part of certain segments of the population across the industrialized world and the allied desire to consume more customized, higher "status" products. But it is also an outcome of the search for increased sales through "niche" marketing—the identification of and marketing to certain tastes and preferences associated with different ethnic, income, and status groups. As it has globalized, the marketplace society has also become increasingly customized. The fact that most of the still mass-produced goods and many of the customized ones are not made in the United States has obvious political-economic implications. America is deindustrializing.

Six "pillars" of the market-access system can be identified. The first is a move away from the dominance of the American model of industrial organization in international negotiations toward a hybrid model in which there is less emphasis on keeping governments and industries "at arm's length" and commitment to encouraging interfirm collaboration and alliances both across and within national boundaries. In this new model foreign firms are allowed to contest most segments of national markets, except in cases where clearly demarcated sectors are left for local firms. A second pillar involves the increased cooperation and acceptance of common rules concerning trade, investment, and money by national bureaucracies with an increasingly powerful role also played by supranational and international organizations (such as the European Commission for the EU and the World Trade Organization for the GATT, respectively). Two consequences are the blurring of lines of regulation between "issue areas" (such as trade and foreign direct investment, which increasingly can substitute for each other) and the penetration of "global norms" into the practices of national bureaucracies.

The third pillar is the increasing trade in services beyond national boundaries and the concomitant increased importance of services (banking, insurance, transportation, legal, advertising, etc.) in the world economy. One reason for this is that high-tech products (computers, commercial aircraft, etc.) contain high levels of service inputs, and servicing the "software" that such products require has led to an explosion in producer services. Another reason is that producers are demanding services that are of high quality and competitively priced. They can turn to foreign suppliers if appropriate ones are not available locally. Banking and telephone industries are two that have experienced a dramatic increase in internationalization as producers have turned to nontraditional (frequently foreign) suppliers. The fourth pillar is international negotiations about trade and investment that are now organized much more along sectoral and issue-specific lines than was the case in the past. One rule no longer fits all. But many of the new rules are essentially ad hoc rather than formal. This has opened up the possibilities of bilateral and minilateral (more than two parties, but not all parties) negotiations, but at the expense of the greater transparency that would come from a consistent multilateral focus.

The final two pillars concern the content of the rules of the market-access regime. One is equivalence today between trade and investment, due largely to the activities of transnational corporations in expanding the level of foreign direct investment to astronomical highs. Local content rules about how much of a finished product must be made locally (within a particular country) and worries about the competitive fairness of firm alliances, however, also have led to new efforts by governments in industrialized countries to regulate the flows of foreign investment. "Leveling the playing field," to use the American parlance, has meant pressure and counter-pressure between governments to ensure at least a degree of similarity in regulation (in, for example, cases of presumed monopoly or antitrust violations). The final pillar involves the shift on the part of firms from a concern with national or home-base comparative advantage to a concern with establishing global or world-regional competitive advantages internal to firms and their networks. This reflects the overwhelming attractiveness of "multinationality" to many businesses as a way of diversifying assets, increasing market access, and enjoying the firm economies of scale that come from supplying larger markets. At the same time, plant economies of scale (reductions in unit costs attributable to an increased volume of output) have tended to decrease across a wide range of sectors, as noted first by Joe Bain in 1959.[59] This means that large firms can enjoy firm economies of scale without having just a few large factories. They are not restricted by the lure of high-average plant economies to one or few production locations. Production facilities can be located to take advantage of other benefits that come from operating in multiple locations, particularly those offered by foreign sites.

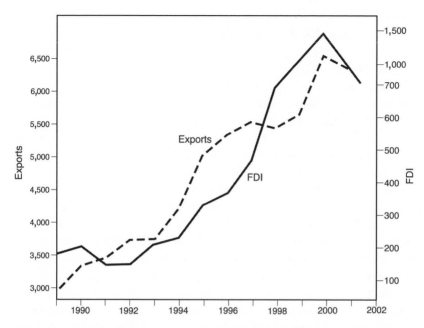

FIGURE 6.3. The Growth of Total World Foreign Direct Investment Relative to Exports, 1989–2001 in billions of current US$.
Source: International Monetary Fund, *Direction of Trade Statistics* (2002); *Balance of Payment Statistics Yearbook* (2001).

Five important consequences seem to set the new transnational order associated with the market-access regime apart from the immediate postwar period. First, foreign direct investment has increased at a faster rate than has the growth of exports (Figure 6.3). The ties that bind the world economy together are increasingly those of direct investment more than trade. In the late 1980s and 1990s, the rate of growth of foreign direct investment in the world economy was three times that of the growth of world exports of goods and services.[60]

Second, national trade accounts can be misleading guides to the complex patterns of trade and investment that characterize the new global economy. Perhaps 50 percent of total world trade between countries as of 2000 was trade within firms. Further, more than half of all trade between the major industrial countries is trade between firms and their foreign affiliates. A third of U.S. exports goes to American-owned firms abroad; another third goes from foreign firms in America to their home countries. And because the new global trading networks involve the exchange of services as much as the movement of components and finished goods, many products no longer have distinctive national identities.[61] The U.S. 1986 trade deficit of $144 billion thus becomes a trade surplus of $77 billion if the activities of U.S.-owned firms outside the United States and foreign-owned firms in the United States are included in the calculations.[62]

Third, as the U.S. territorial economy loses manufacturing jobs and shares of world production to other countries, the global shares of its firms are maintained or enhanced. As the U.S. share of world manufactured exports went from 17.5 percent in 1966 to 14 percent in 1984, American firms and their affiliates increased their shares from 17.7 percent to 18.1 percent.[63] This leads to the question, "Who is U.S.?" in relation to government policies that can favor U.S. firms rather than the U.S. economy.[64] From this point of view, helping "foreign" firms locate in the United States benefits the U.S. territorial economy more than helping "American" firms, which may be owned by Americans or headquartered in the United States but have most of their facilities and employees located overseas. As long as the American economy is growing through increased employment and productivity, these paradoxes will exact little political price. But under recession and as the U.S. government reconstructs the tax code to benefit (nominally) U.S. businesses at the expense of the median taxpayer (as with the administration of George W. Bush), they can be expected to receive more attention.

Fourth, the productive and cultural linkages at the heart of globalization are increasingly anchored in discrete regions and localities within countries rather than to countries as a whole. From the point of view of transnational businesses, for example, the United States is not a unitary space but a disparate congeries of places with quite different costs and benefits from an investment purview. Returns to agglomeration (such as locating near similar firms with pools of skilled labor and common services, as with Hollywood and Silicon Valley), state incentives (such as tax breaks for locating in a given jurisdiction), and access to key resources (such as cheaper labor when labor costs are a high component of total costs) determine the relative attractiveness of different regions. Macroeconomic conditions, then, frequently provide only the broadest of contexts within in which much more geographically specific investment decisions are made.[65]

Fifth, the U.S. government still remains the "enforcer" of last resort to keep the entire market-access regime in place, but often in a more clearly neoimperial capacity in relation to purported allies than during the period from 1947 to 1971. This role can take on several different forms that have varied across administrations and in response to different situations from the 1970s to the present. One is in the form of military intervention to either impose political stability or remove recalcitrant governments. The administration of George W. Bush has had no compunction about following this course of action, using the pretext of the terrorist assaults on New York's World Trade Center and the U.S. Department of Defense in Washington, D.C. (the Pentagon) on September 11, 2001. A second form is to oversee and underwrite financial bailouts for countries facing either bankruptcy or serious monetary crisis. The cases of Mexico in 1983, Indonesia and other Southeast Asian countries in 1998, and Turkey and Argentina in 2002 are examples of this. A third form is to publicize and recruit elite supporters around the world for present globalization (in the shape of the market-access regime) as both inevitable and positive. Even the government of nominally Communist China seems to have accepted many of the precepts of the marketplace society. Whether the U.S. government can afford to continue policing globalization when its benefits do not proportionately trickle back to the U.S. territorial economy and whether the rest of the world will continue to indulge U.S. attempts at using globalization for U.S. ends are probably the major questions facing the long-term sustainability of the market-access regime.[66] In some issue-areas, the U.S. government now has considerable difficulty either persuading or coercing others. For example, antitrust, tax evasion, and illegal immigration are some of the issues that the U.S. government no longer shows any sign of exercising leadership over.[67] A time may be approaching, therefore, when the direct U.S. government role in globalization will be much reduced, but U.S. hegemony's institutionalization in various global forums might augur globalization's continuation without much control by the U.S. government.[68]

The Geography of Globalization

The Cold War era certainly laid the groundwork for what we see around us in the early twenty-first century. But it is since the 1970s that the geography of power around the world has changed the most. In particular, existing territorial states have become less and less "full societies." At one and the same time they are both too large and too small. They are too large for full social identities and many real economic interests. This can be observed in the economic and political divisions between regions in the United States, often only papered over by the declaration of common "national" interests at stake in some far-off corner of the globe. It can also be seen in the efflorescence of national claims among ethnic groups in a wide range of states. But existing states are also too small for many economic purposes. They are increasingly "market sectors" within an intensely competitive, integrated, yet unstable world economy. This is the paradox of fragmentation in the context of globalization that many geographers have noted about the world since the "slow ending" of the Cold War in the 1980s. Though frequently seen as separate processes, globalization and fragmentation are in fact related aspects of a geopolitical order that has been slowly emerging.

In writing about international relations and political economy there has been little commentary on this dual process of fragmentation and globalization.[69] The fact that a state-based hegemony, such as the United States', has been a temporary phenomenon of the nineteenth and twentieth centuries has received short shrift.[70] Most images of world order retain a focus on territorial states and an assumption of "dead space" around and within them that prevents the possibility of even contemplating alternative geographies of power. A writer who does contemplate this, Richard Rosecrance, offers one argument why this is so rare:

> One of the difficulties of most international theory is that it has been analytical rather than historical in character: it has been deterministic rather then contingent. Models have been offered that described one historical age in theoretical terms but failed to account for others. The dynamics of historical development has in this way defeated any purely monistic approach.[71]

On the other side of the debate about globalization are those who make sweeping claims about the "death of distance," the hypermobility of goods and messages, and postmodern nomads who live permanently on the move. In this frame of reference, economies and cultures are no longer rooted in places. There is no geography at all. But this image of the world depends on two fallacious assumptions. The first is that there once was a totalizing age of fixed territories, based on a "norm of sedentarism," that has now been transcended by technologies of time-space compression.[72] In fact, people and things have been in motion, albeit at slower speeds, for much of human history. What is new about contemporary globalization is the increasingly global dominance of images and practices intimately related to the marketplace society and the speed at which transactions traverse the world. The second assumption is that only recently has the global become intricately interwoven with the local. In one sense of course there is no such thing as the "global." It exists only as an emergent property; the global is made up of webs of interaction, movement, surveillance, and regulation between people and institutions with discrete locations in particular places. What is new is the density and geographical scope of the weave among places not the existence of global/local connections as such.

Globalization

British hegemony in the nineteenth century made trade more free and interdependent. American hegemony during the Cold War went a considerable step further in promoting the transnational movement of all of the mobile factors of production: capital, labor, and technology. Free trade could always be limited when production was organized entirely on a national basis. But today production as well as trade moves relatively easily across national boundaries. People are also moving in large numbers but face much greater barriers to movement than capital and trade. In this world, the possibility of a successful self-contained or autarkic national economy has been much reduced. This means that hegemony can itself begin to lose any clear national identity. Economic power, the material basis to military and political power, is no longer a simple attribute of single "container" or "storage bin" states that have more or less of it.

There is varied evidence for this qualitative shift in the character of the world economy and the diminution in the economic importance of existing territorial states as the basic units of account. First of all, since the 1950s, but at a rapidly expanding pace in the 1980s and 1990s, world trade has expanded at a rate well in excess of that of earlier periods.[73] Most of this growth in trade has occurred in the already industrialized regions of the world. It owes much to the declining importance of transportation costs and to institutional innovations such as the GATT (since 1994 the WTO) and the European Union. In a world of large-scale trade there is a premium placed upon maintaining openness and balance rather than territorial expansion and military superiority.[74]

Different world regions have shared unequally in the growth of trade. Expansion of trade in manufactured goods has far exceeded that of primary commodities. By and large, the more industrialized economies have experienced the greatest growth in trade. The hitherto isolated and insulated American economy has become a major participant as a node in this finely balanced *system* of trade. In the late 1970s the main circuits of this system were as follows: (1) a U.S. manufacturing trade deficit with East Asia (cars, electronics, clothing) offset by a surplus with

Europe (computers, aerospace); (2) a net U.S. trade surplus with Latin America balanced by an outflow of U.S. direct investment, primarily to Brazil and Mexico; (3) European manufacturing deficits with the United States and East Asia balanced by surpluses with Africa; and (4) Japan's surpluses with Europe and the United States balanced by payments for energy and raw materials and the export of capital to the United States, East Asia, and elsewhere.[75]

In the 1980s this system started to destabilize because of the debt crisis and an overexpansion of the U.S. trade deficit with Japan and East Asia. Since the 1990s, as the debt crisis became chronic rather than acute, the rise of China as a trading partner of the United States has tended to undermine the balance in the system, along with the intervention of Chinese and Japanese governments to keep the exchange rates of their currencies with the U.S. dollar from rising and thus undermining the competitiveness of their exports. Each party has an interest in keeping the balance within limits, given the extent of cross-border capital flows and mutual dependence on each other's markets. For example, Japanese direct investment in the United States has increasingly substituted products made in the United States for ones imported from Japan. China's dependence on the United States as a final market for many of its exports limits its options in challenging U.S. exchange-rate policy, but U.S. dependence on China for products it no longer manufactures also limits U.S. government leverage over Chinese economic policies.

In this porous world economy promoted by U.S.-style capitalism, it is a mistake to analyze any one country's domestic outlook as if each were a world unto itself. Capital and goods now flow relatively easily from region to region. Indeed, a case can be made that as of 2003, China and Japan allowed the United States to run unprecedented current account deficits by building up huge dollar reserves that they then used to prop up the dollar exchange rate against the yuan and the yen. Given the state of the U.S. federal budget and the yawning U.S. balance-of-payments deficit in 2004, it is more than a little ironic that U.S. military spending, for example, which is designed to project the United States as the world's "sole remaining superpower," has come to depend on China and Japan for a large part of its financing. In late 2004, foreigners owned one-third of U.S. Treasury bonds, of which China and Japan accounted for about one-half. Of course, this does limit U.S. action to force any change in Chinese and Japanese exchange-rate policies. The bottom line for the United States circa 2004 is that domestic manufacturing in the United States, undermined by Chinese and Japanese competition, has been sacrificed to maintain American federal budgetary profligacy and to serve the interests of U.S. (and other) multinational firms locating their factories in China. The imbalances in the world economy are the consequence of the increasing geographical specialization that is economic globalization's driving force. But even as the imbalances threaten to explode, the parties involved are so closely bound together that it pays for them to compromise with one another rather than see the imbalances as a zero-sum or winner-take-all game. This is the essence of a deterritorializing, yet still largely state-regulated, world economy.

Second, American multinational firms have been major agents in stimulating a more open world economy. For example, as mentioned previously, even as the U.S. territorial economy's total share of world exports shrank by one-quarter between 1966 and 1984, U.S.-based firms still accounted for the same proportion of world exports because of their worldwide operations.[76] Even small firms have been "going global." As a first step they often rely on joint ventures, partnerships, and licensing agreements. The expansion abroad may be reluctant, designed to diversify markets and gain access to foreign demand more than to conquer global market share. But it illustrates the general pressure to "compete internationally to be successful," irrespective of firm size.[77] Crucially, however, the Americans have been joined by multinationals from all over the world, from China and South Korea to Western Europe and Japan. By 1985, European firms accounted for fully 50 percent of total world foreign direct investment (FDI). Non-American multinationals now account for a majority of total world FDI. With the exception of capital flows to offshore financial centers, FDI in developing countries, except for China and some Southeast Asian countries, has tailed off over the past twenty years. At the same time, FDI between North America, Japan, and Western Europe has exploded. Between 1983 and 1989 and again between 1992 and 1999, this FDI grew approximately three times faster than the rate of world trade growth. Between 1960 and 1983, world trade and FDI had grown at comparable rates. By the mid-1990s, foreign-owned assets had reached 57 percent of world gross domestic product. In 1980 they had been just 18 percent of the total.[78] The "nationality" of the firms is increasingly unrelated to the distribution of their assets.

Third, even the relatively protectionist Japanese economy, the second largest in the world after the United States, is increasingly internationalized and subject to stresses generated abroad.[79] For example, the "meltdown" of various Asian economies in 1997–1998 had negative effects on Japan because of heavy Japanese involvement in that region through exports, investment, and production. Since the late 1980s, Japanese-owned foreign assets have become comparable to American ones. Paralleling the U.S. experience, much of this is in FDI rather than just in bonds or portfolio investment. The increased openness of the Japanese economy is also evident in the growing role of the yen in international transactions, particularly in Asia; in the importance of the Japanese central bank in global finance; and in the ties being forged through FDI with the European Union, the United States, East Asia, Mexico, and Russia.

Fourth, the world financial system is increasingly globalized. The demands of institutional investors, such as pension funds and insurance companies, for more diversified portfolios; the deregulation of national stock markets; and the floating of currency-exchange rates have led to a transnationalization of finance. Deregulation in the 1980s, particularly in London and New York, encouraged the development of new financial products such as junk bonds, derivatives, and hedge funds. To serve their worldwide clienteles, many financial markets now operate around the clock and without close government supervision. They work with a mix of currencies. The U.S. dollar may well still dominate, but increasingly other currencies, particularly the Euro and the yen, have also acquired reserve functions. These financial trends have redefined the space for national monetary sovereignty by encouraging ever more intensive and rapid cross-border flows of capital. The threat of capital flight constrains governments to follow tight counterinflationary policies and limit fiscal expansion. This sets clear limits to government social spending when seen as inflationary and likely to increase interest rates and dampen private sector growth. Such trends also increase the vulnerability of national banking systems to the looser practices and outright criminality of banks operating outside regulated national channels.

Fifth, various institutions and new social groups have emerged as agents of the globalization of production and exchange. The IMF and the World Bank, for example, have become both more powerful and more autonomous of their member states than was intended when they were founded in the 1940s. The WTO, successor to the GATT, is off to a rough start but nevertheless also provides a forum potentially "greater than the sum of its parts." Private organizations such as the Trilateral Commission and the World Economic Forum attempt to build an internationalist consensus among leading businessmen, journalists, and academics from the United States, Europe, and Japan.[80] Some commentators see the progressive growth of an international "bourgeoisie" or class of the managerial employees of transnational firms whose loyalties are to those firms more than to the states from which they come.[81] Whether such nascent groups will become important actors in the world economy as agents of "transnational liberalism" will depend in large part on the success of transnational organizations such as the Trilateral Commission and the World Economic Forum in maintaining and legitimizing an open world economy.

Sixth, and finally, boundaries between states are either slowly dissolving for a range of flows, as in the case of states within the European Union; becoming opportunities for cross-border collaboration, as with the so-called Euregios between adjacent European countries and the various forums on the Irish border emanating from the Good Friday Agreement of 1998; or shifting their effective locus from the edges of states to the airports and port cities where most migrants, refugees, and asylum seekers attempt entry. For most people, however, interstate boundaries retain a general significance with access to citizenship rights and political identity that they have begun to lose for businesses.[82] Indeed, this is a major source of conflict in many relatively wealthy countries such as the United States, France, and Britain, as immigrants from poor countries become the target of political movements anxious to reinstate border controls to reestablish national cultural homogeneity. One consequence of the terror attacks of September 11, 2001, in the United States has been a "rebordering" of the country, even as the economy still depends on massive inflows of capital and goods from outside. But imposing a simple "inside-outside" set of boundaries on the country in the face of the imperatives of globalization will be no easy task.

This new world economy is neither inherently stable nor irreversible. In particular, total levels of world trade and flows of foreign direct investment could be limited by the growth of world-regional trading blocs, such as the European Union and the North American Free Trade Agreement (NAFTA), which divert trade and investment into more protected circuits and reduce the global flows that have expanded most in recent years, by the failure of many parts of the world to achieve benefits from globalization, and by the difficulty of reforming international institutions (from the United Nations system to the IMF and the World Bank) to make them more open and democratic.

Fragmentation

Under the rigid military blocs of the Cold War and before the emergence of the "market access regime" in the 1970s, improvements in per capita incomes, regional economic policies, and state repression produced a world order in which state and society were mutually defining. With globalization, however, an increasingly uneven process of economic development, the retreat from regional policies in the face of pressures to increase "national" competitiveness in the world economy, and the demise of state socialism in all but a few outposts such as Cuba, Laos, and North Korea have called this equation into question. Interdependent with economic globalization, therefore, has been growth in within-state sectionalism, localism, regionalism, and ethnic separatism.

This growing fragmentation seems to have two aspects to it. One is the redefinition of economic interests from national to regional, local, and ethnic-group scales. The other is the questioning of political identity as singularly a phenomenon of existing states. The first of these is the direct result of the breakdown of the national economy as the basic building block of the world economy.[83] Economic restructuring has involved a collapse of regional-sectoral economic specialization in established industries (cars in Detroit, steel in Pittsburgh, etc.) and the decentralization of production to multiple locations, including many in other states. At the same time, markets are less and less organized on purely national grounds. One important political consequence has been a geographical redefinition of economic interests. Local areas are now tied directly to global markets where they must compete for investment with other localities and regions. Meanwhile, the economically stimulative and regulative activities of national governments have weakened and become less effective. Geared toward a national economy that has fragmented into regional and sectoral parts, government policies can no longer shield local communities or ethnic groups from the impacts of competition or readily redistribute resources to declining or poorer areas.

The net result, as Chapter 7 shows in more detail, has been a substantial upswing in income inequalities within countries, even if in a context of overall rising average incomes at a world scale (accounted for particularly by the spectacular economic growth of China and, to a lesser extent, India). The trend toward increasing polarization (across income categories and regions) within countries has been much greater than that between countries. In other words, relatively more of total global income inequality is now accounted for within countries than between them, although between-country differences among poor countries (as a category) have also increased.

The other aspect of fragmentation has been encouraged by the crumbling of national economies, but relates more to the emergence of new political identities often based on old but revitalized ethnic divisions.[84] The past twenty years have seen the proliferation of political movements with secessionist or autonomist objectives. In Western Europe this trend can be related to the growing redundancy of national governments with the increased power of the European Union and increasing levels of relative deprivation between regions and ethnic groups. In Eastern Europe and the former Soviet Union, the assertion of ethnic identities has more to do with the demise of strong national governments, the exhaustion of state socialism as an ideology that incorporated ethnic elites, and the settling of old political scores from the distant past. In Africa, and to a degree elsewhere, national-level economic development and nation-building are being sacrificed, after the immediate euphoria of independence and the stasis imposed by the Cold War, to ethnic and regional interests. These now have to seek their fortune in a world where their state powers, weak as they may be, are increasingly co-opted by international institutions such as the IMF and the World Bank. As a result, the boundaries between regions and localities within countries are increasingly challenging the boundaries that appear on the world political map as the more meaningful ones from the perspective of everyday social life for many people. In the Sudan, for example, the north-south divide is more important politically than that between Sudan and neighboring states. This process is not restricted to Africa. In Ireland, for example, while the border between north and south maintains its symbolic political importance, the borders between neighborhoods in cities such as Belfast and the economic gap between Dublin and the rural far west of Ireland are more important in people's daily lives. One consequence of increased political-economic and ethnic divisions within countries has been an increase in the devolution of regulatory and administrative functions to regions and localities.[85]

Conclusion

Contemporary globalization is not simply the result of technological change, the spread of modernity, or the intellectual attraction of liberal economics. All of these phenomena could have taken place without the emergence of the particular geographical logic that marks the present world economy. This logic is traceable to the dominant influence exerted on the world economy over the past fifty years by the U.S. government putting into practice on a world scale, and in the face of a variety of countervailing powers, an ideological disposition and a set of policies initially developed within the United States itself.

American hegemony—the sponsorship and naturalization of marketplace society—has gone through two principal phases since the Second World War, when the United States emerged as one of the main victors. In the first Bretton Woods phase, the U.S. government served as the global lender of last resort, instituted a number of international economic and political organizations for multilateral management of the world economy, and integrated a free world economy through organizing alliances against its major adversary: the Soviet Union. By the 1960s, the first part of this system was in serious trouble from an American perspective. Under the Bretton Woods system the U.S. government could not devalue the U.S. dollar to stimulate U.S. national exports and national economic growth. Ironically, therefore, the more open, free-wheeling world economy that came into existence beginning in the 1970s had its origins in the self-serving actions of the U.S. government.

The market-access regime for trade and foreign direct investment that has replaced the old Bretton Woods system has relied on speeding up the world financial system, breaking up national economies into distinctive geographical parts, using the Bretton Woods institutions (particularly the IMF and the World Bank) to discipline states following nonconforming economic policies, and having the United States as enforcer of global norms of political and economic conduct, even if the fiscal consequences for the U.S. territorial economy are grave indeed. Beginning with the Reagan administration in 1981, a series of bold attempts has been made to reassert American centrality to the world economy, even while encouraging globalization. Whether what now seems like a paradox is sustainable, however, is very much open to question. The next two chapters address, respectively, the inequalities and dynamics of the new global economy and the impacts of globalization on the United States itself.

7 The New Global Economy

In recent studies of the world economy invoking the impact of globalization, the idea of "time-space compression" or its equivalents have dominated discussion among geographers and many others.[1] This idea postulates that revolutionary changes in communication and transportation technologies are producing a new global economy. In this chapter I challenge the adequacy of this idea for understanding the course of the contemporary world economy and the new uneven development it is producing. In its place I argue for the importance of the geopolitical role of the United States and the vision of world economic order—*transnational liberalism*—which, post-1970s, the U.S. government has actively sponsored, both unilaterally and multilaterally, in the emergence of the new global space-economy and its geographical structure. In this perspective, technological changes have been enabling and encouraging rather than determining in and of themselves.

I start with a brief discussion of how state-defined space or territoriality has tended to monopolize understandings of economic development. I then offer a critical survey of the various strands of the emerging literature that sees time-space compression as leading the transformation of the world economy into a global space-economy. Two strands are distinguished that focus on the singularity of the present, suggesting that contemporary "time-space compression" augurs a postmodern world in which the fixed territorial spaces of modernity no longer match a new world of kaleidoscopic and jumbled spaces where speed conquers established geopolitical representations. One of these strands maintains a focus on the role of the agents of capital in creating this new world, while the other tends to highlight the impact of new communication and representational technologies such as round-the-clock news reporting, the Internet, and new weapons systems. A third strand sees greater continuity between the present and past in the configuration of global space. In this perspective, new local spaces interlinked with existing territorial spaces produce a mosaic pattern to global development, with local as much as global forces leading the process. It is not obvious what is entirely new about much of this. The world's economic geography has long been a product of a mix of localizing and globalizing pressures. What is new is a very different geopolitical context in which American hegemony now operates without the constraints of the Cold War. In a third section, therefore, I briefly recapitulate the case for the geopolitics of globalization laid out in more detail in previous chapters. In line with this argument, a fourth and final section offers evidence for an emerging pattern of global uneven development—in terms of global income inequalities that show increasing polarization between classes and regions within countries—for which the global market-access regime sponsored by the U.S. government offers a more complete historical explanation than does time-space compression or any related technological-economic explanation.

States and Territorial Space

From one point of view, terrestrial space is inert. It is simply the geographical surface upon which physical, social, and economic practices and ideas exert their influence. But because the impact of practices and ideas is historically cumulative and geographically differentiating, space can be thought of as having long-term effects on the conduct of human life because of the very unevenness in the spatial distribution of physical resources and human capabilities. In this way, space is turned into place or "lived space": the humanly constructed settings for social and political action. Contemporary geography has abandoned the view once characteristic of many of its Anglo-American and German practitioners that physical geography is determining of other features of geographical difference across geographical scales, from the local to the global. Rather, social and economic practices are now seen as primary in creating geographical differences of all kinds.

In the modern political realm, lived space has been almost invariably associated with the idea of state-territoriality; politics is about modes of government within and patterns of conflict and cooperation between the territories or tightly bounded spaces of modern states. Plausibly, however, this rendition of the association between politics and place is both historically and geographically problematic. Not only is the state-territory relationship a relatively recent one, but it is also one that has never completely vanquished other types of political geography (such as network-based kinship and city-state or core-periphery imperial political systems) around the world. Writing about "failed" or "quasi" states in locations as diverse as East Africa or southern Europe, for example, often misses the fact that the absence of a working state bureaucracy throughout a given state's territory does not signify the absence of either politics or of alternative governance arrangements working nonterritorially.

"Political space," therefore, cannot be reduced to state-territoriality for two reasons. First, states are always and everywhere challenged by forms of politics that do not conform to the boundaries of the state in question. For example, some localities have kinship or patronage politics, others have ethnic or irredentist politics oriented to either autonomy or secession, and others support political movements opposed to current constitutional arrangements, including the distribution of governmental powers between different tiers of government within the state. Second, state boundaries are permeable, and increasingly so, to a wide range of flows of ideas, investments, goods, and people that open up territories to influences beyond the geographical reach of current governmental powers.

The point is that territoriality is only one type of spatiality or way in which space is constituted socially and mobilized politically.[2] Territoriality always has two features: blocks of rigidly bordered space and domination or control as the modality of power upon which the bordering relies. This may well be legitimate power—that is, exercised with authority (either bureaucratic or charismatic), but it ultimately rests on demarcation through domination. Yet, both space and power have other possible modalities.[3] *Authoritative* power, involving command and obedience, can also operate over long distances (for example, through the deployment of military assets), but this has less possibility of sustained or legitimate impact on the people with whom it comes into contact. This is a networked form of domination, however; it is based on control over flows through space-spanning networks, not control over blocks of space. To the contrary, *diffused* power refers to power that is not centered or directly commanded but that results from patterns of social association and interaction in groups and movements or through market exchange.[4] It can be territorialized, but only so far as the networks it defines are territorially constrained by authoritative power. Otherwise, networks are limited spatially only by the purposes for which they are formed. In this way, power is generated through association and affiliation rather than through command or domination.[5] When not sustained through collective action, however, the power networks created will disintegrate.

Global corporate elite networks form one of the most important emerging nonterritorial driving forces of the new global economy.[6] These involve both interlocking corporate directorships and global policy groups (such as the International Chamber of Commerce [ICC], the Bilderberg Conferences, the Trilateral Commission, the World Economic Forum, and the World Business Council on Sustainable Development [WBCSD]). While corporate directorships represent the operations of distinctive business interests, global policy groups provide a much more overtly political agenda in representing the goals of different varieties of transnational liberalism, from the laissez faire capitalism of the ICC to the more evidently regulationist WBCSD. Though many corporations still have important "home bases" with respect to the recruitment of executives as well as operations,[7] they are increasingly tied together *politically* through transnational networks that conjoin businesses both directly and indirectly through the various policy groups. For example, the sociologists Carroll and Carson have shown empirically how the five major global policy groups relate to interlocking directorates and how each, in turn, makes a distinctive contribution to a transnational capitalist hegemony by building consensus across global corporate elites and by making the case to publics and governments for their versions of transnational liberalism. These range from unrestricted free trade and monetarism to more regulated versions focused on achieving international collaboration for common goals.[8] Though highly centralized around a few cosmopolitan business leaders, the network extends unevenly across major corporations and around the world.

Consequently, in geographical perspective there is an imbalance between the overwhelming emphasis in the contemporary social sciences on territorial states as the main vehicles of governance and the geographically variegated world that current territorial government is ill-suited to manage and represent by itself. Literature has begun to develop in geography that addresses the sources of this political impasse. Most of this relates to the idea of time-space compression.

Time-Space Compression and the End of History

By early in the twentieth century, it appeared obvious that the German philosopher, and prophet of the world of territorial nation-states, G.W.F. Hegel seemed to have gotten it right a hundred years earlier. As

Hegel had taught, history seemed to have culminated with the advent of the European nation-state and the nation-state seemed to be the highest form of governance, accepted as representing the fundamental essence of Western civilization. Now a new end of history has appeared. This time, however, it is one in which the globe substitutes for the state. The ease with which space is now overcome, militarily, economically, and culturally, is seen as creating a world in which "all that is solid melts into air," to borrow a phrase from Karl Marx. Capital now moves around the world at the press of a button, goods can be shipped over great distances at relatively low costs because of containerization and other innovations, cultural icons represented by such products as blue jeans and Coke bottles are recognizable the world over, and Stealth technology undermines the ability of territorial military power to police its air space. A new postmodern world is emerging in which old rules of spatial organization based on linear-distance decay of transportation costs and territorial containing of externality effects have broken down.

Under the new "flexible accumulation" associated with globalization, the unique attributes of particular places can take on greater value for what they can offer to increasingly mobile capital, from specific types of labor market to fiscal incentives. The need for rapid access to information has privileged those "world cities" that have good connectivity to other places. The local availability of entrepreneurship, venture capital, technical know-how, and design capabilities differentiate "attractive" from "unattractive" sites for investment. At the same time, tastes are increasingly volatile, subject to manipulation through advertising and the decline of status-markers other than those of consumption. Niche markets associated with different social groups increasingly cross national boundaries, giving rise to cross-national markets that can be served by factories located in any one of them or, for labor-intensive goods, produced wherever labor costs are lower.

To David Harvey, one of the most persuasive advocates of time-space compression as the cause of recent globalization, the "condition of postmodernity" does not signify the decreasing importance of space (at least, not for now).[9] Rather, it represents the latest round in capitalism's long-term annihilation of space by time in which capitalists must now pay "much closer attention to relative locational advantages, precisely because diminishing spatial barriers give [them] the power to exploit minute spatial differentiations to good effect. Small differences in what space contains in the way of labor supplies, resources, infrastructures, and the like become of increased significance."[10] Politically, this makes local populations and elites increasingly vulnerable to the depredations of capital without the shield of the state. States are increasingly debordered and hollowed out. Spatial differentiation benefits some places, but all are subject to the threat of withdrawal of capital unless they conform to its demands.

Yet, ultimately, given the logic of time-space compression, the expected world is one where people no longer matter very much, materially or culturally. Implicit in the perspective is an imminent decline in the significance of place, as first technological conditions and then social relations produce an increasingly homogenized global space within which local difference will be purely the result of human volition and probably politically reactionary in prompting nostalgia for past differences. Only in the here and now is there increased differentiation, as new technologies conjoined to the unchanging imperative of capital accumulation work unevenly across the face of the postmodern world. The historical record, however, offers little comfort to this teleology. Wealth and power always seem to pool up in some places and not in others. However, this time around the pattern is a much more localized one than that associated with the era of national-industrial (Fordist) capitalism and its welfare states.

Drawing particularly on the philosopher Henri Lefebvre, Edward Soja argues that *thinking* about the politics of space has changed along with the material impacts suggested by Harvey.[11] In particular, Soja claims evidence for a "spatial turn" in contemporary social science in which the previously dominant historicist approaches are increasingly challenged and displaced by ones in which "lived space" is conjoined with "perceived" and "conceived" space to build a "shared spatial consciousness . . . to take control over the production of our lived spaces."[12] In other words, a critical spatial imagination has been stimulated by recent transformations in the production of space, giving rise to a new "spatial politics" that fundamentally challenges hitherto dominant historical-social conceptions of political change. From this point of view, the end of history is as much intellectual and political as it is material.[13] As yet, however, the "normal" social sciences show little or no evidence of the "spatial turn," notwithstanding the strong logical case that Soja makes for its arrival.[14] To them, to quote writer William Faulkner's famous phrase about the American South, "the past isn't dead, it isn't even past."

At the same time, not much has changed in the distribution of power. It is still concentrated in the hands of relatively few powerful states and dominant market actors. The possibilities of organized resistance to this concentration of power may well be enhanced in local places that have coveted assets, but certainly not in those that the powers-that-be are more than willing to write off as used up or without anything to offer to them. The prospects for resistance, therefore, are geographically contingent at scales other than the national and in various localities, not because of a new world in which spatial consciousness is now predominant but precisely because of the character of the *historical* moment in which we now find ourselves.

A second strand in writing about time-space compression emphasizes more the role of speed in postmodernity than the role of local places or lived space. Indeed, in this understanding, "the power of pace is outstripping the power of place."[15] Accepting the rhetoric of the gurus of the Internet world and the "Third Wave," this perspective sees the world as on a technological trajectory in which global space is being "remastered" by a totally new geopolitical imagination in which accelerating flows of information and identities undermine modernist territorial formations. Drawing on such writers as Paul Virilio,[16] "Places are conceptualized in terms of their ability to accelerate or hinder the exchanges of global flowmations."[17] Space is reimagined not as "fixed masses of territory, but rather as velocidromes, with high traffic speedways, big band-width connectivities, or dynamic web configurations in a worldwide network of massively parallel kineformations."[18] Though there is much truth to this story, the main danger here, as McKenzie Wark notes, is mistaking a trend toward massively accelerated information flow with a deterritorialized world in which where people are no longer matters.[19] In my view, it still matters immensely. Some places are well-connected while others are not; media and advertising companies work out of some locations and cultures and not out of others. The simulations of the media are still distinguishable (for some people) from the perils and dilemmas of everyday life. Pace is itself problematic and potentially disruptive when the images and information conveyed lead to information overload and fatigue more than accurate and real-time decision making. The much-hyped televisual world must still engage with an actual world in which most people have very limited daily itineraries that root them to very particular places. To think that geopolitics is being replaced by chronopolitics is to project the desire for a boundaryless world characteristic of an older utopianism onto an actual world in which the old geopolitical imagination is still very much alive and well. History has not yet ended in instant electronic simulation. History is not the same as the History Channel.

A third strand of thinking is less apocalyptic about recent change in the nature of global space. It sees recent shifts from more to less territorialized modes of social and political organization, such as those global corporate networks mentioned previously, as growing out of previous features of global political-economic organization. In particular, it emphasizes that the spatial organization or spatiality of development is increasingly "constructed through interactions between flow economies and territorial economies."[20] It is not a question of either/or but of how one relates to the other.

In this strand, a number of different territorial-organizational dynamics are distinguished so as to better monitor the trend toward globalization and its challenge to established, largely territorial modes of regulation and governance. Local sources of advantage maintain a role that cannot produce complete locational substitutability for businesses moving investments from place to place. Michael Storper, for example, distinguishes four dynamics that work differentially across economic sectors and world regions:

> In some cases, the opening up of interterritorial relations places previously existing locationally specific assets into a new position of global dominance. In a second set of cases, those assets are devalued via substitution by other products that now penetrate local markets; this is not a straightforward economic process, however; it is culturally intermediated. In a third set of cases, territorial integration permits the fabled attainment of massive economies of scale and organization, devalues locationally specific assets and leads to deterritorialization and widespread market penetration. In a fourth set of cases, territorial integration is met by differentiation and destandardization of at least some crucial elements of the commodity chain, necessitating the reinvention of territory-specific relational assets.[21]

Globalization of trade, foreign direct investment, and production, therefore, are not just about an emerging geography of flows, but also about how flows fit into and adapt to existing territorial or place-based patterns of economic development.

The point is that "globalization does not entrain some single, unidirectional, sociospatial logic."[22] Rather, place-specific conditions still mediate many production and trade relationships. For example, most multinational businesses still betray strong national biases in investment activity, and the intersection of various external economies and "relational assets" (to use Storper's term) give different places different competitive advantages in expanding their economic base. Various modes of local and long-distance regulation and governance emerge

TABLE 7.1. Combinations of Spatial Transaction Costs and
External Economies

	Spatial transaction costs		
External economies	Low	Medium	High
Low	4	5	1
High	3	6	2

Source: Based on Allen J. Scott, "Regional Motors of the Global
Economy." *Futures* 28 (1996): 391–411.

to handle the development process. In particular, a global trend toward devolution of power to lower tiers of government suggests that
localities and regions have either been mobilized by states to organize their response to market forces[23] or have taken on this role themselves absent the effective capacity of states to act any longer on their
behalf.[24]

Whatever the precise outcome in terms of devolution of regulatory
powers, the new global economy under market-access conditions is
based on trade-offs specific to different business sectors between the
benefits/costs of economic transactions over space, on the one hand, and
the benefits/costs of firms clustering together on the other.[25] The former comes down to spatial transaction costs—that is, the costs involved
in bringing together inputs, serving markets, etc.—whereas the latter
involves the external economies gained from locating adjacent to suppliers, competitors, specialized pools of labor, and so forth (Table 7.1).

In one scenario (similar to the situation facing resource-based industries), wholesaling, retailing, transport costs, and/or direct access to
customers drive locational decisions. Little or no incentive exists for
firms to cluster together. The result is locational patterns closely parallel to the distribution of resources and population (1). A second scenario
(2) is one in which both external economies are significant and spatial
transaction costs are high. This defines the situation of industrial districts and high-technology complexes (such as California's Silicon Valley). Intensive relations between firms encourage clustering, but heavy
inputs of resources and sensitivity to consumer markets put limits on
agglomeration. In a third scenario (3), essentially that of branch-plant
industrialization, external economies are internalized within firms (or
interfirm alliances) and realized through dispersal of production to locations with advantageous costs (e.g., lower wage bills) A fourth scenario
(4) is one where any productive activity can be located anywhere. This

would be the ultimate world of utter time-space compression. As yet, it is without any real-world examples. More likely is the fifth scenario (5), where external economies can be obtained at a distance but spatial transaction costs mandate location close to markets or input sources. Most important to the new global economy is the sixth scenario (6). In this case, external economies are high and spatial transaction costs are average. A high incentive to cluster is the net result. These provide the concentrations of innovative manufacturing and service industries that drive the new global economy. Giant metropolitan areas are the major beneficiaries of this process, given their competitive advantages in the services and suppliers that innovative firms need.

It is often not quite clear, however, what is entirely new about all of this. The world's economic geography has long been a product of a mix of localizing and globalizing pressures, as world-systems theorists have long maintained.[26] In the last case, a genuine skepticism about the empirical basis to globalization as a universal process is also conjoined with a fairly economistic rendering of what is happening. From this viewpoint, it is production that is the sole driving force behind the new global economy. This is where greater attention to geopolitical context is needed, not in denying the scale/complexity of the spatial impact of globalization so much as offering a different account of its origins, novelty, and geographical impact. From this point of view, contemporary globalization has its roots in the ideological geopolitics of the Cold War, with U.S. government attempts at both reviving Western Europe and challenging Soviet-style economic planning by stimulating a "free-world economy" committed to lowering barriers to world trade and international capital flows.[27]

The Geopolitics of Globalization

Globalization, therefore, did not just *happen*. It required considerable political groundwork, without which technological and economic stimuli to increased international economic interdependence could not have taken place. From the standard American viewpoint, all states ideally would be internationalized, open to the free flow of investment and trade. This not only contrasted with the closed, autarkic character of the Soviet economy, but it also had as a major stimulus the idea that the depression of the 1930s had been exacerbated by the closing down of international trade. In the five decades after 1945, American dominion was at the center of a remarkable explosion in what I have called "interactional" capitalism.[28] Based initially on the expansion of mass consumption within the most industrialized countries, interactional capitalism later involved the systematic reorganization of the world economy around massive increases in the volume of trade in manufactured goods and foreign direct investment.

Beginning in the 1970s, this system started to change in profound ways that augured the onset of the contemporary explosion of globalization (as detailed in Chapter 6). First came increased levels of international trade, particularly between the major industrialized regions of the world, following the revolutionary effects of the Kennedy Round of the General Agreement on Tariffs and Trade (GATT) in the mid-1960s. This was followed in 1971 by the U.S. abrogation of the Bretton Woods Agreement of 1944, liberating currencies from a fixed exchange rate to the U.S. dollar so as to improve the deteriorating trade position of the U.S. economy. Currencies could now float against one another and this created the globalized financial system now in place around the world. Third came the globalization of production associated with dramatic increases in the level of foreign direct investment. Initially led by large American firms, by the 1970s and 1980s European, Japanese, and other firms had also discovered the benefits of production in local markets (above all, those of their main competitors). These benefits included taking advantage of macroeconomic conditions (exchange rates, interest rates, etc.), avoiding tariff and other barriers to direct trade, and gaining knowledge of local tastes and preferences. Foreign direct investment has soared sevenfold since the 1970s, to around $400 billion per year by the late 1990s.[29]

With the collapse of the alternative Soviet system since 1989 (largely because of its failure to deliver the promise of increased material affluence), the "American" model emerged into prominence at a world scale. An approach set in the 1940s to counter the perceived threat to the American model at home by exporting it overseas has given rise to a globalized world economy that is quite beyond what its architects could have foreseen at the outset of the Cold War. Yet, that is where its roots lie—not in recent technological changes or purely in the recent machinations of American or global big business. Globalization has geopolitical, more than simply technological or economic, origins.

Globalization has also had dramatic effects on global political geography, affecting the political autonomy of even the most powerful states. One effect is the internationalization of a range of hitherto domestic policies to conform to global norms of performance. Thus, not only trade policy but also industrial, product liability, environmental, and social welfare policies are subject to definition and oversight in terms of their impacts on market access between countries. A second effect is the increased global trade in services, once produced and consumed largely within state boundaries. In part this reflects the fact that many manufactured goods now contain a large share of service inputs—from R&D to marketing and advertising. But it is also because the revolution in telecommunications since the 1980s that many services, from banking to design and packaging, can now be provided to global markets. Finally, the spreading geographical reach of multinational firms and the growth of international corporate alliances have had profound influences on the nature of trade and investment, undermining the identity between national territories and economic processes. Symptomatic of the integration of trade and investment are concerns about rules, such as rules on unitary taxation, rules governing local content to assess where value was added in production, and rules governing unfair competition and monopoly trading practices.[30]

None of these policy areas is any longer within the singular control of individual so-called sovereign states. They all must live in an increasingly common institutional environment, including the United States. Unfortunately, as demonstrations at the November 1999 World Trade Organization (WTO) (formerly GATT) meeting in Seattle made clear, the global institutional environment is not one currently very open to democratic demands. Indeed, the globalizing world is marked by a crisis of governance because existing national-state–scale institutions cannot offer the spatial reach needed to regulate increasingly worldwide and world-regional transactions, but existing global-scale institutions are still creatures of the most powerful states and dominant business-interest groups from them.

The globalizing world economy is also marked by a substantially different geography of economic prospects and consumption from that of either the territorialized capitalism of the colonial era or the national development strategies of the Cold War period. The new geography would never have emerged without the fundamental changes in the structure and regulation of the world economy that have taken place under American auspices since the 1970s. The new global economy has three particularly distinctive features. The first is its focus around a world city network rather than dominant national economies. This owes something to the economic logic of high external economies and average spatial transaction costs for businesses, outlined previously. But this just begs the question of why firms that exhibit such a cost structure should be in the ascendance. One answer is that the leading sectors in the new global economy are financial and business services such as banks, advertising agencies, market consultancies, law firms, and insurance agencies; media and communications firms; and the real estate, office, and consumer services that sustain them. These all find their best locations in the largest cities. Manufacturing is increasingly located in their hinterlands or in specialized industrial districts.

What is key to this argument is that the power over other sectors and the definition of the avant garde of consumption are increasingly concentrated in a hierarchy of world cities. This is the new geography of power, not just to coerce other places but, through association with affiliated organizations, to give world cities a directing role in the world economy at large. The "global command centers" for this system are New York and London, but the networks that bind it together stretch far and wide, with denser connectivities in Europe and North America (with significant extensions to East Asia) than elsewhere, particularly with respect to "gateway cities" that access important hinterlands for manufacturing, such as Hong Kong for coastal south China.[31]

A second feature is the centrality of consumption and distribution in a world in which daily life for many people is increasingly globalized. Alongside increased rates of physical mobility, particularly to the world cities, there is phenomenally increased exposure to images, products, and practices that flow through the various media of communication. As Bruce Robbins puts it: "We are connected to all sorts of places, causally if not consciously, including many we have never travelled to, that we have perhaps only seen on television—including the place where the television itself was manufactured."[32] This is the world of Ulf Hannerz's "global ecumene" in which, rather than a juxtaposition of separate cultures rooted in different places, there is a complex system of long-distance flows of images, goods, and people moving according to the exchange values of a global marketplace society.[33] In many parts of the world, particularly in world cities and in places strongly connected to global circuits of migration and trade, the local is increasingly a spatial moment in the global rather than an older or residual community rooted in traditional routines.

In an enthralling survey of the relationships between media, mobility, and identity in this new global economy, David Morley quotes Richard

Wilk's description of contemporary Belize, well off the beaten path of the world city networks:

> The economy is open to foreign capital, the stores are full of imports. Belizians themselves are transnational—their families scattered across the United States and Canada, with most of the young expecting to spend part of their lives abroad. Those who stay at home are bombarded with foreign media.... When Belizians turn off the television they can look out the window at a parade of foreign tourists, resident expatriates and students in search of authentic local experience, traditional medicine, untouched rainforests and ancient ruins.[34]

In this world, consumption of foreign goods is widely available to even the poorest segments of the population. This is not simply "Americanization" in terms of consumption of goods that are made for and marketed by American businesses. This is far from it. Although the marketplace model may have American origins, it has long transcended its particular roots. Indeed, many of the most demanded goods are what can be called Japanese electronics, Italian clothes, or French perfumes, except that many of them are no longer made in the national spaces that we intuitively associate with them. The national image is all that may be left of national production.

Does this mean, therefore, in terms of consumption like those of production, that time-space compression is giving rise to cultural homogenization and standardization? In other words, are markets simply overcoming places instead of supporting and differentiating them? Certainly the marketplace model is central to the long-distance relationships through which distribution connects production and consumption. But beyond this there is persisting place differentiation, not just in the exploitation of place images such as "Italian Design" when it is actually "Made in China." For example, McDonald's famously tries to adapt to different local tastes even as it builds global market share in the fast food business.[35] Starbucks is a peculiarly American (even Pacific Northwest) version of the Italian coffee "bar" that has now even diffused to Italy, where it has had to adjust to local tastes in coffee that differ considerably from the "medium roasts" preferred by most Americans. Japan has become increasingly central as a source of American consumption motifs. Perhaps the most obvious example, along with Japanese television cartoons and Pokemon, is the enthusiasm for sushi. In his study of the commodity chain connecting Atlantic bluefin tuna fishing with the Japanese sushi business (a global commodity chain if there ever was one), Theodore Bestor shows how sushi and other Japanese foods, adapted in many ways, have become mainstream in North America.[36] Japanese food has became an inspiration for nouvelle cuisine:

> Wasabi mashed potatoes, sushi ginger relish, and seared sashimi grade tuna steaks have become commonplace in upscale restaurants in North America and Europe. At a coffee shop in Cambridge, Massachusetts, a painted window sign advertises "espresso, cappuccino, carrot juice, lasagna, and sushi." At the same time, sushi has moved down-market as well. Supermarkets even in remote places like Ithaca, New York, now provide take-out sushi box lunches made on the spot by employees wearing *hachimaki* (headbands) and *happi* coats.[37]

The third feature of the new global economy that clearly sets it apart from previous periods is the pace of economic transactions and the difficulties states face in regulating the subsequent rapid flows of people, goods, messages, and capital. Of course, very much part of the story are the technologies that have made possible the acceleration of transportation and telecommunications—from containerization, the jumbo jet, the fax, and the Internet to cell phones, GPS, and computerized stock and currency trading—many of them originating with U.S. Department of Defense research and development programs and the overwhelming emphasis of U.S. business on substituting capital (by means of technology) for labor. But also part of the story is the dispersal and relative density of the people who now need to be connected as rapidly and efficiently as possible. Again, the spread of marketplace society as the medium for economic transactions favors those sites, such as world cities, that provide access both to services and to surrounding hinterlands. At these locations people come together from a wide range of cultural backgrounds and disparate domains of economic organization, political action, and belief to engage with the new technologies. Pace then favors those places most connected to others, both culturally and technologically. It punishes the less connected. Just as the velocity of money and credit increasingly directs the flow of the world economy, so does the increased difficulty states have in exercising oversight prefigure a world increasingly differentiated at geographical levels other than that of states in terms of market access.

Global Uneven Development

Much of the sociological hype about globalization sees it as synonymous with homogenization, as if the whole world was becoming alike culturally and economically. The literature on time-space compression might also suggest such a prospect, if only on the distant horizon. In fact, there is considerable evidence that globalization is polarizing the world as a whole between geographical haves and have-nots: between regions and localities tied into the globalizing world economy and those outside it (Internet and all), and between those who have received a "leg up" into this economy and those who may have to remain outside it. I will cover these points with respect to trends in income inequality between and within groups of countries, but first I want to provide a broader portrait of contemporary global uneven development.

The first point of note is that the globalizing world economy is not an economy of national territories that trade with one another, as the World Bank and other organizations tend to portray it. Rather, it is a complex mosaic of interlinked global city-regions, prosperous rural areas, resource sites, and "dead lands" increasingly cut off from time-space compression. All of these are widely scattered across the globe, even if there is a basic global north-south structure to the world economy as a whole. Some of the prosperous areas, for example, can be found within even the poorest countries, so it is important to bear in mind the mosaic nature of the emerging world economy throughout the following discussion.[38] The word "mosaic" is used advisedly here, not in the sense that Taylor, for example, associates with a world metageography of territorial states, but as a metaphor for the networked links across places and fractured territoriality that characterizes the new global economy.[39]

The second point is that the major geographical anchors of the new global economy are overwhelmingly located in North America, Europe, and East Asia, whatever the income and employment worries of the First-World protesters in Seattle. For example, during the period 1998–2000, the United States, the European Union, and Japan accounted for 75 percent of the inflows of foreign direct investment (FDI) and 85 percent of the outflows, and for almost 60 percent of inward and nearly 80 percent of outward FDI stocks.[40] Trends suggest, however, that since 1985, the United States has become relatively less important as both a source and a destination for FDI, whereas certain poorer countries have become relatively more important as both destinations and as sources; China, Brazil, South Korea, Mexico, and Malaysia are the outstanding cases.

In this context, therefore, the improved economic performance by some formerly poor countries, predominantly in East and Southeast Asia, is worthy of comment. Since 1987, China has become a major destination for FDI and a major exporter of manufactured goods to the

United States and elsewhere. Much of this is due to the low wages paid to Chinese factory workers who are as skilled as any in the world. U.S. and other multinational companies are thus attracted to China because they have particularly labor-intensive processes of production, but also because China has become tightly connected to East Asian business networks anchored to Hong Kong (since 1995 officially part of China but still with a separate administration), Taiwan, and the Chinese diaspora in Southeast Asia and in North America. China's government opened up its economy in the 1980s at precisely the time when wages had begun to increase for workers in such countries as South Korea and Mexico. Not surprisingly, some of China's growth has been at their expense. But the Chinese government has also helped protect and enhance recent national economic growth by freeing local governments and individuals to partner with foreign industries while keeping capital controls and managing the rate of exchange of the currency—the yuan—against the U.S. dollar. This case illustrates the mix of branch-plant industrialization for export markets, large domestic markets, skilled but relatively low-paid labor forces, and the interventionist governments that have lain behind much of the economic success of East Asia since the 1970s.

At the same time, other world regions are on the edge of or are actually falling out of the world economy because they are not attractive to outside investors. Having borrowed heavily in international financial markets to finance national development projects (and elite lifestyles) in the 1970s and 1980s, these regions have become subject to internationally mandated programs of economic restructuring that reflect the dominant neoliberal ideology of the International Monetary Fund (IMF) and global business policy groups such as the ICC more than appropriateness to local circumstances. Large parts of Africa are exemplary. Characteristically, in these cases the economic attributes are more or less the reverse of the ones exhibited by China. In many such countries, however, economic difficulties have been exacerbated by disastrous interethnic rivalries, the AIDS epidemic, and the general weakness of state institutions.

Global Income Inequality

One way of trying to describe the current pattern of global uneven development is to examine trends in global income inequalities. This is something of a snapshot of a wider range of more complex processes at work. There is considerable controversy over the relationship between income inequality and economic growth. But the general consensus is that, ceteris paribus, higher growth eventually reduces inequality. The main contention is about whether this is delayed or whether there is a direct reflection of higher growth in lowered inequality.[41] My presumption is that with globalization there should be a changing pattern in which within-country income inequalities increase relative to between-country ones in the overall context of a much more geographically differentiated global pattern of economic growth across countries.

Until very recently, global income inequalities usually have been measured by comparing the differences between national averages over time. If the differences increased across groups of countries over time, this was interpreted as an increase in global inequality or vice versa. This approach is still widely used. It is certainly an indicator of the relative performance of different national economies and, as such, has merit. But it does not give an accurate account of inequality between individuals at a global scale. In a globalizing economy, estimating shifts in inequality between individuals across all countries might be a better indicator of global inequality. In this construction, it is how individuals are doing, not national economies, that matters. The problem here is that it gives no idea of the processes whereby individual-level inequalities are increasing or decreasing with respect to the performance of global, national, regional, and local economies in which individuals are embedded. After reviewing results from the two approaches, I provide a synthetic account of current trends in global income inequality.

Global Income Inequalities by Country

The aggregate evidence strongly suggests two important trends in global inequality by country: among the richest countries in the world today, per capita incomes have converged over the past 130 years, with the poorer countries among them growing faster and catching up with the richer; and divergence between rich and poor countries has increased, particularly in the era of globalization after 1970.[42] Underlying examining these particular trends, of course, is the idea that most income inequality lies between countries, not within them.

Turning first to convergence among the richer countries, of course, there is something tautological here, in that countries that were relatively rich and became poorer (such as Argentina) and ones that were poor but became poorer (such as India) are not included in the rendering of growth trajectories. Only those seventeen countries that are today rich as defined by the World Bank and the Organization for Economic Cooperation and Development (OECD) are included. But for these

TABLE 7.2. Average Yearly Growth Rates in GDP per Capita for 17 Advanced-Capitalist and 28 Poorer Countries

	1870–1960	1960–79	1980–94
17 advanced-capitalist countries	1.5	3.2	1.5
(s.d.)	(0.33)	(1.1)	(0.51)
28 poorer countries	1.2	2.5	0.34
(s.d)	(0.88)	(1.7)	(3.0)

Source: Lant Pritchett, "Divergence, Big Time." *Journal of Economic Perspectives* 11 (1997): 5, 13; based on Angus Maddison, *Monitoring the World Economy, 1820–1992* (Paris: OECD, 1995).

countries there is renewed clustering (1980–1994) around the group average of growth rates in gross domestic product (GDP) per capita after a long period of clustering (1870–1960) and a short period of divergence (1960–1979) : from a standard deviation of 0.33 in the years 1870 to 1960, to 1.1 for 1960 to 1979, to 0.51 for 1980 to 1994 (see Table 7.2).[43] Putting this somewhat differently, there is nearly as much convergence in rates of income growth among rich countries in the thirty-four years from 1960 to 1994 as in the ninety years from 1870 to 1960. What is important for present purposes, however, is that the globalization era of 1980 to 1994 shows sustained convergence after a short period of increased divergence between 1960 and 1979. In this understanding, convergence temporarily stopped among the rich countries as the old Bretton Woods/Cold War system frayed and globalization dramatically picked up its pace.

What also seems clear, however, is that as today's rich countries have been converging with one another, the rest of the world has been largely left behind. Assuming a lower bound of P$250 for the poorest country in 1870, Pritchett shows that as the U.S. per capita income went from P$2,063 in 1870 to P$9,895 in 1960 to P$18,054 in 1990; that of the average poor country went from P$740 to P$1,579 to P$3,296, respectively (P$ = 1985 purchasing power parity US$).[44] What is more, in examining growth rates for per capita incomes in twenty-eight poorer countries that assume rather lower initial starting incomes than was probably the case for many of them (Table 7.2), the unmistakable conclusion is of increasing divergence between them and the rich countries, with the lowest growth rates between 1980 and 1994 after some degree of acceleration between 1960 and 1979. Using manufacturing pay data, Galbraith reports a similar finding of increased global inequality, but in his more limited temporal frame of reference as a trend setting in during the 1980s, but not before then.[45] To Galbraith this suggests that the liberalization policies that began in that decade lie behind the higher inequality, not simply the expansion of trade and investment. If higher incomes and growth rates for now-poor countries are assumed to have prevailed in the nineteenth century,[46] then even greater long-term divergence between rich and poor has probably been the case, with the period since 1980 being particularly important in widening the gap.

What these data suggest, therefore, is that divergence between rich and poor countries has increased significantly during the globalization era compared to the immediately previous period. At least at the scale of groups of relatively rich and poor countries and with respect to those included in these data, the world has been splitting into two parts: an increasingly rich world with lessened inequality in income growth among countries and an increasingly poor world with increased divergence among its members. As a result, with only 15 percent of the world's population, the rich countries now account for around 60 percent of world GDP. Putting this in a historical timeframe, if in 1960 the world's twenty richest countries had thirty times more income than the poorest 20 percent, by 1995 that gap had grown to seventy-four times.

Just as convergence among the rich countries has increased since the 1970s, so has divergence among the poorer ones. The standard deviations reported in Table 7.2 show increasing variance among poorer countries in their income growth rates over time, with a significant spike after 1980. Poorer countries are becoming less and less alike with respect to economic growth rates, and this has happened at an increasing rate since 1980. Between 1970 and 1995, the poorest countries had no increase whatsoever in average real incomes, and the better-off ones had only a 0.7 percent average annual increase compared to 1.9 percent for the world's rich countries.[47] Of the 108 countries for which reasonably reliable data are available in the Penn World Tables, eleven grew faster than 4.2 percent (the rate at which a country would have to grow to go from the lower-bound in 1870 [P$250] to match the U.S. level in 1960 [P$9, 895]) in the 1960–1990 period.[48] Almost all of these are East and Southeast Asian economies such as South Korea, Taiwan, and Indonesia. Most countries fared much more poorly than these eleven: forty (more than one-third) had annual GDP growth rates between 0.5 and 1 percent; twenty-eight (more than one-quarter) had rates of 0 to 0.5 percent (e.g., Peru with 0.1 percent); and sixteen had negative growth rates, (e.g., Mozambique at −2.2 percent and Guyana at −0.7 percent). The range of annual rates of GDP growth across the poor countries from 1960 to 1990 was from −2.7 percent to +6.9 percent.[49]

What seems to have been happening since the 1970s is that three groups of poorer countries have sharpened their differences: a fortunate few largely in East and Southeast Asia (with China as the latest and most successful addition) have successfully made themselves export platforms for goods sold largely in the advanced capitalist world, but have also built domestic markets for themselves; some larger countries (such as Brazil) and oil-rich countries (such as Iran and Saudi Arabia) have, respectively, either large domestic markets (and reasonably strong import-substitution sectors) or crucial commodities that underwrite at least a modicum of growth; and "the others" have few commodities in world trade and little in the way of labor-market, consumer-market, or resource advantages to offer the rich countries and their investors.[50]

Global Income Inequalities across Individuals

Some recent studies suggest that, contrary to country-based studies, global inequality in incomes between individuals is decreasing and that this is a positive function of globalization. This claim is based on attempting to convert income data from all countries, usually quintile data rather than information about all individuals, into a global distribution and showing how this has moved toward greater equality in the years between 1970 and 2000. Thus, one study shows how a "bulge" in the distribution of incomes across the world's population (US$ per million people) has increased, indicating both increasing equality and a growing middle class worldwide.[51] This can then be informally "correlated" with information about how much or little a given set of countries has globalized, understood as liberalized trade and currency regulations, to suggest that decreased individual inequality is caused by increased globalization.[52] Unfortunately for this claim, neither China nor India fits the role of model globalizer with freely floating currencies and open national markets.

Using different data and a different method, Bhalla computes an estimate of mean income for every percentile within a country and then aggregates these to obtain a global income distribution.[53] Among a range of results, Bhalla reports a drop in the proportion of the world's population living in poverty (defined using the World Bank norm of less than $2 per day), from 56 percent in 1980 to 23 percent in 2000; a net decline in global inequality in incomes from the 1970s to 2000; and, more specifically, a huge increase in inequality in Eastern Europe (the most equal part of the world in 1960), the sharpest decrease in inequality in the developing world (7 percent for four-fifths of the world's population), and rising inequalities within China and the United States since the 1980s.

Bhalla plausibly argues that most of the change toward decreased individual inequality owes much to the remarkable economic development of China, a country with a very large population (1.3 billion) that went from having fully half of its population absolutely poor in 1960 to a situation where it regularly has had economic growth rates of 6 percent to 7.5 percent per year since the 1980s.[54] India's recent experience, Bhalla suggests, is following closely in the same direction. Neither China nor India, however, is a good example of a country following closely the nostrums of liberalization, even if they are active participants in the new global economy. China's case illustrates the importance of not confusing the spread of the marketplace society associated with globalization with the particular policies pushed by the IMF or proponents of extreme economic liberalization.

These two huge countries star in Stanley Fischer's account of recent trends in global income inequality.[55] He shows that if GDP per head in 1980 is regressed against percent of growth in real GDP per capita from 1980 to 2000, there is an upward sloping curve indicating that, on average, the rich countries are getting richer faster than the poor are getting richer. But he points out that if countries are weighted by population size, the comparison is between richer and poorer people, not richer and poorer countries. Changing the focus produces a downward-sloping curve between the two variables. The main reason is that the poor, on average, are catching up. This is due in large part to China and India, two of the world's poorest countries, having enormous populations that remain hidden when calculating global inequality if their averages are compared to those of smaller countries and they had rapid increases in incomes per capita in the years in question, 1980 to 2000. Along with Brazil and Russia, two other large countries with significant resources and massive economic growth possibilities, China and India could well surpass in total GDP the G6 of industrialized countries (the United States, Japan, France, Germany, Britain, and Italy) before mid-century.[56]

The studies of global inequality between individuals stand, therefore, in marked contrast to the country-based studies. There are some problems with them, however, that deserve attention. First, global individual inequality may be declining because of decreases in between-country inequalities, but within-country inequalities could still be increasing. In other words, not everyone in China and India may be experiencing the average increase in incomes; some groups and regions may lag behind. Second, it is important to look back before the globalization era to see if the changes are that remarkable. For example, country-based studies suggest that the divergence between rich and poor countries actually increased between 1980 and 1994 relative to 1960 to 1979. Also, it is not really necessary to go to the trouble of computing global data sets and claiming that these are about individuals. They are not. They are about deciles or percentiles of national distributions. They are simply more refined indicators of within-country income inequality. Finally, looking at global income inequalities across individuals does not help to understand how inequalities are produced or decline. Inequality does not just happen to individuals by random shock; it is a product first of where you are born and then of what you do for a living, where you work, and how much you are paid.

A Synthetic Account

It seems clear that world income inequalities increased enormously during the course of the nineteenth and twentieth centuries. This was largely the result of dramatic increases in between-country income inequalities.[57] Indeed, even today about 70 percent of the variance in individuals' incomes around the world is accounted for by which country they live in. It was national-capitalist industrialization that brought about these disparities. But as the new global economy replaces the national-oriented economies of the past and national forces give way to global forces in the creation of income, then the correlation between income and nation should decline.

The demographer Glenn Firebaugh makes a strong empirical case for what he calls a "new geography" of global income inequality.[58] In short, what he shows across the period 1975 to 2000 is declining inequality between countries accompanied by increasing inequality within many countries. This suggests that the dominant approaches have largely missed the point, committed as they are to either national units or individual outcomes as the basic reference points for discussing inequality. Obsessed with global divergence or convergence, the authors of these approaches have tended to miss the changing geographical shape of inequality. In particular, they have failed to see that the changing geographical structure of global income inequality, not its global deepening or narrowing, is the central question.

Firebaugh reviews most existing studies of global income inequality and then provides his own estimates of between- and within-country

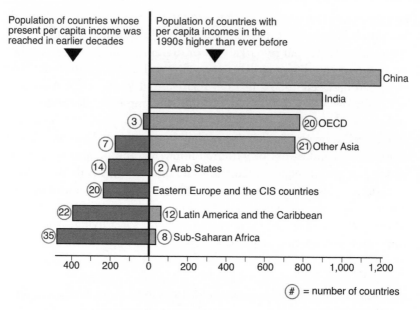

FIGURE 7.1. Countries Whose Per Capita Incomes Peaked in Either the 1990s or Previously
Source: World Bank, *Human Development Report,* 1996.

income inequality.[59] Using the Penn PPP (purchasing power parity) (1960–1989) and World Bank PPP data (1990–1998) (and countries weighted by population size to give individuals equal billing), he computes Theil, MLD (Mean Logarithmic Deviation), and Gini coefficients, which show that between-nation income inequalities declined at an accelerating pace in the 1990s. This happened after a period of increased between-country income inequality in the 1960s, which peaked in the early 1970s, and a subsequent period of declining inequality from the 1970s through the 1980s. China, however, again looms large in the calculations. Without China, "between-nation income inequality was about the same at the end of the 1990s as it was in 1960."[60] Worldwide, it is useful to show both the weight of China and India in estimating global income inequalities and the trends in between-country income inequality in the 1990s compared to prior decades (Figure 7.1). The major industrialized countries(OECD), China, India, and other Asia report per capita incomes peaking in the 1990s, whereas in other parts of the world, where there are both lower rates of economic growth and less demographic heft, per capita incomes peaked before the 1990s.

Using quintile data, Firebaugh also shows that from 1980 to 1995, within-country income inequality increased in all world regions except for Africa.[61] Britain, the United States, Canada, Australia, and New Zealand ("Western offshoots") had bigger increases in inequality than did Western European countries. Inequality also grew rapidly within countries in Asia and Latin America, particularly in the 1980s. Eastern Europe has seen the greatest increase in income inequality, almost doubling from 1989 to 1995. The collapse of Communism, therefore, is certainly an important reason for the resurgence of within-country income inequality at the same time that between-country inequality has been decreasing. Firebaugh suggests a number of other causes elsewhere: spreading industrialization that creates increased wage inequalities between agricultural and industrial workers in poorer countries; increased inequalities within richer countries as a result of deindustrialization and the development of a service sector polarized between high- and low-paying jobs; the growing impact of market access, which creates pressures for common institutional responses from states but also limits their capacity to operate internally in redistributing incomes; and the changing geography of production that enables the increasing flow of information across national boundaries—but access to this is still stratified within countries by educational attainment and the distribution of opportunity to tap into it.[62]

Of course, increased within-country income inequality is distributed socially as well as geographically. But many of the causes Firebaugh identifies are closely related to increased spatial differences in economic growth within countries. Given its importance to the case for declining between-country inequality around the world, it is useful to focus briefly on the case of China.

If the figures of Bhalla, Firebaugh, and others are correct, then in China some 400 million people have been lifted out of poverty (using the World Bank definition) over the past thirty years.[63] But at the same time, overall economic growth in China has produced enormous income inequalities within the country that are among the fastest growing in the world. When the Chinese government began to move away from central planning in 1978, the mean ratio of urban to rural incomes was 2.5:1; by the mid-1980s this ratio had narrowed to 1.8:1 mainly as a result of privatizing agriculture and government policies that favored rural areas. Since then, however, income from agriculture has stagnated and the boom in manufacturing industries has benefited urban residents to the extent that urban residents have average incomes fully three times those of rural areas. The vast increases in consumption in China since the 1980s, not the least of cars and other consumer durables, are overwhelmingly concentrated in urban areas.[64] Life in the countryside continues at a pace and with levels of consumption much the same as thirty years ago. The Chinese government is very well aware of the potential social conflict that such a gap may portend. Indeed, social unrest in the countryside and in interior cities has already begun. Official figures may, in fact, overstate rural incomes, so the gap may be even larger than that reported above. Some estimates put the rural/urban income ratio in China at around 6:1. The ratio between the wealthy coastal provinces in the hinterlands of Hong Kong, Shanghai, and Taiwan, both rural and urban, and the much poorer interior is of a similar magnitude.

The central government has devolved powers to local governments as one part of its strategy for opening up the country to FDI and collaborative development projects. Those areas that have been most successful in their entrepreneurship are increasingly guarded about defending what they have achieved. Even if the Chinese government wished to interfere with the geese that are laying the golden eggs, it could not hope to tempt much development away from the coastal hinterlands unless infrastructure and services are dramatically improved elsewhere and unless the inefficient state-owned industries that dominate the interior cities are either reinvigorated or closed down. Though restrictions on rural-to-urban migration have been relaxed, the absolute size of the rural population (about two-thirds of the total population of 1.3 billion) also puts limits on the feasibility of migration as a solution to the "development gap" between rural and urban and coast and interior. If the present trend is any guide, spatial income inequality in China will continue to grow (Figure 7.2).[65]

Global Income Inequality and Global Uneven Development

Here it is best to return to the main theme of the section: how do trends in global income inequality relate to the changing geography of the world economy? First, recall the three groups of poorer countries identified by Pritchett: the fortunate few in East and Southeast Asia; the miscellany of large (Brazil) and oil-exporting countries; and the poor countries that have become poorer.[66] Even though Pritchett arrives at this classification by using country averages, using quintiles or percentiles would not change this picture very much at all. The first and the third groups are of particular interest.

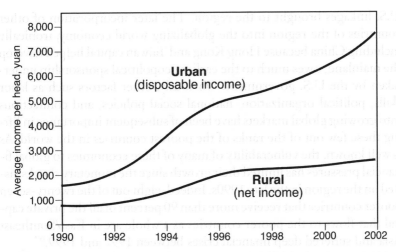

FIGURE 7.2. Average Per Capita Incomes in Rural and Urban China, 1990–2002
Source: National Bureau of Statistics of China, 2003.

Focusing initially on the first group, there are all kinds of explanations for the so-called NIC (newly industrializing countries) phenomenon usually associated with this group, from their relatively high education levels to good infrastructure, strong governments, ethnic homogeneity, Confucian cultural traditions, and high savings rates. Early in the twentieth century they had many of these characteristics but were as poor relative to the advanced capitalist countries as African countries are to them today. Bruce Cumings was perhaps the first to suggest what was most important in priming the "pump" of economic growth in East Asia and setting this region apart from elsewhere in the poor world of the 1960s and 1970s.[67] Of course, once primed the pump has had to work with local resources and capacities.

To Cumings, the priming came from the combination of the U.S. geopolitical devotion to the region during the Cold War and from previous investment in infrastructure (railways, ports, etc.) under the Japanese Empire.[68] The U.S. government certainly poured capital into such free-world outposts as Taiwan and South Korea in the form of military aid and infrastructure investment, building on what was already there. The immediate purpose was the containment of Communist China, but to this was allied the goal of anchoring the Asia-Pacific region, above all Japan, into the U.S.-based world economy. Initial investment in the region from outside was premised on the "stability" that

U.S. linkages brought to the region. The later incorporation of other countries of the region into the globalizing world economy, ironically including China because Hong Kong and Taiwan capital helped develop the mainland, owes much to the earlier geopolitical sponsorship undertaken by the U.S. government. Obviously, other factors such as labor skills, political organization, national social policies, and connections into growing global markets have been of subsequent importance in lifting these few out of the ranks of the poorest countries in the world. As is well known, the vulnerability of many of these economies to global financial pressures has limited their growth since the monetary shocks visited on the region in the late 1990s. Indeed, eight out of the twenty-seven poorer countries that receive more than 90 percent of all the private capital that flows to the poorer countries as a whole are in East/Southeast Asia and suffered deep financial crises between 1997 and 1999.[69]

Without the Cold War to attract even minimal attention from the U.S. government and other powerful global actors, many other countries now face the possibility of actually dropping out of the world economy altogether, retreating into more localized economic zones with only limited connections to the globalizing world. Many countries in Africa and elsewhere no longer have well-established niches within the world division of labor, having lost the positions they occupied as important primary producers within the territorial-imperialist capitalism of the early twentieth century. For example, the African share of world coffee exports dropped from 29 percent to 15 percent between 1974 and 1994.[70] The following four factors seem of primary importance in relation to Africa's lost role in the world economy, suggesting that no single factor offers a complete explanation: the loss of comparative advantage and declining terms of trade for many primary commodities, particularly since 1970; vulnerability to world markets with the collapse of colonial ties; political cronyism and corruption; and the overvaluation of currencies for political ends, particularly to support urban populations at the expense of rural populations.[71] The U.S. geopolitical imagination during the Cold War had only a limited place for Africa and other regions at some remove from the primary conflict of the day. But at least the countries of these regions had potential leverage in the omnipresent threat posed by the former Soviet Union and its political-economic ideology. This has now passed and with it has gone the incentive to stimulate investment in large areas that are consequently the most extensive "dead lands" of the current world: without either economic or geopolitical advantage within the globalizing world economy.

In the second place, however, the focus solely on divergence between countries is potentially misleading. It obscures the point made most forcefully by Firebaugh that the main feature of the new global economy is the significant rise in within-country income inequalities as between-country inequality goes down (almost entirely because of recent tremendous economic growth in China and India).[72] This is a global trend from China to the United States. Therefore, it is not just a feature of a national "stage" of development in which new industrialization temporarily increases wage inequalities between rural and urban workers. Obviously, there is some of this in China, but there is also something much more global about this trend. It represents a new economic geography in which localities and regions increasingly find their place within a global economy, not within separate national ones.

Conclusion

Not one single word can adequately describe the new global economy. It is not organized territorially as were the old European empires, the Soviet Union, or the United States as it "made itself" in the nineteenth century. So "empire" will not do. The order upon which it is based, however, is a hegemonic one complete with a continuing, if increasingly conflicted, hegemonic leader: the United States. But it is simultaneously a transnational liberal order based on the relatively untrammeled access of businesses to opportunities wherever they can find them. In the final analysis, transnational liberalism finds its strongest political support among those interests whose network ties define the new geography of power behind the new global economy. This is not to say that all of the governments of countries operating under this transnational liberal hegemony are or have been liberal or democratic ones. They need only allow relatively free access to capital and oppose too much state-based economic development to qualify for entry and potential U.S. government patronage. China's seemingly unlikely passage from Communist adversary to membership in the WTO and other institutions of global capitalism is only the strangest example of recruitment into the ways of transnational liberalism and the marketplace society abroad.[73] As Bruce Cumings has noted, one of liberalism's strengths is the "accretion of norms" as practice is compared to ideals and practices are thereby adjusted.[74] Along with it, however, have come coercion and a vast global militarization that brought a U.S. military presence, vast investments in infrastructure, and the inculcation of liberal norms. Some regions have received undoubted benefits from this—the countries of Western Europe with the Marshall Plan, Japan, and the countries of East Asia, such as Taiwan, South Korea, and now China—but others have been and continue to be left out. As a result:

> A deepening spatial segregation between rich and poor both within countries and in the world as a whole defines our era, and enhances central power just as it peripheralizes those left behind, creating new polarizations of wealth and poverty that have only increased in the past two decades.[75]

This is America's geopolitical gift to the world.

8 Globalization Comes Home

T he world economy that the United States has created beyond its territorial boundaries is no longer one in which all of America sees a positive reflection. Though the American economy has largely recovered from the worst negative trends of the 1970s and 1980s, there is nevertheless a widespread unease about what the world economy delivers to the United States. As this chapter claims, there is good reason for this. The United States now faces an impasse in its relations with the global economy. This is not to say that the United States uniformly is a victim of its own hegemony. But during the 1990s, it mainly was the financial sector, wholesale and retail sales, and a bubble economy associated with Internet services and telecommunications that drove growth. Many other sectors have experienced little other than decline, particularly in relation to job growth and global market share provided from plants in the United States.

Though America might seem to have done well from 1990 to the early 2000s, or at least better than in the 1970s and 1980s, many Americans have not done very well at all. Whether they've done well depends on where they live and for which industries they work. Major metropolitan areas have experienced the largest shares of total national economic growth, but they also illustrate most visibly the growing national polarization in incomes and wealth between rich and poor. The 1990s were a good decade for America's rich. It was more problematic for everyone else. The second section of the chapter, therefore, moves from the impasse of the United States in the world economy to an examination of the consequences for groups and places within the United States and to the macroeconomic context in which these have occurred. The analysis parallels that for the new global economy as a whole discussed in Chapter 7. The main point is that the identity between the United States and world economies that served to underpin domestic support for American hegemony for so long has broken down.

America's Impasse

A common view is that since 1985 the United States has experienced something of an economic renaissance. The recent general trajectory of the U.S. economy certainly has been more favorable when compared to the dark years of 1970 to 1985, when low economic growth combined with high inflation, and relative to other major industrial countries. In the late 1990s, as the U.S. stock market boomed and new informational technologies promised a seemingly endless era of growth—the so-called new economy—the United States seemed to reestablish its centrality to innovation in manufacturing and services in the world economy.[1] Overall, however, the idea that the American economy stands on top of the world is questionable. Some signs in 2003–2004 pointed toward a significant upturn in U.S. economic growth compared to other countries, but much of this may be due to cost cutting and employees working longer hours more than a profound "productivity revolution."[2] Part of the story of American economic growth since the 1980s has been of one false dawn after another, so skepticism is warranted as to the sustainability of the 2003–2004 "turnaround."

Over the fifteen years from 1989 to 2002, the best measure of economic performance, growth in gross domestic product (GDP) per capita, averaged 1.6 percent for the United States, much the same as in Japan but much less than in Germany (1.9 percent). At the same time, the main measure of what causes economic growth, change in level of multifactor productivity (efficiency of using capital, labor, and technology), grew more slowly in the United States than in either Japan or Germany (respectively, annual averages of 0.9 percent, 1.3 percent, and 2.6 percent). The U.S. unemployment rate averaged 5.8 percent, lower than Germany's 7.8 percent but higher than Japan's 2.4 percent.[3] In the recession between 2000 and 2003, the U.S. unemployment rate climbed back above 6 percent as the country lost approximately 2.7 million jobs. In only one way did the United States outperform either of these other industrial countries during between 1989 and 2002: job creation. Many of the new jobs, which replaced the mainly manufacturing sector jobs lost in the United States in the 1990s and between 2000 and 2003, however, pay much less. In Los Angeles, for example, state payroll records show that of the 300,000 new jobs created between 1993 and 1999, most paid less than the $25,000 average per year of the metropolitan area in 1993 and only one in ten paid $60,000 or more per year; the number of jobs paying $15,000 or less grew at an annual rate of

TABLE 8.1. Major U.S. Economic Indicators, Average Annual Increases for the 1960s, 1970s, 1980s, and 1990s

	1960s	1970s	1980s	1990s
	Average Annual Increase*			
Real GDP	4.4%	3.3%	3.1%	3.1%
Productivity	2.9%	2.0%	1.4%	1.9%
Employment	1.9%	2.4%	1.7%	1.3%
S&P 500	6.6%	−0.5%	12.9%	15.9%
	Average Level**			
Inflation	2.3%	7.1%	5.6%	3.0%
Unemployment	4.8%	6.2%	7.3%	5.8%

*Based on year-over-year quarterly growth. S&P refers to inflation-adjusted total returns.
**Based on quarterly data.
Source: Cletus C. Coughlin and Daniel L. Thornton, Federal Reserve Bank of St. Louis, "Yes, the '90s Were Unusual, But Not Because of Economic Growth." *Business Week*, April 24, 2000:32.

4 percent, more than twice the rate for all other income categories.[4] Working Americans also typically work far longer hours than do workers in other industrial countries. This plus a higher percentage of the population in the labor force account for the higher average GDP per capita in the United States, not simply higher productivity or efficiency in using the factors of production.[5] People in other industrialized countries typically have more leisure time and more and better public goods.

Popular "common sense" relies more on comparisons with the past experiences of the United States than with other countries. But here again, the 1990s were not exceptional (Table 8.1). On average, the economy grew no faster than in the 1970s and 1980s and much slower than in the 1960s. Across the key indicators of average productivity growth, unemployment, and even inflation, the decade was no match for the 1960s. It looks even less impressive when taking into account the fact that inflation, productivity, and unemployment are now measured in ways that definitely understate inflation and unemployment while raising employment relative to previous decades.[6] In only two respects did the 1990s shine, which reflected the power of U.S. financial markets and the role of the U.S. dollar as an effective global monetary standard. The first is economic stability. Inflation and economic growth both remained steadier over time than previously, probably as a result of the U.S. government's capacity to use interest rates to manipulate relative prices. The second is the stock market. The 15.9 percent real average annual return posted by the S&P 500 stock index was far above that of the 1960s and the miserable 1970s. Its collapse since 2000, however, illustrates the degree to which its ascent in the 1990s did not have much of a connection to the true state of the U.S. economy.

Notwithstanding the hoopla over the long expansion of the U.S. economy from 1991 to 2000 and the explosion of the stock market, the American economic model is no longer a national or global paragon. It must now struggle alongside all of the others, producing somewhat higher growth than in the period 1970 to 1985, but with wider income inequality than in most industrial countries. It is sometimes asserted that America has traded higher inequality for faster growth. Yet over the period 1989 to 1998, average individual incomes have risen by similar amounts in Japan, Germany, and the United States, despite America's much bigger income differentials. In the United States, the richest 20 percent earn nine times as much as the poorest 20 percent, compared with ratios of four times in Japan and six times in Germany. Despite a higher average income in the United States, the poorest 20 percent in Japan are about 50 percent better off than America's poorest 20 percent.[7]

A plausible account of the phenomena of income stagnation and fading promise would stress, first, the cutting of the Fordist knot that tied together production and consumption. The globalization of labor markets has meant that businesses without fixed local markets are relatively free to move at will to wherever they can obtain the best "deal." Under such conditions, expansionism beyond national borders no longer guarantees a return for most of those people left at home. Only those who earn their livings from investments are beneficiaries. At the same time, this also discourages businesses from investing in capital, especially in productivity-enhancing equipment.[8] This in turn accounts for the decline in capital/output ratios in the United States (a measure of the relative importance of labor and technology in production measured by how many units of capital have to be invested on average to obtain one unit of output) since the early 1980s through the mid-1990s. This now does seem to have turned around, particularly in the manufacturing sector where technology has increasingly been a substitute for labor. The rate of growth in the amount of capital available to each worker in the United States fell from its peak in the early 1980s through the mid-1990s, which suggests that the American economy was producing its goods and services in a more labor-intensive way than in the past. In other words, work was substituted for capital; toil increased as investment in capital equipment declined. While productivity increased starkly in 2003 (and more slowly from 1995 through 2002), it is by no means clear that this resulted from increased returns on investment in technology. It could be the result of people working harder. The long-term dilemma is that without sufficient capital investment, median incomes will not rise, and without rising incomes, labor will not be able to purchase the products of globalized production. This is the great conundrum facing American marketplace society.

At first this might sound surprising. For example, has there not been a vast investment in computer technology that has presumably improved productivity and reduced the burden on labor? Will this not feed back into the welfare of American workers? In fact, considerable evidence suggests that computer technology has not yet produced the productivity gains widely predicted, particularly in the service sector where much of the growth in the U.S. economy has been concentrated. Information overload, rapid obsolescence, the lack of impact of information processing in many industries, and technical-interface conflicts have conspired to reduce the overall effect of the new technology in the U.S. economy.[9] Where computerization has had undeniable positive effects (e.g., in the operations of firms such as Wal-Mart), it is does not seem to be the long-term benefit of the U.S. labor force in terms of increasing the standard of living.

There has been an increasing breakdown of the geographical matching of production and consumption, as manufacturing jobs succumb to technology or move overseas and are replaced by lower-paying jobs, which leads American consumers to purchase goods and services that they do not produce. This breakdown has been exacerbated by increasing pressures on governments to facilitate "market access" and to make "their" businesses "lean and mean" for the rigors of global competition. There are fewer and fewer "policy buffers" between countries and the global business cycle.[10] Even large and previously "sheltered" economies, such as the United States', find themselves subject to economic shocks that are increasingly beyond the management powers of central government. At the same time, to conform to the discipline of financial markets, countries must restrict their welfare-state expenditures; however, as Rodrik has persuasively suggested, economies traditionally more open to trade and investment have had bigger relative welfare expenditures.[11] The United States, with its minimalist welfare state (by industrial country standards), is therefore faced by a prospective social problem as welfare cutbacks parallel increased openness of the national economy.

TABLE 8.2. Major U.S. Capital Flows, 1970–2000 ($ Billion, at Current Prices; [–] Denotes Outflows)

	1970	1980	1990	2000
Balance on G+S+I *	4	11	−59	−391
Exports G+S+I	63	344	697	1419
Imports G+S+I	−59	−334	−757	−1809
Unilateral Transfers	−3	−8	−33	−54
U.S. govt. grants/pensions	−2	−7	−20	−22
Private gifts	−1	−1˙	−13	−33
U.S. Assets Abroad	−8	−87	−74	−581
Govt. assets	−2	−13	−4	−1
Direct investment	−4	−19	−30	−152
Foreign securities	−1	−4	−29	−125
U.S. bank and other lending	−1	−51	−11	−302
Foreign Assets in the U.S. Net	6	58	122	1024
Foreign official assets, net	–	15	34	38
Foreign private assets, net	6	43	88	987
Direct investment	–	17	48	288
U.S. Treasury securities	–	3	−3	−53
Other U.S. securities	4	5	35	486
U.S. bank and other liabilities	2	18	8	266
Residual	1	27	44	−2

*G+S+I = goods plus services plus investment.
Source: Bureau of the Census, U.S. Department of Commerce, *Statistical Abstract of the United States: 1998, 1992*; and U.S. Bureau of Economic Analysis, *Survey of Current Business*, 2001.

The sense of a more fragile and unstable economic future has given rise to a questioning of the "common sense" of the American ethos. Free trade and international economic competition are openly criticized in ways that would not have been thought possible thirty years ago. Criticism draws on the sorry condition of the U.S. balance of payments in the 1980s and 1990s. The figures suggest an economy increasingly dependent on imports of goods and capital from elsewhere rather than a powerhouse economy dominating the rest of the world and invulnerable to foreign decision makers (Table 8.2). Trade and competition are vital corollaries of the extension of the frontier nation into the world at large. But the setting of wages at the lowest-cost location—without addressing the collective consequences for Americans of expanding production overseas and without commensurate increases in the earnings capacity for American consumption—is seen as a violation of the American promise to its own population. Interestingly, criticism comes from both left and right ends of the political spectrum, as seen most dramatically

TABLE 8.3. Trade Openness of Major Industrial Economies (Exports + Imports as a Percentage of GDP), 1960–2000

Country	1960	1970	1980	1990	2000
Canada	33.0	44.4	52.3	60.4	86.8
United States	**08.5**	**11.9**	**17.8**	**22.0**	**26.2**
Japan	14.7	21.2	28.7	36.5	20.1
West Germany*	28.1	43.1	66.2	76.3	67.0
France	22.6	36.3	45.1	52.6	55.7
Italy	22.5	42.1	43.6	51.0	55.8
United Kingdom	42.9	53.0	56.3	62.6	57.9

*Germany in 2000.
Source: OECD National Accounts, Volume 2, Detailed Tables (Paris: OECD, 1979, 1992, 2002).

in the protests against the World Trade Organization (WTO) meeting in Seattle in 1999. Labor unions, environmental activists, and far-right militia groups take exception to the idea that the United States and its regions are just locations for investment and disinvestment rather than parts of the abstract space of economic promise bequeathed to them by the frontier nation. This attitude is manifested in the increase in isolationist positions on both economic and military issues. These positions question such core U.S. commitments as global diplomatic activism, leadership of liberal international organizations such as the WTO, membership in the United Nations system, and various alliance structures such as NATO. Though there is a range of "isolationisms" that give priority to different issues—from protecting existing jobs and environmental regulations to worrying about foreign cultural influences—all of them share a basic antipathy to the globalist status quo.[12] Lurking within them is the wish to squeeze the genie (globalization) unleashed by the frontier nation back into the territorial bottle (the United States).

One dimension of globalization is particularly in question: the faith in the benefits of free trade. Increasingly heard are criticisms of a free-trade regime in which wages are set at the lowest-cost location without attention given to the collective consequences of expanding production without commensurately increasing the earnings capacity for global consumption. This is both a global and an American problem, and Americans are no longer sheltered from its effects. Even though the United States is less open to and less dependent on foreign trade than any other major industrial country (Tables 8.3 and 8.4), its relative

TABLE 8.4. Trade Dependence of the Major Industrial Economies (Exports as a Percentage of GDP), 1960–2000

Country	1960	1970	1980	1990	2000
Canada	17.2	22.0	28.4	29.2	46.0
United States	**05.2**	**05.8**	**07.1**	**10.5**	**11.2**
Japan	10.7	10.6	14.6	18.1	10.8
West Germany*	19.0	20.9	32.4	39.7	33.7
France	14.5	16.7	23.9	25.2	28.5
Italy	13.0	17.7	22.8	23.8	28.4
United Kingdom	20.9	21.8	29.1	29.4	28.1

*Germany in 2000.
Source: OECD National Accounts, Volume 1, Main Aggregates (Paris: OECD, 1990, 2002).

position has changed significantly in the years since 1960. Less skilled and lower-income workers particularly tend to oppose liberalization of trade, immigration, and foreign direct investment, and were its major critics between the 1960s and the 1990s. This reflects the reality of their situation. As of 1998, however, two-thirds of Americans, not just low-wage earners, thought that trade has been a "principal cause" of lower U.S. living standards.[13] The negative perception of globalization, therefore, extends well beyond those perhaps most immediately affected by it.

The basic issue in the overall status of the U.S. economy is its relative autonomy compared to its relative capability. On the one hand, an indicator of interdependence or susceptibility to external shocks (the ratio of U.S. trade and exports to gross national product [GNP] or GDP) has increased dramatically since 1970 (Figure 8.1). On the other hand, an indicator of capability within the world economy (the ratio of U.S. GNP or GDP to total core [industrial world] GNP or GDP) declined almost linearly between 1950 and 1980 but since then has fluctuated with marked increases in the early 1980s and in the late 1990s (following a significant drop from 1985 to 1995). With the U.S. economy as the "motor" of the world economy in both the early 1980s and again in the late 1990s, these results are not surprising. The sustainability of the late 1990s "bounce," however, now depends more on the recovery of other industrialized economies as much as it does on overall U.S. economic performance. The United States has been spending way beyond what it produces and saves, and a drop like that after the 1980s, therefore, is very much in the cards. Fred Bergsten has used the term "scissors effect" to describe the joint consequences for the U.S. economy of increased

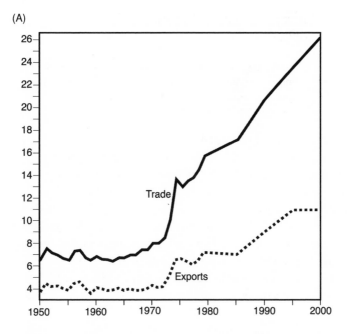

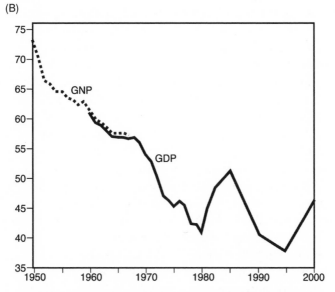

FIGURE 8.1. The "Scissors Effect": Ratios of (A) U.S. Trade and Exports to GDP (1950–2000) and (B) United States to Total Core (Industrial World) GNP (1950–67) and GDP (1960–2000).
Source: Organization of Economic Cooperation and Development, *National Accounts*, 2002.

economic interdependence and declining, if more recently, somewhat resilient capability:

> The United States has simultaneously become much more dependent on the world economy and much less able to dictate the course of international events. The global economic environment is more critical for the United States and is less susceptible to its influence.[14]

In the late 1980s, I provided a detailed analysis of why U.S. economic autonomy and capability had declined.[15] Bringing this up to date, and with respect to autonomy, the massive and ever-widening U.S. current account and trade deficits show the country as the world's largest debtor and importer relative to exports with Japan and China as its single largest creditors. But beyond this, the increased interdependence and velocity of world financial markets affect the United States as they do other countries. The United States does have some obvious advantages. The most important of these is that the country's major traders hold their reserves largely in U.S. currency and thus help to finance the U.S. deficits, given that the savings rate in the United States is too low to do so domestically. Controlling the world's major transnational currency, the one in which much of the world's trade is denominated, also gives the United States the capacity to allow the dollar to fall in order to boost exports and affect the relative real prices of its rivals' products. These advantages, however, are not absolute. For one, losing foreign cooperation could lead to a dramatic fall in the value of the dollar because at least one-third of U.S. Treasury debt is owned by official foreign agencies. For another, "talking down the dollar" can lead to a crash rather than a managed decline in value. The idea that the U.S. economy has "empire-like power," as alleged by numerous writers, therefore needs relating to the actual performance of the U.S. economy rather than to abstract accounts of the powers the United States potentially has available to it.[16] While these powers may have aided financial institutions, multinationals investing outside the United States, and the monetary position of the United States, they have not translated into an automatic superior general economic performance for the U.S. economy.

With respect to capability, the main problem lies with the relative decline in GNP potential or the capacity to produce. This is partly a function of the changing labor force (more dependents, lower skills, etc.), but it is largely a product of declining national productivity. In 1990 this was indexed at 1.4, compared to 4.3 in 1965. By 2000 it had improved somewhat to 1.9. As a consequence, real GNP or GDP growth has slumped from 4.4 percent in the 1960s, to 3.3 percent in the 1970s, to 3.1 percent in the 1980s, to 3.1 percent in the 1990s. Part of the answer to this pattern is that the service industries whose share of total GDP and whose employment rate is growing most in the United States show much lower increases in productivity than do those manufacturing industries whose share in total GDP and employment rates are shrinking dramatically.[17] But globalizing capital and labor markets are also undoubtedly part of the answer. On the one hand, the increasing uniformity of regulations and accessibility across different national economies makes it easier for businesses to move investment from one to another. On the other hand, labor is now increasingly available on a global basis. In particular, skilled labor can be imported if a local economy provides insufficient qualified workers. Competition from lower-paid (often overseas) labor and legal restrictions have jointly affected the ability of labor unions to organize the workforce. As a result, not just average wages but also average benefits (such as pensions and health insurance), which tend to be considerably higher for union members, have gone down. This makes production more flexible and also less dependent on relatively immobile local populations. The net effect is to turn wages from the source of demand they were under Fordism to the cost of production they have become in a more globalized economy.[18] As a result, there is a potential global "leveling" of incomes. It is not a coincidence that the "golden age" of middle-class incomes and lifestyles for American workers correlated with relatively high levels of membership in labor unions and limited global capital mobility.[19]

Globalizing labor markets can be seen at work in two separate ways. One is in the increasing choice of locations available to businesses that have a wide range of labor-market requirements at different phases of production or that are attracted to diverse markets in order to spread investment risks. As countries "liberalize" their economies, they reduce regulations and constraints on business practices. They thus impose fewer constraints (environmental regulations, labor force restrictions, product liability claims, etc.) on mobile businesses. The other way globalizing labor markets can be seen is in the recruitment and migration of both skilled and unskilled workers. In the first case movement happens both within transnational corporations and in sectors such as healthcare where contracts reflect, respectively, the needs of businesses and global labor shortages. In the second case movement occurs when large numbers of unskilled workers from poorer countries fill jobs unattractive to locals in industrial and other wealthy economies. These trends not only have economic consequences in terms of potentially reducing the bargaining power of resident workers, but they also have cultural and social impacts as societies such as the United States become increasingly multicultural with marked ethnic divisions of labor. Since 1990, however, there is evidence that international migration of both skilled and unskilled labor into the United States has declined relative to the previous decade, whereas the movement of foreign direct investment has tended to increase. Therefore, the first feature of globalizing labor markets is now more important relative to the United States than the second one.

The virtue of the expansionism inherent in the American experience has recently come into question in the United States. Elsewhere the benevolence of American omnipotence has long been openly problematic. What has focused minds has been the seemingly negative impact that the globalization brought by American global hegemony is now having at home. On one side the dramatically increased polarization of incomes and wealth between the rich and everyone else has been attributed by many commentators and some politicians to the effects of globalization, particularly the loss of the relatively high-paying assembly line jobs that characterized Fordist America.[20] It seems more than a coincidence of timing that U.S. median male earnings and median household incomes both peaked in 1973 and have stagnated ever since with a massive earnings gap opening up during the same period between the richest 1 percent of the population (who garner their incomes largely from stocks and real estate) and everyone else (whose incomes come from work) (Figure 8.2). Real-wage slowdown is particularly concentrated in the less-traded services: given that jobs in this sector are the only ones usually available with the shrinkage of higher-paying manufacturing jobs, globalization is working through this displacement to affect average earnings. Though U.S. unemployment has been consistently lower than Europe's since 1973, this difference is largely accounted for by the growth of part-time employment and low-paid customer service jobs in the United States relative to Europe. For example, between 1965 and 1998, jobs in retail and service sectors—the two lowest-paying sectors—rose from 30 percent to 48 percent of all production and nonsupervisory jobs in the United States.[21] Wal-Mart is not only where many Americans shop, mainly for imported goods, but it is also where many of them could soon be working—at poverty wages.

This represents an unstable economic situation. From the late nineteenth century through the 1980s, the massive economies of scale in American manufacturing production allowed the country to profit from

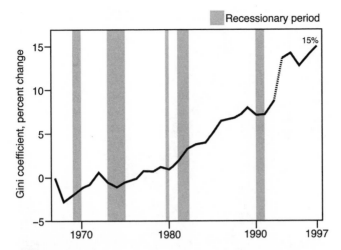

FIGURE 8.2. Household Income Inequality by Gini Coefficient, 1965–97

Note: The Gini coefficient measures the degree of concentration of households across the income distribution. The percent change shows the extent to which incomes are becoming less (if positive) or more (if negative) equally distributed across all households.

Source: U.S. Bureau of the Census, *Statistical Abstract of the United States* (Washington DC: U.S. Department of Commerce, 1998).

a virtuous circle of expanding production, expanding incomes, and expanding consumption. In the contemporary global economy, the United States serves as the giant purchasing machine for products increasingly made elsewhere. Economic growth in the recent past (2000–2004) has been almost entirely consumption driven.[22] As incomes rise elsewhere for those who make these products, however, mass markets alternative to the United States will inevitably emerge. The United States will then lose much of its leverage in relation to the world economy as the "buyer of last resort." In other words, the productivity from larger economies of scale in places actually producing goods—that is, rising output per worker—will give rise to increasing revenues that can pay higher wages and fatten profits that, in turn, can be put toward research and marketing of new products. From this viewpoint, just being the world's biggest consumer is unsustainable. It is no longer possible in such a situation for the United States to retain access to the profits and incomes that its mass market once made possible.

From a different angle, the point has been made that there is increasing pessimism on the part of Americans about achieving one of the

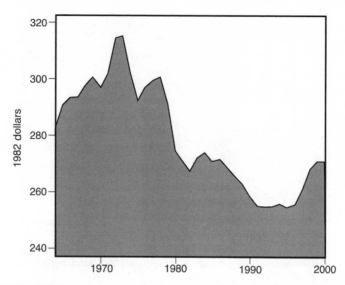

FIGURE 8.3. Private-Sector Nonfarm Average Weekly Earnings, 1965–2000.
Source: U.S. Department of Labor, Bureau of Labor Statistics, *Total Private Average Weekly Earnings in 1982 U.S. dollars,* 2002. http://www. bis.gov/datahome.htm.

fundamental "promises" of the American historical experience: the high likelihood that one's children will have a higher standard of living than one does. The generations coming to maturity after the Second World War and employed in the burgeoning Fordist industries of the epoch enjoyed continuing real growth in their incomes. From 1973 to 1999, however, this pattern was replaced by net declines in real weekly earnings for U.S. workers (Figure 8.3). This is not to suggest that this promise is necessarily a good thing in the context of growing concern about the sustainability of high levels of economic growth under conditions of environmental degradation, but only that the promise of increasing incomes is very much a part of the American marketplace ethos. Its potential loss is of major cultural and political significance.[23] It is this "compact" between populace and expanding economy that has bonded so many Americans to the norms of marketplace society.

It would be mistaken, however, to presume that the myth of American exceptionalism is simply fading away as a result of the excesses of globalization. Shopping is still not only the major national pastime but also absolutely central to economic growth.[24] "Consumers in America spend because they feel they must spend. More than in the past, the necessities of life, real and perceived, eat up their incomes."[25] This spending is huge—roughly $7.6 trillion a year in goods and services and around two-thirds of total national economic activity. Increasingly, however, it is less and less discretionary and relatively more financed by nonwage income, such as that from mortgage refinancing or credit. Writing of the period between 2000 and 2003, Robert Brenner notes: "US economic growth in the past three years has been driven by increases in demand generated by borrowing against the speculative appreciation of on-paper wealth, far more than in demand generated by increased investment and employment, driven by increasing profits."[26] He is referring specifically to the financing of current consumption from the cash released by mortgage refinancing and house-price inflation. A major force that also boosts spending is that the average household now has two adults at work instead of one as in the early 1970s. Even as doubts about the returns on the old ethos spread, the rhetoric of techno-capitalism is combining with American exceptionalism to suggest new frontiers that lie in cyberspace rather than in geographical space. At the same time, many Americans seem to accept, and even relish, the social inequalities that the economic boom of the 1990s has entailed. Increasingly, as huge inequalities in wealth are taken as natural measures of market-based demonstration of success and worth, conservative politicians and pundits are excoriating the federal government, journalism, academia, and Hollywood as being populated by a motley "new class" systematically engaged in undermining faith in the "American way." Relationships to this "market populism," to use Thomas Frank's term, were at the center of the 2000 and 2004 American presidential elections, which made obvious the geographical polarization of the country between the largely skeptical coasts and the true believers in the American "heartland" in between.[27] Neither the frontiers of cyberspace nor market idolatry, however, completely offsets the depredations of globalization and the image of an America now on the receiving end of powerful forces from both beyond and inside its borders.

Marketplace Society Comes Home to Roost

It is misleading to portray the United States and its population as simply one more set of "victims" of globalization. First, many Americans and some American localities have benefited mightily from the growth of trade and foreign investment. This is particularly the case for those workers and places with successful export firms and those benefiting from flows of foreign direct investment. Critically, for example, the growth of trade with the Asian Pacific Rim has particularly benefited the western states of the United States with respect to transportation, finance, resource and food exports, and strategic alliances as the Asian countries have inserted themselves into the circuits of globalized production. Second, the contemporary world economy is largely a product of U.S. design and ideology. From its origins as a new state in the late eighteenth century, political-economic expansionism has lain at the heart of the American experience. In a position to realize its old ambitions after the Second World War, U.S. government and business became enthusiastic supporters of a shrinking world in which capital would know no boundaries. Americans now live with the consequences: a world much more open to trade and investment and diverse cultural influences, but also a world that has increased economic competition and insecurity. In the 1990s, established manufacturing industries were largely sacrificed as service and financial sectors came to dominate the United States economically and politically in the new global economy.[28] Therefore, the relative well-being of different groups and localities has much to do with the domestic sectors that now lose in global competition and those that have a continuing or growing competitive advantage.

The Geography of Winners and Losers

From the late nineteenth century until the years after the Second World War the United States had a regionally structured national economy. The bulk of manufacturing and related employment was located within a belt running from Long Island in the east to Illinois in the west and bounded to the south by the Ohio River and to the north by the Canadian border (with an extension into Ontario). In their classic work, Perloff et al. show that this geographical pattern, with the exception of new industrial investment in California and the textile industry in the piedmont South, lasted from the 1890s into the 1950s.[29] Most of the classic manufacturing industries located in the industrial core had all stages of production on-site or nearby. In other words, there was a low level of separation of functions within production and a low level of variation in locational requirements between functions. This was based upon technological conditions (high transport costs, poor long-distance communication, etc.) and the lack of international competition in U.S. markets. The spatial division of labor was thus based on sectoral specialization such as cars in Detroit, steel in Pittsburgh, paint in Cleveland, beer in Milwaukee, etc. The other regions specialized in resource extraction and agriculture with "islands" of more specialized economic activity (such as film-making in Los Angeles) that were scattered according to various rationales relating to climate, local resources, and the serendipity of prior historical development.

By the 1960s costs were rising in the core, so business turned to the periphery to take advantage of low-cost, nonunion labor; growing markets; and low-cost sites on major transport routes. As a result, manufacturing industries began to close down in the industrial core and move their operations southward and westward. Some commentators have argued that this was a purely internal rebalancing between core and periphery within the U.S. economy. In this view, regions go through life cycles with rising scale economies in their youth and declining scale and external economies as they age. Consequently, interregional competition was producing a more dispersed pattern of industrial location and a concomitant diminution in interregional income inequality.

The problem with this interpretation is twofold. It was only when the U.S. position in relation to the world economy changed after the 1960s that the old geographical pattern began to disintegrate.[30] During the 1960s, trade negotiations, particularly the Kennedy Round in the General Agreement on Tariffs and Trade (GATT), lowered many tariffs on manufactured goods traded between the world's most industrialized countries. This was to have a dramatic impact in the United States. U.S. companies that had taken their massive national market for granted were now faced with foreign competitors hungry for market share in the United States. Increasing competition from foreign firms was the initial catalyst, therefore, in the geographical restructuring of the U.S. economy by forcing U.S. manufacturing firms into strategies such as relocating to the South and West and abroad to meet the competitive challenge. As the Fordist firms of the industrial core started to shift to outsourcing or externalizing many functions to other smaller firms, they were able to enjoy cost advantages by decentralizing production while retaining central corporate control. This led to a new uneven development in the United States with the seeming paradox of a delocalization or concentration of *control* over many firm functions and a localization or decentralization of firm operations to the most "attractive" locations for particular *functions*. The logic of the various local mixes of spatial transaction costs and external economies described previously (in Chapter 7) was at work in the United States.

The second point relates to the nature of competition. In the context of increased competition from foreign firms, localities and cities have to compete with one another, not large regions or sections, to get more or keep what they have. As firms become more competitive with one another without the protective cocoon of high tariffs and quotas, places become oriented to retaining and attracting the mobile capital that often primes the pump of local development. As a result, one political consequence of the increased openness of the American economy has been that the American states and various municipalities have embarked on programs to set up their own investment and trade policies without going through Washington D.C. For example, California, which has the seventh largest economy in the world, has its own health and pension policies and has tried to establish its own immigration policy.

The new uneven development in the distribution of manufacturing industry, beginning in the late 1960s but increasing its pace thereafter, has had a number of effects not just on the geography of production but on consumption as well. These include the increased polarization in occupational structure between cities and suburbs as new high-tech industries locate in the latter and old plants close down in the former; a deindustrialization of old industrial cities with replacement by jobs in relatively high-paying producer and relatively low-paying consumer services; new branch plants on green field sites in the South and West; a concentration of headquarters functions in the largest cities such as New York, Chicago, and Los Angeles, with high-skilled groups provided with services by much lower paid people, often recent immigrants to the United States; the emergence of new centers for certain service industries, such as banking in Charlotte, N.C., and Miami; and major new high-tech industrial districts such as Silicon Valley in California. In sum, a new spatial division of labor stimulated by foreign competition and made possible by new informational and communications technologies and new nonspatial scale economies created a pattern of localized restructuring.

Not surprisingly, given this process of global competition and localized growth and decline, there is a very localized aspect to the pattern of income decline and polarization.[31] If in the period between 1945 and the early 1970s the major regions of the United States had converged in incomes, reflecting a nationwide process of growth in the middle class, the period since then has seen a trend toward the regional distinctiveness in development and incomes that had characterized earlier epochs in American history. This time around, however, the geographical pattern is much spottier, with city-suburban and metropolitan-small city differences more significant than simply regional ones.[32] Some broader regional trends are apparent, however. As a result of its economic domination by declining heavy manufacturing industries, the Midwest region has experienced the highest levels of job loss in middle-income categories, with only lower-income manufacturing and service sector jobs available as substitutes. At the other extreme, California and New England have benefited most from increased domestic and foreign trade and investment, particularly in high-tech industries and informational technology. The Northeast and West totally dominate with respect to new capital investment, reflecting concentrations of skilled workers, existing clusters of technological innovation, and the presence of capital locally in the hands of those who have profited from previous rounds of investment. Six states—California, Massachusetts, New York, Texas, Washington, and Colorado—accounted for 75 percent of venture capital in 1999, up from their 50 percent share in 1995. Technology advances, as measured by new patents, are overwhelmingly concentrated in these states. Venture capital comes from the wealth accumulated by established high-tech entrepreneurs. These people tend to live in areas such as Silicon Valley, Boston, and Seattle, and to favor investing in local companies that they can easily watch over.[33]

If anything, the picture for many U.S. manufacturing industries, the places they are located in, and the people who work in them has grown more dismal since the late 1990s. After recovering from a huge fall in the late 1980s from the historic high in 1979, U.S. manufacturing employment climbed back to 17.6 million in 1998. Since then it has simply collapsed, shedding almost 3 million of those jobs by 2003.[34] This owes much to U.S. and other companies relocating operations abroad, particularly to China; to the substitution of technology for labor in U.S.-based operations; and to the overall loss of manufacturing industry in the United States as U.S. firms go out of business. Symptomatic of the trend, between 2002 and 2003 the U.S. economy had a "jobless recovery" from the 2000–2001 recession as gains in productivity drastically outpaced increases in employment.[35] This is a structural change. In the past, laid-off workers could expect to be recalled once business picked up, but not today. Many U.S. manufacturing industries have either gone out of business or shrunk permanently in employment terms.[36] Therefore, the likelihood of closing the "job gap" through the revival of high-paying manufacturing jobs looks exceedingly unlikely.[37]

The emerging geographical structure of the new American economy, reflecting the centrality of service and high-tech sectors as its leading edges, is a heavily city-oriented one. Some writers argue that cities are increasingly part of global networks in which they are service centers for multinational companies that have "gone global."[38] The network flows of information, decisions, personnel, and capital that draw cities together and give them their purposes are channeled to only a limited extent by national boundaries. New York and London, the two cities that sit astride the entire global network for the widest range of functions, are the decision centers for a worldwide hierarchical system of cities. Research by Peter Taylor shows, however, that beyond New York, Chicago, Los Angeles, San Francisco, and Miami, most U.S. cities are still "relatively separated from world cities in other countries."[39] Taylor suggests that this may be so for two reasons. One is that foreign service firms are typically noncompetitive beyond New York and a few other U.S. cities in which they locate to serve non-U.S. clients. Another is that many U.S. firms expand to other U.S. cities beyond their home base instead of going transnational because the U.S. market is so large.

What is clear is that U.S. cities are at the heart of the emerging U.S. economy. The leading industries in terms of contribution to U.S. GDP growth in the 1990s have been those in information technology, processing, and telecommunications, on the one hand, and users the products of these industries in finance, insurance, and real estate (FIRE), on the other. The largest cities have reaped much of the benefits of this new economy and many of the costs during the downturn of 2001 to 2003. Collectively, these large-city based sectors generated fully 26 percent of U.S. GDP in 1996.[40] Their concentration in large cities has been matched by their contribution to massive suburban development around these cities, producing the so-called edge cities where office centers and residential developments spill over into countryside as much as fifty miles from the historic cores of such cities as Atlanta, Washington D.C., Houston, and Los Angeles. The flip side to this trend is the increasing marginality and destitution in those central-city neighborhoods that have lost the old line manufacturing jobs and don't have the spatial or educational access to the newer jobs appearing at the urban fringe or in downtown office blocks.

Across U.S. metropolitan areas the net effect of the dual trends toward growth in informational and finance capitalism and the decline of traditional manufacturing industries has been a polarization between two sets of cities. Older, specialized industrial cities in the U.S. Northeast and Midwest have done poorly in economic growth and in retaining population (Table 8.5). The cities that have done better are overwhelmingly smaller and more diversified and are located outside the historic industrial core. Many are involved in the new dynamic high-tech

TABLE 8.5. Winners and Losers in the American Urban System: Extremes of
Growth and Decline, 1980–1990

Large (+250,000) metropolitan statistical areas (State)	Population's (000's)		% Change	Economic basis to growth/decline
	1980	1990		
Highest Growth				
Fort Pierce (FL)	151	251	66.1	R&R*
Fort Myers (FL)	205	335	63.1	R&R
Las Vegas (NV)	463	741	60.1	Recreation
Orlando (FL)	700	1073	53.3	R&R
West Palm Beach (FL)	577	864	49.7	P&R
Melbourne (FL)	273	399	46.2	R&R
Austin (TX)	537	782	45.6	Govt/HT†
Daytona Beach (FL)	259	371	43.3	R&R
Phoenix (AZ)	1509	2122	40.6	Services/R&R
Modesto (CA)	266	371	39.3	Services
Most Rapidly Declining				
Davenport (IA)	384	351	−8.8	Agric. Service
Pittsburgh (PA)	2423	2243	−7.4	Industrial
Youngstown (OH)	531	493	−7.3	Industrial
Huntington (WV)	336	313	−7.1	Resources
Charleston (WV)	270	250	−7.1	Resources
Saginaw (MI)	422	399	−5.3	Industrial
Peoria (IL)	356	339	−4.8	Industrial
Flint (MI)	450	430	−4.4	Industrial
Buffalo-Niagara Falls (NY)	1243	1189	−4.3	Industrial
Beaumont (TX)	373	361	−3.2	Resources

*R&R = Recreation and Retirement
†HT = High Tech
Source: Larry S. Bourne, "The North American Urban System: The Macro-Geography of Uneven Development." *North America: A Geographical Mosaic*, ed., Frederick W. Boal and Stephen A. Royle (London: Arnold, 1999), Table 12.7, 185.

manufacturing sectors; others are recreational, retirement, or government centers. The range in population growth or loss rates over the decade of the 1980s was tremendous, suggesting a definite geography of winners and losers in the new U.S. economy; this weakened in the 1990s, though, as rates of growth dampened (except for Las Vegas and some other cities) and rates of decline slowed throughout the Northeast and Midwest. Regional and local patterns solidified, however, suggesting limited prospects of any ready reversal in urban fortunes.[41]

The overall economic picture varies so much from place to place that providing some specific examples can give a more nuanced portrayal of what has been happening. For example, Detroit is synonymous with the industry that makes one of the main icons of American consumer culture: the automobile. Traditionally dominated by the Big Three of General Motors, Ford, and Chrysler, the U.S. automobile market has splintered since the 1970s in the face of aggressive foreign competition. This shift partly reflects changes in consumer demand, particularly in the 1970s and 1980s when the American companies failed to offer low gas consumption models at a time when oil prices increased dramatically. Japanese and some European producers, such as Volkswagen, moved into the vacuum. By 2003, the Japanese firm Toyota had surpassed both Chrysler and Ford and became second in U.S. sales behind GM. On profitability Toyota was already number one. Many of the U.S. companies use cash rebates and low-interest loans to drive their sales; this gives them a price advantage over the Japanese vehicles, but it also lowers their profit margins.

To meet the foreign challenge, the U.S. firms have changed the way they operate, moving many production operations to external suppliers in the United States and abroad, engaging in joint ventures with some of their competitors, and relocating assembly plants to places with lower costs. Japanese firms, in response to the "voluntary export restraint" agreements negotiated by the Japanese and U.S. governments in the 1980s on car imports from Japan, set up their own assembly plants in the United States. They located these in places in Ohio, Kentucky, and other states that offered deals on services and that were without Detroit's (and Michigan's) long history of antagonistic labor relations. In reaction, the Big Three have adopted many of the "lean production" processes pioneered by the Japanese, but they have proved less adroit at serving large segments of the U.S. market with their models and in terms of vehicle reliability.[42] Japanese producers have also benefited from the years of yen weakness against the U.S. dollar because they import 30 percent to 50 percent of the components priced in yen from Japan and then sell the vehicles in dollars. The exchange-rate windfall is one reason that Toyota, Honda, and other Japanese firms producing cars in the United States are more profitable than the Big Three. Chrysler has merged with Daimler-Benz (the German company) but is in a subordinate position with regard to management decisions. As a consequence of all of these changes, Detroit (and its hinterland) has lost the central position it once had in the automobile industry and in the hearts of American consumers.[43]

A second example comes from the city of Syracuse in New York. Manufacturing was long the backbone of this city, providing substantial and rising incomes to its working population and providing the taxes that sustained city services. Slowly over the past thirty years every one of the major manufacturers in the city has closed its doors, because each went out of business altogether, went out of manufacturing, or moved production elsewhere. The latest of the shutdowns was in September 2003, when the Carrier Corporation, a maker of air conditioning equipment, announced that it would phase out what is left of its local production and lay off the remaining 1,200 workers. The reason given was that the company sells 80 percent of its shipping container refrigeration units, hitherto made in Syracuse, in Asia and so it makes more sense to manufacture these where they are purchased.[44] Of course, production costs, particularly the wage bill, will be lower in Asia. Whatever the precise reason, Carrier is effectively becoming an Asian company, at least insofar as the manufacture of container refrigeration units is concerned. Syracuse, in turn, continues to lose population but, more significantly, can no longer provide jobs with the promise of increasing incomes and other compensation. One of the main remaining employers in the city is a huge shopping mall, the Carousel Center, devoted to selling goods, many of which are made in China and elsewhere abroad, to a population with declining average real individual earnings.

A third example is a state that by many measures has performed very well economically compared to much of the rest of the United States during the globalization era: California. Yet, in October 2003, in a "recall" election, voters ousted the incumbent governor, Gray Davis, who had been reelected the previous November, and elected the action-film celebrity Arnold Schwarzenegger in his place. Voters told poll takers that they were concerned about the state's economy, particularly the state budget, even though they themselves were doing relatively well. On the negative side of the economic ledger were the state budget deficit in 2002–2003 of $38 billion, an electric power crisis in 2001 (engineered by Enron and other power suppliers but negotiated by Davis), and the bursting of the so-called dot-com bubble in Silicon Valley after five years of seemingly endless growth (whose revenue-generating potential was estimated by the state government as also endless). But on the positive side were increased military spending (40 percent increase from 2000 to 2003) after the collapse of the early post–Cold War years, house building, an upturn in the computer hardware sector, and a resurgence in banking and finance. Employment losses in the period from 2001 to 2003 were concentrated in the coastal areas, particularly around San Francisco and San Jose. Job growth moved inland toward Merced in the San Joaquin Valley, and eastward toward Riverside and San Bernardino counties in southern California. To a considerable extent, inland gains reflect coastal losses as people and businesses move to take advantage of more affordable housing and cheaper land for factories and warehouses. Movement of investment and people within the state has compensated for the absence of much new investment from outside of California. Because of trends in the economy toward a polarized income structure, higher average incomes generated by employment in high-tech and FIRE sectors, and much lower average incomes in personal services (often provided by recent and frequently undocumented immigrants), California perhaps lives up to its reputation as the bellwether for the United States as a whole: Los Angeles today, the whole of the United States tomorrow.[45]

The new openness of the U.S. economy to external pressures since the 1970s has had radically different political impacts in different parts of the country depending on economic mix and vulnerability to foreign competition. It is not surprising that the most fervent proponents of free trade tend to be from California and New England; those counseling greater degrees of protectionism and opposing the development of more free trade accords with other countries tend to come from the Midwest and those parts of the South with the most to lose from a further globalization of labor markets by mobile capital.[46] The pattern is likely to be much more variegated than this, however, because the interests at stake are typically more localized today than in the past. The consequences of localized economic restructuring might be expected to show up, therefore, in a relatively motley geographical pattern of votes by congressional representatives on trade and investment legislation.

That this is in fact the case is shown, for example, in the votes for two pieces of legislation relating to trade and investment issues that were introduced in the U.S. Congress in 1985: the Textile Import Quotas Bill (HR1562) of October 10. 1985, a bill imposing quotas on textile imports, and the Plant Closings Notification Bill (HR1616) of November 21, 1985, a bill requiring employers of 50 or more employees to give workers at least 90 days notice of any plant shutdown or layoff involving at least 100 employees or 30 percent of the workforce. The first bill, which passed the House of Representatives 252 to 159 (Republicans 75–97; Democrats 187–62), has no apparent regional pattern in the votes for and against. Because of the scattered locations of textile-related industries, there is also no sectional or regional "position" to vote for or against (Table 8.6). A three-region (Northeast, West, South) analysis of variance does not support a sectional interpretation. The

TABLE 8.6. Sectionalism Redux? U.S. House of Representatives Votes on Two Trade-Related Bills in 1985

Trade Area	Percent Yes	
	A	B
Philadelphia (NE)	100	80
Boston (NE)	100	80
Buffalo (NE)	50	50
Chicago (NE)	50	70
New York (NE)	75	60
Detroit (NE)	60	40
Pittsburgh (NE)	100	85
San Francisco (W)	50	75
Cleveland (NE)	80	70
Omaha (W)	0	0
Cincinnati (NE)	50	50
Minneapolis (W)	25	65
Indianapolis (NE)	25	50
Kansas City (W)	0	40
Denver (W)	0	15
St. Louis (W)	90	55
Baltimore (NE)	80	50
Louisville (S)	90	50
Richmond (S)	85	0
New Orleans (S)	70	30
Birmingham (S)	100	20
Atlanta (S)	100	0
Memphis (S)	100	30
Dallas (S)	55	30
Analysis of Variance	Actual F = 1.69	6.76
($P = 0.05$)	Critical F = 3.42	3.42

Regions: NE = Northeast; W = West; S = South

Note: Votes by trade area (rounded to nearest 5%) supporting (A) HR 1562 Textile Import Quotas, a bill imposing quota restrictions on textile imports, and (B) HR 1616 Plant Closings Notification, a bill requiring employers of at least fifty employees to give at least ninety days notice of any plant shutdown or layoff involving at least one hundred employees or 30% of the workforce.

Source: John Agnew, "Beyond Core and Periphery: The Myth of Regional Political-Economic Restructuring and Sectionalism in Contemporary American Politics." *Political Geography Quarterly* 7 (1988), Table 6, 137.

second bill, rejected by the House 203 to 208 (Republicans 20–154; Democrats 183–54), does have a sectional effect. Here the northeastern/midwestern congressional delegations tended to support the bill and others voted against it. The fact that this bill was strongly supported by labor unions, which have had their greatest strength in the old industrial core, probably has much to do with this result.

The changed pattern of geographic concentration of much economic activity, from the greater clustering of vertically integrated firms under Fordism to the much more decentralized pattern evident today, however, makes the sectional vote something of an anomaly. Much more variegated votes on trade and investment issues are now the norm. This is important politically. The first bill with its localized support passed; the second sectionally based one failed. As Ronald Rogowski shows, "Deconcentration increases protectionist influence; it means increased pressure-group activity, more district-level contests among pressure groups, a shift of power to interests that were formerly more concentrated, and increased volatility of policy."[47] Rogowski demonstrates that "moderately dispersed" interests are the ones that win most congressional support over concentrated and highly dispersed ones. Consequently, as the number of districts with moderate vulnerability to foreign trade has increased, the traditional U.S. support for free trade comes under greater pressure than when industrial activity was geographically concentrated and representatives from elsewhere could outvote those from the heavily industrial areas.

Macroeconomic Context

Americans still spend more and more even as they produce relatively less. Consumption has lost none of its sparkle. Indeed, it has been American spending (and Chinese production) that has kept the world economy afloat and growing since the mid-1990s. This is possible because of massive credit inflows from abroad (see Table 8.2). Therefore, there is a fundamental imbalance in the world economy created by the gap between American consumption and American production. This is reflected above all in the country's current-account deficit. The current-account deficit is the amount that the United States must borrow annually from foreigners to spend more than it produces. This has been rising quickly and in 2003 stood at the historic high of more than 5 percent of GDP. Consequently, the United States, which as recently as 1985 was a creditor country, has become the world's biggest debtor.[48] Why has spending outstripped domestic sources of funding? Are the large current-account deficits sustainable?

In the 1990s, U.S. firms fueled much of the spending spree based on foreign borrowing with massive debt-financed investments. This diminished after the stock market crash of 2000. Since then the U.S. investment rate has fallen, so most of the capital flowing into the United States now goes to finance private consumption and government, not investment. The other two sources of spending beyond domestic means, therefore, are households and government. These have continued un-abated, with the latter particularly important during the administration of George W. Bush. The debt-service ratio for households in 2003 was at a historic high, as what people owed constituted an increasingly large part of their annual incomes. The previous peak in 1985 registered 100 percent of disposable income; 2003 saw this trumped at 120 percent.[49] With low-interest rates this can be sustained for a time, but eventually the bill comes due once interest rates increase and easy credit dries up. At this point, consumers will need to spend less and save more. At the same time, government has also been on a borrowing binge to cover revenue shortfalls from the economic downturn of 2000–2003, huge regressive tax cuts, and heavy increases in spending on the military, social security, Medicare, and subsidies to agribusiness. In the short term the federal government deficit has stimulative economic effects. The longer-term picture, however, is different. Extending tax cuts, the coming retire-ment of the "baby boom" generation, the aging of the population, and the open-ended War on Terror will all increase pressure on the federal budget. One of the few positive signs for the United States, compared to Europe and Japan, is that because of immigration the United States has a more "youthful" population with potentially more people available to pay for all those retirees. Unlike the late 1980s, however, when similar budget deficits emerged, this time around there will be no "Cold War dividend," in the form of reduced military expenditures, and no dra-matic increase in the stock market with associated rise in revenues, and there will be an exponential growth in entitlement spending on health care and pensions for the elderly.

Turning to the sustainability of current-account deficits, one view is that they are sustainable because the United States is a more or less permanently attractive destination for foreigners' savings. The United States provides higher investment returns at lower risk than elsewhere. U.S. financial markets are the most attractive in the world for their range of financial products and for the sophistication of their trades. More-over, the structural role of the U.S. dollar in a world mainly of floating exchange rates gives the U.S. economy a major fillip.[50] Current-account deficits can be financed by selling government debt securities. Because the U.S. dollar is the main currency for international transactions, for-eigners tend to hold their reserves in dollars. This means that when the value of the U.S. dollar falls, the U.S. debt burden decreases because debt to others is recouped in dollars. In essence, the United States faces no exchange-rate risk. Having persuaded so many countries to liberalize their financial markets in the 1980s and 1990s, the United States is now able to have them finance its deficits as their nationals (and governments) pour their reserves (in dollars) into U.S. debt instruments.[51] From this viewpoint, therefore, the party can go on more or less indefinitely while others pay the bill for American profligacy.

A different view is that ever-increasing current-account deficits are not sustainable and that after they reach about 4 percent to 5 percent of GDP, all manner of consequences arise, irrespective of the special status enjoyed by the United States because of its dollar. Three different scenarios are within the realm of possibility. Perpetual profligacy is not. The first scenario is adjustment postponed: if U.S. demand accelerates, pulling GDP growth along with it, the current-account deficit widens, but the rest of the world will foot the bill because of the collective stake in U.S. economic stability. At some point in the future, however, household savings are more likely to rise than fall, given their extremely low current rate. As a result, U.S. savings will start to provide credit in place of foreign investors. This alternative seems implausible, if only because the U.S. federal deficit and a low interest rate will inevitably lead foreign private investors to look elsewhere for better returns. Only foreign governments with large dollar holdings, such as Japan and China, will be left. Even they, however, show signs of wanting to diversify their currency holdings into the Euro, if only to be less beholden to U.S. policy.

A second scenario, therefore, is brutal adjustment: a collapsing U.S. dollar (against the yen and the Euro) follows U.S. attempts at promoting exports through a devalued dollar by making China and Japan's currencies appreciate against the dollar. This would threaten economic recovery in Japan and Europe and, in turn, would raise interest rates in the United States. This would increase the debt service load of poorer countries and undermine U.S. economic recovery. It might also reduce the long-term attractiveness of the United States as a haven for foreign investment.

That leaves a third possible outcome: a smooth adjustment. This scenario requires a rebalancing of world demand with Europe, Japan, and China all experiencing dramatic increases in demand relative to the United States. Instead of sending money to the United States, the other countries would then combine appreciation of their currencies against the dollar with greater spending. Needless to say, this would require coordinated fiscal stimulus in other countries and government and household spending reductions in the United States. Since the early 1990s, the U.S. government has largely abandoned any kind of concerted macroeconomic coordination with the other major industrial countries.

The U.S. federal government shows little or no sign of contemplating this third scenario. It would involve a direct assault on the "guns and butter" federal budget and require raising interest rates to ration credit. But the United States does not want consumption to be constrained. Thus the first and second scenarios remain. The first I have already suggested is implausible. The second, then, is the most likely. It is likely to be exacerbated by two trends in U.S. trade and foreign policy. The first trend is that the United States has begun to abandon multilateral trade agreements for bilateral ones in which the U.S. government tries to force through special deals for the United States against its trading partners.[52] But it has proved much more difficult to do this against countries such as China than against countries such as Japan. This is because the United States has a complementary trade relationship with the former but a competitive one with the latter. This means that the United States simply has less leverage over China because it needs what China exports, whereas with Japan, it and the United States are selling each other the same kinds of things. Consequently, in monetary policy the U.S. government cannot use trade as a weapon against China in the way it can against Japan and Europe. If China starts to shift its reserves away from the U.S. dollar, therefore, the U.S. government has limited possibility of punishing China without also punishing the U.S. economy. The second trend is that the U.S. government wants to follow an increasingly unilateral foreign policy, as witnessed by the war on Iraq when many of its erstwhile allies (and much of its own population) opposed the war. Can the U.S. government sustain such a foreign policy when it increasingly depends on foreigners to finance its current consumption? This seems highly unlikely. A hegemony (and certainly an empire) cannot be built on debt. The asymmetry in the world economy between an America that borrows and yet pretends to follow its own unilateral course is not one that can persist for very long.

Conclusion

In 1950 the United States' territorial economy dominated the world in terms of its shares of manufactured output, merchandise trade, and foreign investment. Of course, this was in the shadow of the Second World

War when most of the world's major industrial economies, other than the United States', remained devastated. Many Americans in the years following, however, assumed that this was the "natural" state of affairs. But by 2000, the relative share of the U.S. economy in world manufacturing had declined by around 50 percent from its postwar peak and ts trade position had weakened enormously. From providing almost one-half of the world's foreign direct investment in 1960, the United States now provides under 25 percent. In large part these changes are the result of the globalization of the world economy, with its increasing fragmentation of production and the geographical separation of different stages of processing. In this global context, the U.S. national economy has experienced a number of profound realignments, from the increased "global shift" of U.S.-based businesses through the relative decline of the manufacturing sector as a source of jobs and GDP and the rise of the service sector, to the geographical restructuring of population and jobs in new economic spaces, generally in terms of a movement from the Northeast and Midwest to the South and the West. The explosion of flows between the largest metropolitan areas has boosted the role of cities in the overall economy of the country, but with increasingly polarized incomes and wealth between those in rising sectors such as information technology and FIRE and those trapped in personal service jobs. Indeed, in this context, writing of the United States as a separable economy makes little sense compared to times past.

Nevertheless, these trends have occurred in a macroeconomic context in which the United States has acquired an increasingly asymmetric position in the world economy: borrowing from foreign creditors to fund domestic spending in excess of what could be financed internally. The United States can do so because of the dominant position of the U.S. dollar as a transnational currency. This position is probably unsustainable, however, unless American demand declines and that of other key economies increases. Allowing that to happen would require the U.S. government to abandon its strategy of propping up American hegemony—and U.S. marketplace society—by manipulating the U.S. dollar and a unilateralist foreign policy. Yet, for many people and places inside the United States, this no longer suffices because they do not benefit. In the past there was no such dilemma. America's national economic well-being and its global status were mutually reinforcing. Serving one now no longer guarantees the other. Globalization and the new geography of power have cut the connection between them. As the country begins a new century, that is the root of America's impasse.

9 Conclusion

The terms "globalization" and "imperialism" signify two features of contemporary world politics that are regarded as antagonistic to each other. The former stands for a seemingly autonomous process of globe shrinking or stretching (depending on how you look at it), whereas the latter indicates a self-conscious extraction and movement of profit from some places to others through political domination and coercion more than economic rationality. If advocates of the first tend to have a postmodern, depoliticized view of the world, those of the latter tend to have a profoundly modernist geopolitical view in which dominant states (above all, the United States, usually looming as a monstrous or Satanic presence) are constantly trying to turn a politically divided world into an empire.

In this book, I have offered an alternative theoretical perspective to these two views by arguing that the United States has not acquired an empire in any meaningful sense, and largely has not pursued one except as a default move when all else fails. Rather, the United States has produced the singularly most effective worldwide hegemony in history based on a set of practices I have labeled "marketplace society." If it is the networked geography of power associated with this hegemony that suggests most strongly why continuing to think in the territorialized terms of empire is mistaken, then it is U.S. sponsorship and action on behalf of globalization that indicates that it is anything other than spontaneous. But this worldwide hegemony is hardly the outcome of the state's "Grand Plan". It is mistaken to think of American hegemony as a singular gift of the U.S. government. American society has been much more instrumental in spinning the materials of hegemony, out of which the government has woven a not always coherent plan.

This book is an account of how American hegemony came about, its effects on the world, and how it has come back to haunt its creators. I began with a discussion of how the 2003 U.S. invasion of Iraq illuminates the debate over empire versus hegemony as distinctive ways of understanding the U.S. role in the world. I then turned to a theoretical examination of the connections between statehood, hegemony, globalization, and the geography of power. A subsequent chapter traced the "rise" of American hegemony, from the founding of the United States in the late eighteenth century to the growth of a national "marketplace society" in the nineteenth and early twentieth centuries. Then I disputed the view that American hegemony has mainly political-constitutional roots, suggesting that the U.S. system of government is in fact dysfunctional from hegemonic and imperial standpoints. This led into a narrative account of the worldwide imposition of U.S. hegemony in the twentieth century with a detailed analysis of the geography of the world economy this has produced. The two final chapters examined, respectively, the nature of the new global economy and its impacts on the United States itself.

Two points are worth reiterating about this narrative. The first is that it identifies a consumption-based economic model first developed on a large scale in the United States as the dynamo at the heart of American hegemony. This model is a set of material practices and associated ideas, not just an "ideology" to a "deeper" infrastructure. This departs considerably, therefore, from those accounts that privilege either production in itself or military competition. In this account those are servants of the consumption model and not vice versa.[1] Second, though the United States has dominated the world in many ways since the mid-twentieth century, it has itself become increasingly subject to the logic of globalization that its governments and other institutions helped release. It cannot be seen as the singular beneficiary of globalization. Indeed, I argue that recent American imperial temptations are a response to weakness, not strength, within the world economy.

American hegemony has now entered a period of crisis. Two critical features of this crisis, however, imply that the way out will not be through empire (either American or other) or by means of reinstating or strengthening state sovereignty tout court. These are worth examining at length because they involve the political consequences for a globalizing world in which the American role as administrator of its hegemony is much reduced. In the first place, globalization is producing a world economy in which there is a fundamental mismatch between global economic and political geographies. This is most often expressed as the problem of the "democratic deficit" but more generally relates to the issue of establishing some degree of popular control over the increasingly fast-paced and spatially fragmenting world economy. The contemporary democratic deficit can be considered under three headings: sovereignty, flows versus territories, and nonterritorial identities. As various forms of democracy developed in the nineteenth and twentieth centuries, they all tended to be associated with either capturing or influencing national-state governments because the fate of the population was seen as largely bound up with the economic growth and cultural autonomy of the territories those governments controlled. Globalization calls each of these associations into question.

Modern state sovereignty is strongly interwoven with modern democratic theory and its claims. Democracy in large part is about controlling or leveraging states in the interest of various *domestic* groups. The geographical boundaries of the state define the boundaries of the "social contract" upon which modern citizenship rests. Thus, claims about political and social rights are bounded by the sovereignty of particular states. The state itself is thereby understood as a sovereign agent "located at the centre of the body politic wielding absolute power and authority. Explicitly or implicitly, the sovereign is endowed with a distinctive, identifiable will and a capacity for rational decision-making."[2] The contemporary dilemma is that the successes in the struggle for democracy have been largely confined to the democratization of the national state and its extension of social and political rights (including those of the "welfare state") to its own citizens. Yet, the trend toward the globalization of markets and finance opens up the territories of the state to substantially increased international competition. This can lead to the rolling back of the state in precisely those areas of greatest democratic achievement, for example, welfare rights, unemployment benefits, public health, and the regulation of work conditions (despite these being areas that largely remain the preserve of national states in formal terms). Such rights are considered as financially untenable, once minimalist norms of labor regulation follow the opening up of domestic markets.[3] As states begin to enforce the new standards, state sovereignty appears increasingly as a barrier more than a stimulus to the deepening of democracy. Rather than being the instrument for an infrastructural power that states alone can provide to bounded territories, sovereignty in a deterritorializing world becomes the instrument for a hollowing out of states to the benefit of those businesses, social groups, and markets that are best able to exploit the new technologies, financial and production arrangements, and security agreements.[4]

Democratic theory and practice are predominantly organized by reference to discrete territorial blocs of terrestrial space. Most representative governments are based upon territorial constituencies, and their administrative agencies organize themselves into hierarchical service areas, with smaller units aggregated into progressively larger ones. Territoriality has been a vital means of organizing governance.[5] Democratic struggles, from those governing working hours in the nineteenth century to the civil rights movements in the twentieth century, have generally focused on achieving changes in laws and rules that have well-defined spatial jurisdictions. Increasingly, however, localities and city-regions find themselves differentially incorporated into the emerging global economy. Worldwide commodity and financial chains now stretch across the globe, drawing small areas and metropolitan areas into webs of flows of capital, goods, messages, and people that are not primarily organized territorially but as nodes in networks. Somewhat paradoxically, globalization relies on localized processes of growth and development because of the lowering of barriers to the movement of capital, goods, and technology, and the increased importance in many dynamic sectors of localized external economies of production (specialized labor forces, supportive industries and institutions, etc.).[6] This evolving world of flows is not well served by territorial models of governance in which localities and city-regions are subordinated to national states that may sometimes belong to world-regional higher-order organizations such as the European Union, and global organizations such as the World Trade Organization (WTO), the International Monetary Fund (IMF), and the World Bank. There is a growing mismatch between the geographical anatomy of the emerging world economy and the territorial basis to democratic governance.

Democratic politics has long been underwritten by the assumption that national political identities are superordinate in the minds and behavior of citizens. Indeed, democratic politics and nationalism grew up together. Not only did the extension of democratic politics often occur as a "reward" for services to the nation (for example, in the widening of the franchise in many countries after the First World War, or the construction of the National Health Service in Britain after the Second World War), but struggles for democracy and national independence often went hand in hand (as in the postcolonial independence movements in India and Africa). Although national and ethnic identities associated with discrete territories retain considerable attractive power, they must today share the political arena with a much more complex set of identities, only some of which have an explicit territorial dimension. Some identities involve a direct shift in economic interests and political allegiances to levels other than the national (such as the regional) or world-spanning class identities (such as with employees of global companies). Others involve new sources of identity, such as gender, sexual orientation, and other "social movement" identities, that have risen in importance at the very moment when national identities have ceased to have the *inclusive* hold they once had over large populations. The new sources of identity are probably the result of cultural globalization, the increase in shared media images, and the choice of identities available from a marketable stock. But they also result from the declining efficacy of singular national identities in a world in which national membership no longer guarantees the status and rewards it once could.[7] From this perspective, heretical identities can flourish when powerful pressures toward conforming to singular national identities are reduced. To the extent that national identities reflect the power of states to channel or command other identities into a chosen path, the decreased power of states in the realms of communication, education, and adult socialization (as in military conscription) allow for a greater variety and combination of identities. The "communitarian" current in contemporary political theory is largely devoted to trying to reestablish the ground for a stable, inclusive territorial-political identity upon which an inclusive democratic politics can be based. The likelihood and *desirability* of doing so under conditions of globalization is akin to the fabulist's attempt at getting the genie back into the bottle from which it had escaped.[8]

In the second place, the United States has an increasingly ambivalent position within its own hegemony. As I have pointed out in Chapter 8, the United States is now more on the receiving rather than the delivering end of the forces liberated by globalization. "History is finally presenting America with its bill."[9] The United States today is undoubtedly the world's most significant military power. But what this adds up to in a world of increasingly asymmetric warfare is unclear, as the indeterminate outcomes of recent wars in Afghanistan and Iraq indicate. Economically, the United States now depends on draining savings from the rest of the world. But this does not redound to the advantage of most Americans, who find themselves with less job security, spending more and more of their incomes on "necessities," and with less prospect of the intergenerational social mobility that gave the marketplace society its popular appeal. The U.S. commitment to external expansion to manage conflicts at home and serve the commercial ethos of dominant social groups has come back to haunt its creators. The United States now appears as an "ordinary" country subject to external pressures more than simply the source of pressure on others.

The U.S. relationship to the external world, therefore, has changed profoundly since the days of Madison and Jefferson. Moving from a peripheral to central position within the world geopolitical order, the United States brought to that position its own ethos. Its absolute economic predominance and a number of key institutional changes produced in the critical years during and after the Second World War allowed the successful projection of the American ethos beyond its shores. Expansion seemed to produce not only economic but also political returns for the American system. The benefits proved more ephemeral for the majority of Americans than ever was contemplated. Globalization of the world economy under American auspices has shifted control over parts of the American economy to ever more distant seats of power. The increasing fragmentation and entropy of the American governmental system suggest that regaining control will be an almost impossible task. Many Americans consequently find themselves with the increased sense of insecurity and loss of control that others have long experienced. From its origin as a country, America's promise has been that through expansion most everyone would benefit. That everyone no longer does calls into question the very system that produced that promise in the first place. Max Horkheimer's prescient observation about Nazi Germany seems apropos in the U.S. case: "Again and again in history, ideas have cast off their swaddling clothes and struck out against the social systems that bore them."[10]

Recent aggressive militarism in response to the terror attacks of September 11, 2001, a burst of measures to protect domestic manufacturing industries and agribusiness, and retreat from many types of multilateral commitment are indicative of the U.S. government's reactions to perceived military and economic threats. This America is becoming an enemy of globalization because of the perception of being threatened (yet again) by external "enemies." In part, the reactions are a lashing out at perceived enemies, however inadequately the enemies are defined. Indeed, the potential list includes many still unknown ones, as recounted in the famous speech by U.S. Secretary of Defense Rumsfeld:

> There are things we know that we know. There are known unknowns. That is to say, there are things we know we don't know. But there are also unknown unknowns. There are things we don't know we don't know. . . . Each year, we discover a few more of these unknown unknowns.[11]

Aside from the opaqueness of Rumsfeld's style, this pronouncement seems to indicate commitment not only to a war without end but to a war that cannot possibly be won because there are simply too many "known unknowns." Unwittingly, therefore, it reveals both that the administration of George W. Bush did not really know what it was doing—in Iraq or elsewhere—and, as a result, its ignorance turned almost any group into potential terrorists and committed the United States to measures, such as preemptive war and limitless military spending, that are unsustainable if the United States is to remain a marketplace society with even a modicum of democracy. The imperial hubris is also staged as a performance for a U.S. domestic audience: that something, anything, is being done to prevent a repeat of September 11 and to limit foreign economic competition. It is the appearance of doing something, not necessarily achieving anything, that has driven U.S. foreign policy in a unilateral direction. But how successful can the United States be in turning its back on the world it has created?

In responding to this question, three points are worth emphasizing. The first relates to U.S. legitimacy, the second concerns U.S. power, and the third involves the nature of hegemony in the twenty-first century. First of all, as Immanuel Wallerstein contends:

> In the history of the world, military power never has been sufficient to maintain supremacy. Legitimacy is essential, at least legitimacy recognized by a significant part of the world. With their preemptive war, the American hawks have undermined very fundamentally the U.S. claim to legitimacy. And thus they have weakened the United States irremediably in the geopolitical arena.[12]

This is particularly true in the American case because the success of its hegemony has depended overwhelmingly on consensual "compellance": having others enroll in its exercise.

The United States, however, is seen increasingly, even among its erstwhile allies, as something of a "rogue state." For example, most of its economic competitors are unified in opposing, and gaining WTO support against, U.S. protectionist measures in manufacturing and agriculture. Official U.S. opposition to multiple international treaties governing crimes against humanity, antiballistic missile systems, and climate change has further isolated the country in the eyes of the world. Even more obviously, the lack of support by other governments for the U.S. invasion of Iraq in 2003 suggests a significant erosion of U.S. legitimacy. During the 1991 Gulf War, thirty-two countries sent troops to support U.S. forces in liberating Kuwait from Iraqi occupation. In the 2003 invasion of Iraq, only three countries, the United States, Britain, and Australia, sent forces into combat. Of course, the 1991 war was under United Nations sponsorship, while the 2003 war was not. What is most important is that the United States emerged from 2003 with a disparate and fragmented "coalition of the willing" (as the administration of George W. Bush dubbed those countries whose governments supported its invasion in various ways), but without that supportive alliance of major industrialized countries that had underpinned U.S. foreign policy since the Second World War (Figure 9.1).

The main U.S. alliance, the North Atlantic Treaty Organization (NATO), was completely sundered by the U.S. government's obsession with Saddam Hussein. With its open-ended war on terrorism and difficulties in policing a conquered Iraq, the United States now has dire need of capable allies. Otherwise it must provide troops on an indefinite basis to occupy a country without the propaganda cover of operating under a UN mandate. Yet, major allies such as France and Germany have been alienated by a lack of consultation and because of the U.S. government's total inability to offer a reasonable justification for why an invasion of Iraq would make any kind of contribution in bringing to justice the perpetrators of the September 11, 2001 terror attacks.

The retreat from consensual compellance makes the United States have to use its own resources as well as what it can leverage from its control of the U.S. dollar. But is U.S. power up to what is demanded of it? In practice, U.S. power is much less effective than claimed by either its proponents or its critics. As Mary Kaldor puts it: "If America were truly an empire, surely it would be able to extend democracy to other regions, to impose its system on the rest of the world?"[13] The constraints are both geopolitical and economic. The Bush administration's foreign policy has no ordering of strategic priorities. The War on Terror recalls the older wars on drugs periodically declared by the U.S. government, which leapt around from one front to another. At the same time a vast investment is underway in rebordering the United States through funding a so-called missile shield. Little or no attention is given to curing hostility by, for instance, helping to resolve the Israel-Arab conflict. That defies simple technical fixes.

Economically, the United States has seen the return of the "twin deficits" problem of the Reagan presidency: massive government overspending to pay for huge increases in military expenditure plus increased demands for entitlement spending from powerful domestic lobbies

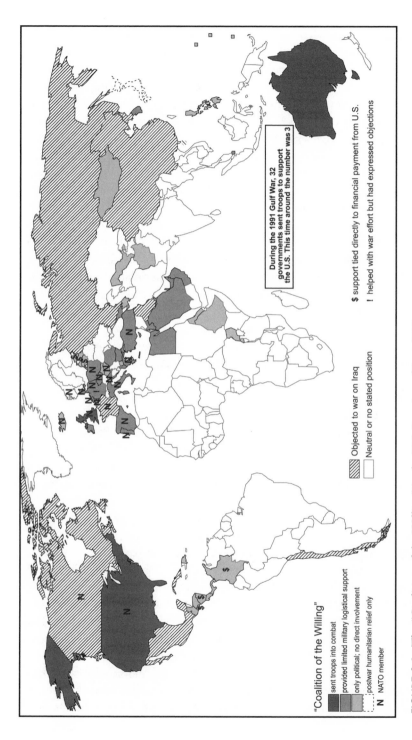

"Coalition of the Willing"

- sent troops into combat
- provided limited military logistical support
- only political; no direct involvement
- postwar humanitarian relief only
- N NATO member

Objected to war on Iraq

Neutral or no stated position

During the 1991 Gulf War, 32 governments sent troops to support the U.S. This time around the number was 3

$ support tied directly to financial payment from U.S.

! helped with war effort but had expressed objections

FIGURE 9.1. The "Coalition of the Willing" in the U.S. Invasion of Iraq, 2003.
Source: Chase Langford and author.

(especially the growing number of elderly) in the face of dramatic cuts in taxes for the rich, producing a large federal deficit; and a national economy increasingly driven by foreign credits because of large trade and general current account deficits. The U.S. government always had two major advantages in financing its profligacy in years gone by: the Cold War and the dollar. The Soviet threat gave the United States bargaining leverage with its allies in Europe and Japan. The dollar's international role gave the United States the capacity to import credit in its own currency and export its troubles by manipulating the dollar's value through increasing its supply, adjusting interest rates, or lowering its value against the currencies of America's competitors. Both of these advantages have now eroded. The open-ended terrorist bogey is no substitute for the Soviet Union. The advent of the Euro and the absolute dependence of the U.S. economy on foreign creditors represent important challenges to America's monetary superiority. Eventually, "it will take higher interest rates to lure foreign savings. Higher rates seem likely to force American politics into harsher choices—between guns and butter, or growth and consumption."[14]

Concurrently, the geographical structure of the world economy has changed with the rise of China and other countries as active participants in the trade, financial, and cultural exchanges driving globalization. The United States is deeply tied into this evolving system and can no longer act as if it is autonomous of it. The irony here is that this dependence reflects in part the very victory in the Cold War that official America so fervently desired but may now have reason to regret. The end of the Cold War brought about the collapse of the most important ideological opposition to the idea of marketplace society as the global ideal. Since then China, Russia, and other countries that were hitherto bastions of state-command capital goods producing economies have converted to the consumption model pioneered in the United States and sponsored by the U.S. government. Some of these—China in particular—seem set to displace the United States as the anchor of globalization if it sets off too far on the wild-goose chase of an endless war on terrorism.

Finally, the above two points both still rest on the assumption of a world divided into territorial states that remain its singular actors. But the burden of the argument in this book has been that this is *not* the spatial ontology or geographical structure that U.S. hegemony has helped to bring about. Rather, in a world in which transnational institutions and actors are increasingly powerful, it is misleading to continue to territorialize understandings of hegemony. From one point of view, a new class of capitalists who may be American, Chinese, or German in formal nationality but whose operations, interests, and identities are increasingly networked globally is in formation. The hegemony of marketplace society is increasingly on their shoulders, not on the U.S. government's. Capital circuits and consumption desires now multiply between national territories, so to speak, rather than within them.

The distinguishing trait of the new transnational bourgeoisie that is now the primary instrument of globalization is that its interests lie in capital accumulation wherever it can be realized rather than in any given national space or local place.[15] The spread of multinational businesses, cross-border mergers and acquisitions, strategic alliances, and production-consumption chains spanning great distances are all indicators of an emerging historic bloc bringing together the global capitalists, their managers and servants in international organizations, and the various transnational forums they jointly run. The main strength of the bloc lies in its ability to muster the values of the marketplace society. Its weakness lies in the difficulty of establishing any sort of global regulatory apparatus to impose stability that might substitute for the states that have carried out this activity in the past. What does seem clear, as this book has argued, is that reinstating a "classic" state sovereignty to command a territorial piece of the global economic pie in the face of this new class and its global allies will prove increasingly difficult. Even for many Americans, therefore, the "In God We Trust" on the dollar bill promises increasingly to be more of a vain hope than the copper-bottomed guarantee they have long regarded as a national birthright.

Notes

Chapter One

1. A sampling of the most recent books would include: Andrew Bacevich, *American Empire: The Realities and Consequences of U.S. Diplomacy* (Cambridge, MA: Harvard University Press, 2003); Niall Ferguson, *Colossus: The Price of America's Empire* (New York: Penguin, 2004); Chalmers Johnson, *The Sorrows of Empire: Militarism, Secrecy, and the End of the Republic* (New York: Metropolitan Books, 2003); Michael Mann, *Incoherent Empire* (London: Verso, 2003); and Emmanuel Todd, *After the Empire: The Breakdown of the American Order* (New York: Columbia University Press, 2003). Whatever their individual merits, and the Bacevich, Johnson, and Mann books have many, all accept the idea that the contemporary United States is best thought of as an "empire."

2. This is the conventional wisdom across otherwise such disparate accounts of world politics as classical realism, neo-realism, world-systems theory, and much of what today goes for Marxism (particularly that of a Leninist cast). In my view, how American power has been realized is not reducible to some universal and eternal calculus of behavior that follows automatically from the U.S. government having achieved a globally dominant position because of U.S. economic and military prowess.

3. John Agnew, "The Territorial Trap: The Geographical Assumptions of International Relations Theory." *Review of International Political Economy* 1 (1994): 53–80. It is the presumption that political power is invariably territorialized, be it in territorial states or empires, that I find particularly problematic about use of the word empire in a world in which power is not invariably territorialized.

4. Presciently, the German (and Nazi) legal philosopher Carl Schmitt suggested in 1932 that "not only was the United States a new power but that there was also something distinctly new about its power" (William Rasch, "Human Rights as Geopolitics: Carl Schmitt and the Legal Form of American Supremacy." *Cultural Critique* 54 (2003): 122, citing Carl Schmitt, *Positionen und Begriffe im Kampf mit Weimar-Genf-Versailles, 1923–1939* [Berlin: Duncker and Humblot, 1988, 184–203]). In Schmitt's view, Rasch continues (122–23), "By being predominantly economic . . . America's expropriations were deemed to be peaceful and apolitical. Furthermore, they were legal, or rather they presented themselves as the promotion and extension of universally binding legality per se." In consequence, "to oppose American hegemony is to oppose the universally good and common interests of humanity." Rasch concludes: "This—the equation of particular economic and political interests with universally binding moral norms—*this* is the intellectual achievement

232 Notes to Chapter One

Schmitt could not help but admire, even as he embarked on his disastrous attempts at fighting his elusive, because nonlocalizable, enemy, which proved to be mere shadowboxing in the end."

5. I thus generally accept the claim to a significant restructuring of world capitalism since the 1970s made by neo-Gramscian and postimperialist theorists such as, respectively, Robert W. Cox, *Power, Production and World Order* (New York: Cambridge University Press, 1987) and David G. Becker et al., *Postimperialism: International Capitalism and Development in the Late Twentieth Century* (Boulder, CO: Lynne Rienner, 1987), but with an emphasis on the central role of cultural practices involving consumption rather than just the simple production-driven logic they endorse. They also fail to note the roots of the transformation in the particular character of American hegemony.

6. On the history of globalization as a long-term process emanating from different world regions rather than as either a singularly Western or capitalist phenomenon, see, for example, A. G. Hopkins (ed.), *Globalization in World History* (New York: Norton, 2002). Leslie Sklair, *Globalization: Capitalism and its Alternatives* (Oxford: Oxford University Press, 2002) makes the useful distinction between what he calls "generic globalization" and "capitalist globalization." These terms come close to what I mean, respectively, by globalization and liberalization, although I do not see any aspect of recent globalization (such as changes in communication and transportation technologies) as somehow independent of the capitalist context within which it has developed. It is just that the specific policies and practices associated with transnational liberalism are not the same as globalization tout court.

7. David Harvey, *The New Imperialism* (Oxford: Oxford University Press, 2003, p. 207) makes the point succinctly: "The unilateralist assertion of U.S. imperial power fails entirely to recognize the high degree of cross-territorial integration that now exists within the capitalistic organization of the circulation and accumulation of capital."

8. The phrase "marketplace society" as used in this book marks a fusion between the similar ideas about "market society" in C. B. Macpherson, *The Political Theory of Possessive Individualism: From Hobbes to Locke* (Oxford: Oxford University Press, 1962) and "marketplace society" in William Appleman Williams, *The Roots of the Modern American Empire* (New York: Vintage 1969) but extended to incorporate the United States as a place in which market society reached its fullest expression from the late nineteenth century on. Williams' use of the term "empire" betrays a more nuanced understanding of American hegemony than his adoption of the word might imply.

9. This is the fundamental argument of Karl Polanyi, *The Great Transformation* (Boston: Beacon Press, 1944) but it is also an important theme in the writings of Max Weber and Antonio Gramsci. It seems lost on both enthusiasts for and critics of American "empire."

10. The "birth" of modern consumer society has older origins in eighteenth-century England even if it is in late nineteenth-century America that it first reaches beyond a relatively narrow segment of the population. See, for example, Neil McKendrick et al., *The Birth of a Consumer Society: The Commercialization of*

Eighteenth-Century England (Bloomington, IN: Indiana University Press, 1982) and John Brewer and Roy Porter (eds.), *Consumption and the World of Goods* (London: Routledge, 1992).

11. A powerful argument to this effect is made by T. H. Breen, *The Marketplace of Revolution: How Consumer Politics Shaped American Independence* (New York: Oxford University Press, 2004).

12. Karl Marx, [1844] Introduction to *The Critique of Hegel's Philosophy of Right*, edited by J. O'Malley (Cambridge: Cambridge University Press, 1970) p. 3.

13. To Paul Kennedy, *The Rise and Fall of the Great Powers* (New York: Random House, 1986), for example, state territories are like giant (mercantilist) storage bins of resources for use against one's military adversaries. To David Harvey, *The New Imperialism*, U.S. foreign policy is essentially about laying the groundwork for resolving the accumulation dilemmas of U.S. capital. In neither account does the moment of consumption in the capital process figure prominently.

14. Capital as a process transforms money (M) into a commodity (C) and back into money (M') (plus profit). This is a major point made by Kojim Karatani, *Transcritique: On Kant and Marx* (Cambridge, MA: MIT Press, 2003). A useful comment on and critique of this argument is provided in Slavoj Žižek, "The Parallax View," *New Left Review*, 25 (2004): 121–34.

15. See, in particular, Albert O. Hirschman, *The Passions and the Interests: Political Arguments for Capitalism before its Triumph* (Princeton, NJ: Princeton University Press, 1977).

16. E. Wharton, [1913] *The Custom of the Country* (New York: Bantam, 1991) p. 96.

17. Karl Marx, *The 18th Brumaire of Louis Bonaparte* (New York: International Publishers [1852] 1963), pp. 15, 16, 135. Peter Stallybrass, "Marx's Coat," in *Border Fetishisms: Material Objects and Unstable Spaces*, ed. Patricia Spyer (London: Routledge, 1998), uses Marx's experience of having to pawn his own coat when times were financially constrained to make this point about the double-edged nature of capitalist consumption.

18. Christopher A. Bayly, "The Origins of the Swadeshi (Home Industry): Cloth and Indian Society, 1700–1930," in *The Social Life of Things: Commodities in Cultural Perspective*, ed. Arjun Appadurai (Cambridge: Cambridge University Press, 1986), p. 314. Objects can be valued entirely in and of themselves. More often than not, however, they also serve social uses of one sort or another. See, in particular, Chandra Mukerji, *From Graven Images: Patterns of Modern Materialism* (New York: Columbia University Press, 1983).

19. Pierre Bourdieu, *Distinction: A Social Critique of the Judgment of Taste* (Cambridge, MA: Harvard University Press, 1984).

20. The essence of the argument of Georg Simmel, *The Philosophy of Money* (London: Routledge, 1978) is that it is *demand* which endows persons and things with value. This does not mean that it is freely chosen, in the sense of the autonomous individual, only that there is popular agency in the hegemonic valuations of marketplace society, unlike in customary and command societies.

21. Jürgen Habermas, *The Structural Transformation of the Public Sphere* (Cambridge, MA: MIT Press, 1991) makes a strong case for the connection between

the rise of marketplace society and the development of a "public sphere." He has been criticized for failing to note its longer-term pernicious effects on the public sphere. See, for example, Nancy Fraser, "Rethinking the Public Sphere: A Contribution to the Critique of Actually Existing Democracy," in *The Phantom Public Sphere*, ed. Bruce Robbins (Minneapolis: University of Minnesota Press, 1993). A brilliant account of the politics of mass consumption in the United States after the Second World War when the country was finally able and willing to imprint itself on a larger world is Lizabeth Cohen, *A Consumers' Republic: The Politics of Mass Consumption in Postwar America* (New York: Random House, 2003).

22. Jim Cullen, *The American Dream: A Short History of an Idea that Shaped a Nation* (New York: Oxford University Press, 2003).

23. Immanuel Wallerstein, *The Decline of American Power* (New York: New Press, 2003), p. 195.

24. John Agnew, *Geopolitics: Re-Visioning World Politics*, Second Edition (London: Routledge, 2003).

25. The De Tocqueville quotation is from Cullen, *The American Dream*, p. 5.

26. Leslie Sklair, *Globalization: Capitalism and Its Alternatives*, makes a powerful case for the rise of a worldwide system of transnational practices based on the "culture-ideology of consumerism" he associates with transnational corporations and a transnational corporate class. This bears a similarity to what I have in mind with the phrase "marketplace society" but I wish to extend that to include the treatment of people as well as things and, of course, I trace it back to American hegemony.

27. William Leach, *Land of Desire: Merchants, Power, and the Rise of a New American Culture* (New York: Pantheon, 1993), p. xiii.

28. See Agnew, *Geopolitics*, Chapter 7 and 8.

29. Michael Hardt and Antonio Negri, *Empire* (Cambridge, MA: Harvard University Press, 2000).

30. Chalmers Johnson, *Blowback: The Costs and Consequences of American Empire* (New York: Henry Holt, 2000), p. 223.

Chapter Two

1. Bernard Bailyn, *The Ideological Origins of the American Revolution* (Cambridge, MA: Belknap Press of Harvard University Press, 1967); Gordon S. Wood, *The Creation of the American Republic, 1776–1787* (Chapel Hill, NC: University of North Carolina Press, 1969); Hannah Arendt, *On Revolution* (New York: Penguin, 1963).

2. William Lee Miller, *Lincoln's Virtues: An Ethical Biography* (New York: Random House, 2002), 190.

3. Walter Karp, *The Politics of War: The Story of Two Wars Which Forever Altered the Political Life of the American Republic (1898–1920)* (New York: Harper and Row, 1979); Thomas Schoonover, *Uncle Sam's War of 1898 and the Origins of Globalization* (Lexington, KT: University Press of Kentucky, 2003).

4. David W. Noble, *Death of a Nation: American Culture and the End of Exceptionalism* (Minneapolis: University of Minnesota Press, 2002), xliv.

5. George Monbiot, "Out of the Wreckage." *Guardian* (London), February 25, 2003: 19.

6. Stephan Haggard, "The Institutional Foundations of Hegemony: Explaining the Reciprocal Trade Agreements Act of 1934." *International Organization*, 42 (1988): 91–119.

7. Walter Russell Mead, *Special Providence: American Foreign Policy and How It Changed the World* (New York: Routledge, 2002).

8. Peter Trubowitz, *Defining the National Interest: Continuity and Change in American Foreign Policy* (Chicago: University of Chicago Press, 1998).

9. Michael Lind, *Made in Texas: George W. Bush and the Southern Takeover of American Politics* (New York: Basic Books, 2002).

10. Harold Meyerson, "The Most Dangerous President Ever." *The American Prospect*, May 2003: 25–28.

11. See, e.g., Lawrence F. Kaplan and William Kristol, *The War Over Iraq: Saddam's Tyranny and America's Mission* (New York: Encounter Books, 2003), and for insightful comments on this sort of thinking, its antecedents, and opposition to it inside and outside the Bush administration see, e.g., William Pfaff, "The Question of Hegemony." *Foreign Affairs*, 80/1 (1999), 221–232; Seymour Hersh, "Selective Intelligence: How the Pentagon Outwitted the C.I.A." *The New Yorker*, May 12, 2003: 44–51; Jonathan Eyal, "The War Is a Sign of Things to Come as U.S. Yearns for Global Invincibility." *The Irish Times*, March 24, 2003: 16; Michael Howard, "The Bush Doctrine: It's a Brutal World, so Act Brutally." *Sunday Times* (London), March 23, 2003: 21; Jean-Jacques Mével, "Rumsfeld et Powell à couteaux tirés." *Le Figaro*, April 25, 2003: 3; "The Shadow Men." *Economist*, April 26, 2003: 21–23.

12. Simon Jenkins, "Bin Laden's Laughter Echoes Across the West." *Times* (London), March 19, 2003: 22; Thomas Powers, "The Vanishing Case for War." *New York Review of Books*, December 4, 2003: 12–17.

13. Eamonn McCann, "Home Front Defeat on Cards of Aspiring U.S. Imperialists." *Belfast Telegraph*, March 20, 2003: 18. More generally, see Benjamin J. Barber, *Fear's Empire: War, Terrorism, and Democracy* (New York: Norton, 2003).

14. Powers, "The Vanishing Case for War," 17.

15. I owe this point to Sankaran Krishna, "An Inarticulate Imperialism: Dubya, Afghanistan and the American Century." *Alternatives: Turkish Journal of International Relations*, 1 (2003): 69–80.

16. Raymond Williams, *Keywords: A Vocabulary of Culture and Society* (London: Harper Collins, 1983), 45. More generally, see Roger Simon, *Gramsci's Political Thought: An Introduction* (London: Lawrence and Wishart, 1991).

17. Stephen P. Rosen, "An Empire, If You Can Keep It." *The National Interest*, 71 (Spring 2003), 51.

18. See, e.g., Andrew Bacevich, *American Empire: The Realities and Consequences of U.S. Diplomacy* (Cambridge, MA: Harvard University Press, 2002); and Neil Smith, *American Empire: Roosevelt's Geographer and the Prelude to Globalization* (Berkeley: University of California Press, 2003).

19. For an analogous but more wide-ranging discussion of degrees of hierarchy and territoriality in security relationships, see David A. Lake, *Entangling Relations: American Foreign Policy in Its Century* (Princeton, NJ: Princeton University Press, 1999), 17–34.

20. This is not to endorse the revival of the term *homo sacer* in the form advocated by Giorgio Agamben (*Homo Sacer: Sovereign Power and Bare Life* [Stanford, CA:

Stanford University Press, 1998]) which sees power as invariably territorialized and the us/them distinction as necessarily following the same lines.

21. Carlo Galli, *La guerra globale* (Rome: Laterza, 2003).

22. Carlo Galli, *Spazi politici: L'éta moderna e l'éta globale* (Bologna: Il Mulino, 2001).

23. Robert E. Goodin, "How Amoral *Is* Hegemon?" *Perspectives on Politics*, 1 (2003): 123–124.

24. Goodin, "How Amoral *Is* Hegemon?" 125.

25. M. Leonard, "Euro Space: Combine and Conquer." *Wired*, June 2003: 132.

26. Niall Ferguson, *The Cash Nexus: Money and Power in the Modern World, 1700–2000* (New York: Basic Books, 2001), and Niall Ferguson, *Empire: How Britain Made the Modern World* (London: BBC Books, 2003). Also, see Niall Ferguson, *Colossus: The Price of America's Empire* (New York: Penguin, 2004).

27. See, e.g., John Pilger, *The New Rulers of the World* (London: Verso, 2002); W. Blum, *Rogue State: A Guide to the World's Only Superpower* (London: Zed Books, 2002); and any one of many books on world politics by Noam Chomsky, such as *Hegemony or Survival: America's Quest for Global Dominance* (New York: Metropolitan Books, 2003). In each case current U.S. foreign policy is seen as a cunning plot to subjugate the rest of the world, that is, to establish a global *imperium*, but without attending to the distinction between the U.S. government and U.S. influence tout court, to the divisions in U.S. domestic politics, or to the difference between hegemony (as I have defined it) and empire or dominance.

28. Paul Kennedy, *The Rise and Fall of the Great Powers* (New York: Random House, 1986).

29. Amitav Ghosh, "The Anglophone Empire: Can Occupation Ever Work?" *The New Yorker*, April 7, 2003: 46–47.

30. Michael Hardt and Antonio Negri, *Empire* (Cambridge, MA: Harvard University Press, 2000).

31. Antonio Negri, *Guide: Cinque lezioni su Impero e dintorni* (Milan: Raffaello Cortina, 2003), 18, my translation.

32. John Agnew and Stuart Corbridge, *Mastering Space: Hegemony, Territory, and International Political Economy* (London: Routledge, 1995).

33. Robert W. Cox, "Structural Issues of Global Governance: Implications for Europe," in *Gramsci, Historical Materialism and International Relations*, ed. Stephen Gill (Cambridge, England: Cambridge University Press, 1993); and Agnew and Corbridge, *Mastering Space*.

34. Ellen Meiksins Wood, *Empire of Capital* (London: Verso, 2003).

35. Chalmers Johnson, "The War Business: Squeezing a Profit from the Wreckage in Iraq." *Harper's Magazine*, November 2003: 53–58.

36. Alberto Ronchey, "L'illusione di fare da soli: Il vero limite della 'dottrina Bush.'" *Corriere della Sera*, April 24, 2003: 1; Jeffrey E. Garten, "Ripple Effects: Anti-Americanism May Harm U.S. Firms." *International Herald Tribune*, April 16, 2003: 9.

37. See, e.g., Karl E. Meyer, *The Dust of Empire: The Race for Mastery in the Asian Heartland* (New York: Public Affairs, 2002).

38. Joseph Nye, *Bound to Lead: The Changing Nature of American Power* (New York: Basic Books, 1990).

39. Joseph Nye, "Limits to American Power." *Political Science Quarterly*, 117/4 (2002–2003): 545–559.

40. Agnew and Corbridge, *Mastering Space*, Chapter 7.

41. Michael Ignatieff, "Empire Lite." *Prospect*, February 2003: 36–43.

42. This is apparent in U.S. official pronouncements about the role of the UN prior to the attack on Iraq in 2003.

43. Richard Pells, *Not Like Us: How Europeans Have Loved, Hated, and Transformed American Culture since World War II* (New York: Basic Books, 1997).

44. Meghnad Desai, *Marx's Revenge: The Resurgence of Capitalism and the Death of Statist Socialism* (London: Verso, 2002), 305.

45. Michael Mann, "The Autonomous Power of the State." *European Journal of Sociology* 25 (1984): 185–213.

46. Allen J. Scott, *Regions and the World Economy* (Oxford: Oxford University Press, 1998).

47. Philip G. Cerny, "Globalization and the Changing Logic of Collective Action." *International Organization* 49 (1995): 621.

48. David M. Andrews, "Capital Mobility and State Autonomy: Towards a Structural Theory of International Monetary Relations." *International Studies Quarterly*, 38 (1994): 193–218; Eric Helleiner, *States and the Reemergence of Global Finance: From Bretton Woods to the 1990s* (Ithaca, NY: Cornell University Press, 1994). An excellent review of the pros and cons of the role of finance in challenging state sovereignty is provided in Eric Helleiner, "Sovereignty, Territoriality and the Globalization of Finance," in *States and Sovereignty in the Global Economy*, ed. David A. Smith, Dorothy J. Solinger, and Steven C. Topik (London: Routledge, 1999).

49. Goodin, "How Amoral *Is* Hegemon?"

50. Nye, "Limits to American Power."

51. Jack Snyder, "Imperial Temptations." *The National Interest*, 71 (2003): 29–40.

52. Paul Starr, "The Easy War." *The American Prospect*, March 2003: 21.

Chapter Three

1. Paul Ricoeur, *Lectures on Ideology and Utopia* (New York: The Free Press, 1986), 198. Of course, as George Steinmetz ("Introduction: Culture and the State," in *State/Culture: State Formation after the Cultural Turn*, ed. George Steinmetz, 20–23 [(Ithaca, NY: Cornell University Press, 1999]), points out, such "foundationalist decontextualization" is characteristic of all orthodox positivist, Marxist, and rational-choice theories of states and world politics, not just a seemingly unlikely candidate such as the hermeneuticist Ricoeur.

2. This is the standard view not only in various realist accounts but also for the liberalism in which a state-based pooling up of political power is seen as a condition to be overcome. Most mainstream texts in international relations theory take the standard view. See, e.g., K. Waltz, *The Theory of International Politics* (New York: Addison Wesley, 1979); K. J. Holsti, *The Dividing Discipline: Hegemony and Diversity in International Theory* (Boston: Allen and Unwin, 1985); and D. A. Baldwin (ed.), *Neorealism and Neoliberalism: The Contemporary Debate* (New York: Columbia University Press, 1993).

3. Robert W. Cox, "Structural Issues in Global Governance: Implications for Europe," in *Gramsci, Historical Materialism and International Relations*, ed. Stephen Gill, 264 (Cambridge, England: Cambridge University Press, 1993).

4. John Allen, "Spatial Assemblages of Power: From Domination to Empowerment," in *Human Geography Today*, ed. Doreen Massey, John Allen, and Philip Sarre, 194–218 (Cambridge, England: Polity Press, 1999); and John Allen, *Lost Geographies of Power* (Oxford: Blackwell, 2003).

5. See, e.g., Hannah Arendt, *The Human Condition* (Chicago: University of Chicago Press, 1975); Michel Foucault, *Power/Knowledge* (Brighton: Harvester, 1980); Gilles Deleuze, *Foucault* (London: Athlone Press, 1980); and Bruno Latour, "The Powers of Association," in *Power, Action, and Belief*, ed. J. Law, 264–280 (London: Routledge, 1986). For a careful and cogent exploration of Foucault's approach to power, emphasizing how agency can be theorized even in the absence of the autonomy associated with individualist and nonsociological conceptions of personhood, see Mark Bevir, "Foucault and Critique: Deploying Agency Against Autonomy." *Political Theory* 27, no. 1 (1999): 65–84.

6. John Agnew and Stuart Corbridge, *Mastering Space: Hegemony, Territory and International Political Economy* (London: Routledge, 1995); Andrew Jones, "Retheorizing the Core: A 'Globalized' Business Elite in Santiago, Chile." *Political Geography* 17, no. 3 (1998): 295–318.

7. Allen, "Spatial Assemblages of Power."

8. David Held, Anthony McGrew, David Goldblatt, and Jonathan Perraton, *Global Transformations: Politics, Economics and Culture* (Stanford, CA: Stanford University Press, 1999).

9. See, e.g., Michael Shapiro, *The Politics of Representation* (Madison, WI: University of Wisconsin Press, 1988), 93; R.B.J. Walker, *Inside/Outside: International Relations as Political Theory* (Cambridge, MA: Cambridge University Press, 1993); David Campbell, *Writing Security: United States Foreign Policy and the Politics of Identity* (Baltimore, MD: Johns Hopkins University Press, 1992); Stuart Hall, "The West and the Rest: Discourse and Power," in *Formations of Modernity*, ed. S. Hall and B. Gieben (Cambridge, England: Polity Press, 1992); and Gearóid Ó Tuathail, *Critical Geopolitics: The Politics of Writing Global Space* (Minneapolis: University of Minnesota Press, 1996).

10. Agnew and Corbridge, *Mastering Space*, 13–45.

11. Alexander Wendt, "Anarchy Is What States Make of It: The Social Construction of Power Politics." *International Organization* 46 (1992): 391–425. On power as a *medium* brought about by social mobilization see, in particular, Anthony Giddens, *The Consequences of Modernity* (Cambridge, England: Polity, 1990); and Michael Mann, *The Sources of Social Power. Vol. I: A History of Power from the Beginning to A.D. 1760* (Cambridge, England: Cambridge University Press, 1986).

12. Richard K. Ashley, "The Poverty of Neorealism." *International Organization* 38 (1984): 225–286.

13. John Gerard Ruggie, "Territoriality and Beyond: Problematizing Modernity in International Relations." *International Organization* 47 (1993): 139–174; John A. Agnew, "The Territorial Trap: The Geographical Assumptions of International Relations Theory." *Review of International Political Economy* 1 (1994): 53–80.

14. David Held et al., *Global Transformations*.

15. See, e.g., on Hobbes's important role in justifying this, Norman Jacobson, "The Strange Case of the Hobbesian Man." *Representations* 63 (1998): 1–12; and Quentin Skinner, "Hobbes and the Purely Artificial Person of the State." *Journal of Political Philosophy* 7 (1999): 1–29.

16. Otto Gierke, *Political Theories of the Middle Age,* trans. F. W. Maitland (Cambridge, England: Cambridge University Press, 1922).

17. Agnew, "The Territorial Trap."

18. Marie-Françoise Durand, Jacques Lévy, and Denis Retaillé, *Le monde: Espaces et systèmes* (Paris: Dalloz, 1992); Jacques Lévy, *Europe: Une géographie* (Paris: Hachette, 1997).

19. Agnew and Corbridge, *Mastering Space,* 15–23.

20. Karl Polanyi, *The Great Transformation* (Boston: Beacon Press, 1944).

21. Michael Storper, "Territories, Flows, and Hierarchies in the Global Economy," in *Spaces of Globalization: Reasserting the Power of the Local,* ed. Kevin R. Cox, 19–44 (New York: Guilford Press, 1997); and Peter Dicken et al., "Chains and Networks, Territories and Scales: Towards a Relational Framework for Analysing the Global Economy," *Global Networks* 1 (2001): 89–112.

22. Roxanne Lynn Doty, *Imperial Encounters: The Politics of Representation in North-South Relations* (Minneapolis: University of Minnesota Press, 1996).

23. See, *inter alia,* John Gaventa, *Power and Powerlessness* (Oxford: Clarendon Press, 1990); Steven Lukes, ed., *Power* (New York: New York University Press, 1986); Peter Morriss, *Power: A Philosophical Analysis* (Manchester: Manchester University Press, 1987); and Stefano Guzzini, "Structural Power: The Limits of Neorealist Power Analysis." *International Organization* 47 (1993): 443–478.

24. See, e.g., Robert A. Dahl, "Power," in *International Encyclopedia of the Social Sciences,* ed. David Sills, 405–415 (New York: The Free Press, 1968); Max Weber, *Economy and Society* (Berkeley: University of California Press, 1972), Chapter 10.

25. See Guzzini, "Structural Power."

26. See, e.g., Stephen D. Krasner, "Regimes and the Limits of Realism: Regimes as Autonomous Variables." *International Organization* 36 (1982): 497–510; James Rosenau, *The Study of Global Interdependence: Essays on the Transnationalization of World Affairs* (London: Pinter, 1980); Stephen Gill and David Law, "Global Hegemony and the Structural Power of Capital." *International Studies Quarterly* 33 (1989): 475–499; Peter M. Haas, ed., "Knowledge, Power and International Policy Coordination." *International Organization* 46 (1992): 1–390; Kathryn Sikkink, "Human Rights, Principled Issue-Networks, and Sovereignty in Latin America." *International Organization* 47 (1993): 411–441.

27. This move is as characteristic of constructivist theories as it is of realist and liberal ones as, e.g., with Alexander Wendt, *Social Theory of International Politics* (Cambridge, England: Cambridge University Press, 1999). For a brilliant critique of this and a much more thorough sociological basis to a social theory of world politics to be found in Georg Simmel's "sociational framework," see Lars-Erik Cederman and Christopher Daase, "Endogenizing Corporate Identities: The Next Step in Constructivist IR Theory." *European Journal of International Relations* 9 (2003): 5–35.

28. Naeem Inayatullah and Mark E. Rupert, "Hobbes, Smith and the Problem of Mixed Ontologies," in *The Global Economy as Political Space,* ed. Stephen Rosow, Naeem Inayatullah, and Mark E. Rupert (Boulder, CO; Lynne Rienner, 1993).

29. Harrison White, *Identity and Control: A Structural Theory of Social Action* (Princeton, NJ: Princeton University Press, 1992).

30. White, *Identity and Control*, 201.

31. Ashley, "The Poverty of Neorealism," 240.

32. Thomas J. Biersteker and Cynthia Weber, ed., *State Sovereignty as Social Construct* (Cambridge, England: Cambridge University Press, 1996). The sociologist John Meyer and his colleagues have argued convincingly that nation-states are exogenously constructed entities, deriving from worldwide models constructed and propagated through sponsorship by powerful countries and subsequent global cultural diffusion. See, e.g., John W. Meyer et al., "World Society and the Nation State." *American Journal of Sociology* 103 (1997): 144–179; and John W. Meyer, "The Changing Cultural Content of the Nation-State: A World Society Perspective," in *State/Culture: State-Formation after the Cultural Turn*, ed. George Steinmetz (Ithaca, NY: Cornell University Press, 1999).

33. Reinhart Koselleck, *Critique and Crisis: Enlightenment and the Pathogenesis of Modern Society* (Oxford: Berg, 1988); Paul Hirst, *From Statism to Pluralism* (London: UCL Press, 1997), 216–235. However, the Peace of Westphalia should by no means be regarded as the singular founding moment of modern statehood. If anything, it favored absolutist over modern, capitalist statehood (see, e.g., Benno Teschke, *The Myth of 1648: Class, Geopolitics, and the Making of Modern International Relations* [London: Verso, 2003]).

34. Ash Amin and Nigel Thrift, "Institutional Issues for the European Regions: From Markets and Plans to Socioeconomics and Powers of Association." *Economy and Society* 24 (1995): 50–51.

35. See, e.g., Joseph Nye, "The Changing Nature of World Power." *Political Science Quarterly* 105 (1990): 177–192.

36. Timothy W. Luke, *Screens of Power: Ideology, Domination and Resistance in Informational Society* (Urbana, IL: University of Illinois Press, 1989), 47.

37. Luke, *Screens of Power*, 51.

38. Some writers note the emergence of the "global-Western state" or the "market state" as the quintessential political form of the contemporary global "constitutional order," for example, respectively, Martin Shaw, *Theory of the Global State: Globality as Unfinished Revolution* (Cambridge, England: Cambridge University Press, 2000) and Philip Bobbitt, *The Shield of Achilles: War, Peace, and the Course of History* (New York: Knopf, 2002), but without tracing its American roots. In neither case is a changing geography of power detected, probably because each remains attached to an idealized territorial state as the agent and container of social and political action irrespective of the "constitutional order" in question.

39. Some commentators claim that Britain was more committed to public-goods hegemony than the United States has been, whereas others argue that the United States has increasingly and successfully substituted coercion for hegemony since the 1970s; still others state that both have been empires for which the word "hegemony" is simply a euphemism. For well-articulated views see, on the first two, Beverly J. Silver and Giovanni Arrighi, "Polanyi's 'Double Movement': The *Belle Époques* of British and U.S. Hegemony Compared." *Politics and Society* 31 (2003): 325–355; and, on the third, Niall Ferguson, "Empire or Hegemony?" *Foreign Affairs* 82, 5 (2003): 154–161. Needless to say, the argument of this book is that the United States has laid

the groundwork for the first only true marketplace or capitalist hegemony. Many of the chapters in Patrick Karl O'Brien and Armand Clesse, ed., *Two Hegemonies: Britain 1846–1914 and the United States 1941–2001* (Aldershot: Ashgate, 2002) come close to this position but largely in terms of trade and monetary policy rather than with respect to marketplace society more broadly construed. For a succinct overview of the case for American singularity as a hegemon with which I am in almost total accord, see Patrick O'Brien, "Myths of Hegemony." *New Left Review* 24 (2003): 113–134.

40. Much of the anthropological literature on "the market" tends to associate both its practical incidence and the power of market rhetoric with "the West." For example, James G. Carrier, ed., in *Meanings of the Market: The Free Market in Western Culture* (New York: Berg, 1997), ix, identifies "the West as market-land." This geographical label could stand some deconstruction of its own.

41. Alternatively, marketplace society is associated with the rise of instrumental behavior at the expense of customary or command behavior as individuals look to markets rather than communities or authority as a solution to the challenge of social change. In any actual situation, of course, the flow of behavior is not simply unidirectional or without contradiction. On this see the arguments, for example, in Peter Temin, *Taking Your Medicine: Drug Regulation in the United States* (Cambridge, MA: Harvard University Press, 1979), 162–192; and Naomi Lamoreaux, "Rethinking the Transition to Capitalism in the Early American Northeast." *Journal of American History* 90 (2003): 437–461.

42. This point is made forcefully in Jim Cullen, *The American Dream: A Short History of an Idea that Shaped a Nation* (New York: Oxford University Press, 2003).

43. A reformulation of central elements of the arguments of Karl Polanyi, the Hungarian economist and journalist, and Antonio Gramsci, the Italian Communist thinker and organizer, can help provide a theoretical argument for (1) the vital importance of civil society in advanced capitalism and (2) the survival of capitalism through replacing irreconcilable conflict (between capital and labor) with the cooperative antagonism characteristic of postmodern capitalist hegemony. Michael Burawoy has recently provided a brilliant theoretical synthesis along these lines. See Michael Burawoy, "For a Sociological Marxism: The Complementary Convergence of Antonio Gramsci and Karl Polanyi." *Politics and Society* 31 (2003): 193–261.

44. Charles Sellers, *The Market Revolution: Jacksonian America, 1815-1846* (New York: Oxford University Press, 1991), 21.

45. Antonio Gramsci, *Selections from the Prison Notebooks* (New York: International Publishers, 1971).

46. Silvio Suppa, *Parsons Politico: Una lettura dell'americanismo* (Bari, Italy: Dedalo, 1984), 35.

47. Antonio Gramsci, "Americanismo e Fordismo," in *Quaderni del carcere*, Vol. III (Turin, Italy: Einaudi,1975), 2137–2181. To Gramsci, Fordism was not the universal phenomenon it has become in many recent neo-Marxist accounts. It had definite roots in the American experience.

48. Dick Howard, *The Specter of Democracy* (New York: Columbia University Press, 2002), Chapter 12, footnote 19.

49. Howard, *The Specter of Democracy*, 231.

50. Howard, *The Specter of Democracy*, 232.

51. Gramsci, "Americanismo e Fordismo," 2165, refers to "the 'Puritan' initiatives of American Fordist industrialists."

52. James E. Block, *A Nation of Agents: The American Path to a Modern Self and Society* (Cambridge, MA: Harvard University Press, 2002), 1.

53. Block, *A Nation of Agents*, 34.

54. The anthropologist Mary Douglas (*The World of Goods* [New York: Basic Books, 1979]) might classify the United States as predominantly a "weak grid, weak group society," in that group values are imposed through self-choice.

55. Thus, one of the primary requirements for successful long-distance social networks, such as those that presently constitute the emerging global network economy, ones based on many "weak ties," was first elaborated as a large-scale prototype in the United States. See Mark Granovetter, "The Strength of Weak Ties." *American Journal of Sociology* 78 (1973): 1360–1380; and Mark Buchanan, *Nexus: Small Worlds and the Groundbreaking Theory of Networks* (New York: Norton, 2002), Chapter 2. The obsession of commentators such as Robert Putnam with "reestablishing" strong associations and communities in the United States seems oblivious to the fact that the peculiar genius of American society has been precisely the absence of such strong communities (see, e.g., Robert D. Putnam, *Bowling Alone: The Collapse and Revival of American Community* [New York: Simon and Schuster, 2000]).

56. Another way of putting this would be to say that the United States was where movement and speed first overcame distance on a continental scale. More generally, see Paul Virilio, *Speed and Politics: An Essay on Dromology* (New York: Semiotext[e], 1986).

57. Sellers, *The Market Revolution*, 32.

58. Suppa, *Parsons Politico*. There is not a little danger, therefore, in exaggerating the common character of the "welfare state" that characterized "Atlantic Fordism" when the American version was always much less extensive and intensive than that which more state-centered Europeans produced after the Second World War, even when the influence of the American industrial model is correctly given central billing (see, e.g., Bob Jessop, *The Future of the Capitalist State* [Cambridge, England: Polity Press, 2002]).

59. Walter LaFeber, "The United States and Europe in an Age of Unilateralism," in *The American Century in Europe*, ed. R. Laurence Moore and Maurizio Vaudagna, 27–28 (Ithaca, NY: Cornell University Press, 2003).

60. As noted by Massimo L. Salvadori, "Utopia and Realism in Woodrow Wilson's Vision of the International Order," in *The American Century in Europe*, ed. R. Laurence Moore and Maurizio Vaudagna (Ithaca, NY: Cornell University Press, 2003), Wilson's vision has outlived in practice those of his main foreign opponents, from Clemenceau and Lloyd George to Lenin and Mussolini.

61. Mark Rupert, *Producing Hegemony* (Cambridge, England: Cambridge University Press, 1995). Even if instrumentally motivated, David W. Noble, *Death of a Nation: American Culture and the End of Exceptionalism* (Minneapolis: University of Minnesota Press, 2002), 298, plausibly argues that from the 1940s American political leaders replaced the "national landscape" with "the international marketplace" as the "timeless space" in which they located the American ideal. According to his account these had previously been in tension with one another.

62. Agnew and Corbridge, *Mastering Space*, 37–44.

63. Mark Rupert, *Ideologies of Globalization: Contending Visions of a New World Order* (London: Routledge, 2000), Chapters 2 and 3. David Singh Grewal, "Network Power and Globalization," *Ethics and International Affairs* 17 (2003): 89–98, argues that the resulting "network power" constitutes a kind of "informal empire." Yet, he also argues that this must necessarily rest on theorizing power in such a way that "does not resemble the command of a political superior" (p. 90). The choice of the word "empire," therefore, leaves much to be desired.

64. In Chapter 6, I discuss the economic policies of the Reagan years in much more detail than is possible at this point.

65. Martin Carnoy and Manuel Castells, "Globalization, the Knowledge Society, and the Network State: Poulantzas at the Millennium." *Global Networks* 1 (2001): 5.

66. Michael Hardt and Antonio Negri, *Empire* (Cambridge, MA: Harvard University Press, 2000) also Americanize globalization, but they do so in terms of the reach of American constitutionalism and not in terms of the spread of marketplace society and the new geography of power this has entailed. In Chapter 5, I show that American constitutionalism has had a limited possibility of transcending its particular roots. The argument of this book is that the same is manifestly not the case for marketplace society.

67. DeAnne Julius, *Global Companies and Public Policy: The Growing Challenge of Foreign Direct Investment* (New York: Council on Foreign Relations Press, 1990); Manuel Castells, *The Information Age. Vol. I: The Rise of the Network Society* (Oxford: Blackwell, 1996).

68. On the empirical dimensions of the "explosion" see, e.g., Stephen Castles and Mark J. Miller, *The Age of Migration: International Population Movements in the Modern World* (London: Macmillan, 1993). On the consequences for citizenship in Europe and North America, see W. Rogers Brubaker, ed., *Immigration and the Politics of Citizenship in Europe and North America* (Lanham, MD: University Press of America, 1989).

69. Andrew Linklater, *The Transformation of Political Community* (Cambridge, England: Polity Press, 1998).

70. Y. N. Soysal, *Limits of Citizenship: Migrants and Postnational Membership* (Chicago: University of Chicago Press, 1994).

71. David Jacobson, *Rights Across Borders: Immigration and the Decline of Citizenship* (Baltimore, MD: Johns Hopkins University Press, 1996).

72. Elizabeth Meehan, *Citizenship and the European Community* (London: Sage, 1993); Rainer Bauböck, *Transnational Citizenship: Membership and Rights in International Migration* (Aldershot, England: Edward Elgar, 1994); Rainer Bauböck and John Rundell, ed., *Blurred Boundaries: Migration, Ethnicity, Citizenship* (Aldershot, England: Ashgate, 1998).

73. Engin F. Isin, "Citizenship, Class and the Global City." *Citizenship Studies*, 3 (1999): 267–282.

74. David Harvey, *The Condition of Postmodernity* (Oxford: Blackwell, 1989); Doreen Massey, "Politics and Space/Time," in *Place and the Politics of Identity*, ed. Michael Keith and Steve Pile, 156–157 (London: Routledge, 1993); Ali Rattansi, " 'Western' Racisms, Ethnicities and Identities in a 'Postmodern' Frame," in *Racism, Modernity and Identity*, ed. Ali Rattansi and Sallie Westwood, 32–33 (Cambridge, England: Polity Press, 1994).

75. Giovanna Zincone, "The Powerful Consequences of Being Too Weak: The Impact of Immigration on Democratic Regimes." *Archives Européens de Sociologie* 38 (1997): 104–138; Dominique Schnapper, "The European Debate on Citizenship." *Daedalus* 126, 3 (1997): 199–222.

76. Jeannette Money, "No Vacancy: The Political Geography of Immigration Control in Advanced Industrial Countries." *International Organization* 51 (1997): 685–720.

77. Benjamin J. Cohen, *Organizing the World's Money* (New York: Basic Books, 1977), 3.

78. Patrick Brantlinger, *Fictions of State: Culture and Credit in Britain, 1694–1994* (Ithaca, NY: Cornell University Press, 1996), 241.

79. Eric Helleiner, "Historicizing Territorial Currencies: Monetary Space and the Nation-State in North America." *Political Geography* 18 (1999): 309–339.

80. Eric Helleiner, *States and the Re-emergence of Global Finance: From Bretton Woods to the 1990s* (Ithaca, NY: Cornell University Press, 1994), Chapter 4; Richard O'Brien, *Global Financial Integration: The End of Geography* (New York: Council on Foreign Relations, 1992).

81. Benjamin J. Cohen, *The Geography of Money* (Ithaca, NY: Cornell University Press, 1998).

82. A. Rotstein and C. Duncan, "For a Second Economy," in *The New Era of Global Competition*, ed. Daniel Drache and Meric Gertler (Montreal: McGill-Queen's University Press, 1991).

83. This is the view across a wide range of theoretical and political positions; see, e.g., Daniel Deudney, "Nuclear Weapons and the Waning of the Real-State." *Daedalus* 124 (1998): 209–251; Lawrence Freedman, "International Security: Changing Targets." *Foreign Policy* 110 (1998): 48–63; Mary Kaldor, *New and Old Wars: Organized Violence in a Global Era* (Cambridge, England: Polity Press, 1999).

84. Kaldor, *New and Old Wars*.

85. S. Feldman, *Israeli Nuclear Deterrence: A Strategy for the 1980s* (New York: Columbia University Press, 1982); Robert Jervis, *The Meaning of the Nuclear Revolution* (Ithaca, NY: Cornell University Press, 1989); J. Mueller, *Retreat from Doomsday: The Obsolescence of Major War* (New York: Basic Books, 1989).

86. With the end of the Cold War, it is the U.S. possession of nuclear weapons that provides one of the main incentives for others (states and renegades) to want to acquire them. As Philip Bobbitt reports (in *The Shield of Achilles*, p. 14): "When he was asked what the lesson of the Gulf War [1991] was, the Indian chief of staff is reported to have said: 'Never fight the United States without nuclear weapons.'" It seems likely that renegades such as terrorists or states captured by apocalyptic visionaries would be first users of nuclear devices in the twenty-first century. Bobbitt (p. 15) is correct to suggest that there is nothing "intrinsic to such weapons" that forbids their use.

87. Mueller, *Retreat from Doomsday*.

88. D. Skidmore and V. Hudson, ed., *The Limits of State Autonomy* (Boulder, CO: Westview Press, 1993).

89. This point is made by a large literature in international political economy. See, e.g., Richard Rosecrance, *The Rise of the Trading State: Commerce and Conquest in the Modern World* (New York: Basic Books, 1986); and Peter F. Cowhey and Jonathan

D. Aronson, *Managing the World Economy* (New York: Council on Foreign Relations Press, 1993). For a direct evaluation of the "changing benefits of conquest," see Stephen G. Brooks, "The Globalization of Production and the Changing Benefits of Conquest." *Journal of Conflict Resolution*, 43/5 (1999): 646–670.

90. Timothy W. Luke, "The Discipline of Security Studies and the Codes of Containment: Learning from Kuwait." *Alternatives* 16 (1991): 315–344.

91. Castells, *The Information Age. Vol. I*; Susan Strange, *The Retreat of the State: The Diffusion of Power in the World Economy* (Cambridge, England: Cambridge University Press, 1996); Allen J. Scott, *Regions and the World Economy: The Coming Shape of Global Production, Competition and Political Order* (Oxford: Oxford University Press, 1998).

92. These remain key tenets of the realist orthodoxy in international relations theory, particularly as related to security studies. For a recent example, see John Orme, "The Utility of Force in a World of Scarcity." *International Security*, 22 (1997–98), 138–167. More generally, see Hedley Bull, *The Anarchical Society: A Study of Order in World Politics* (London: Macmillan, 1977).

Chapter Four

1. Cited in E. H. Carr, *What Is History?* (New York: Knopf, 1961), 82.

2. Emma Rothschild, "Empire Beware!" *New York Review of Books*, March 25, 2004: 37–38.

3. William Appleman Williams, *The Roots of the Modern American Empire* (New York: Vintage, 1969).

4. Max M. Edling, *A Revolution in Favor of Government: Origins of the U.S. Constitution and the Making of the American State* (New York: Oxford University Press, 2003), 219.

5. Edling, *A Revolution in Favor of Government*, 223.

6. Edling, *A Revolution in Favor of Government*, 224.

7. Benedict Anderson, *Imagined Communities: Reflections on the Origins and Spread of Nationalism* (London: Verso, 1983).

8. Joseph M. Lynch, *Negotiating the Constitution: The Earliest Debates over Original Intent* (Ithaca, NY: Cornell University Press, 1999).

9. Joyce Appleby, "Presidents, Congress, and Courts: Partisan Passions in Motion." *Journal of American History* 88 (2001): 408–414.

10. See, e.g., James Buchan, *Crowded with Genius: The Scottish Enlightenment, Edinburgh's Moment of the Mind* (New York: HarperCollins, 2003).

11. Charles Sellers, *The Market Revolution: Jacksonian America, 1815–1846* (New York: Oxford University Press, 1991), 5.

12. John Agnew, *The United States in the World Economy: A Regional Geography* (Cambridge, England: Cambridge University Press, 1987).

13. T. H. Breen, *The Marketplace of Revolution: How Consumer Politics Shaped American Independence* (New York: Oxford University Press, 2004).

14. See, e.g., Carville Earle, *The American Way: A Geographical History of Crisis and Recovery* (Lanham, MD: Rowman and Littlefield, 2003).

15. Garry Wills, *"Negro President": Jefferson and the Slave Power* (New York: Houghton Mifflin, 2003). Of course, if the South had been able to count slaves on a

one-to-one basis then they would have had even greater representation. That they could not was the result of a compromise with northerners. Women and children were likewise included in population counts, but one to one in their case, and they also did not have the right to vote.

16. Daniel Deudney, in *Bounding Power: Republican Security Theory from the Polis to the Global Village* (Princeton, NJ: Princeton University Press, 2004), makes a plausible case for seeing the United States before the Civil War as a distinctive "Philadelphian Union" that only after 1865 became a recognizable modern nation-state. The western expansion of the union constantly threatened the balance of power between north and south, depending on whether states entered as slave or free. Only after an extremely violent war of secession was it possible for a nationwide marketplace society to emerge as the economic-cultural glue that, along with a burgeoning nationalism, held the country together.

17. Peter S. Onuf and Leonard J. Sadosky, *Jeffersonian America* (Oxford: Blackwell, 2002), 218–19.

18. John A. Agnew, "Introduction," in *American Space/American Place: Geographies of the Contemporary United States*, ed. John A. Agnew and Jonathan Smith (Edinburgh: Edinburgh University Press, 2002).

19. Robert W. Tucker and David C. Hedrickson, *Empire of Liberty: The Statecraft of Thomas Jefferson* (New York: Oxford University Press, 1990), ix.

20. William Lee Miller, *Lincoln's Virtues: An Ethical Biography* (New York: Random House, 2002), 88.

21. Thomas D. Schoonover, *Dollars over Dominion: The Triumph of Liberalism in Mexican–United States Relations, 1861–1867* (Baton Rouge: Louisiana State University Press, 1978).

22. Richard H. Sewell, *A House Divided: Sectionalism and Civil War, 1848-1865* (Baltimore: Johns Hopkins University Press, 1988).

23. Agnew, *The United States in the World Economy*, Chapter 3.

24. Donald W. Meinig, *The Shaping of America. Volume I: Atlantic America* (New Haven, CT: Yale University Press, 1986).

25. Barrington Moore, Jr., *Social Origins of Dictatorship and Democracy* (Boston: Beacon Press, 1966), 133.

26. See, e.g., Richard Franklin Bensel, *The Political Economy of American Industrialization, 1877–1900* (New York: Cambridge University Press, 2000); David R. Meyer, *The Roots of American Industrialization* (Baltimore: Johns Hopkins University Press, 2003); and most important, from my point of view, Timothy B. Spears, *100 Years on the Road: The Traveling Salesman in American Culture* (New Haven, CT: Yale University Press, 1995). Spears shows how salesmen drew big-city hinterlands and the continental United States as a whole into an increasingly single market and how their role in everyday life (for example by encouraging "brand loyalty") was central to the consumer culture that increasingly knitted together such a disparate national society towards the close of the nineteenth century. The *Robbins* decision of 1887 by the U.S. Supreme Court judged local ordinances and state laws restricting traveling salesmen as in violation of the freedom of interstate commerce and thus struck a major constitutional blow in favor of a national marketplace.

27. Alan Trachtenberg, *The Incorporation of America: Culture and Society in the Gilded Age* (New York: Hill and Wang, 1982), 20–21.

28. William Leach, *Land of Desire: Merchants, Power, and the Rise of a New American Culture* (New York: Pantheon, 1993).

29. Olivier Zunz, *Why the American Century?* (Chicago: University of Chicago Press, 1998), 75.

30. T. J. Jackson Lears, "From Salvation to Self-Realization: Advertising and the Therapeutic Roots of the Consumer Culture, 1880–1930," in *The Culture of Consumption: Critical Essays in American History, 1880–1980*, ed. Richard Wightman Fox and T.J. Jackson Lears, 3 (New York: Pantheon, 1983).

31. On this process, see, e.g., most famously, Thorstein Veblen, *The Theory of the Leisure Class* (original edition, 1899; New York: Mentor, 1953), and most recently, Robert Frank, *Luxury Fever* (New York: Free Press, 2003).

32. Eric Helleiner, "Historicizing Territorial Currencies: Monetary Space and the Nation-State in North America." *Political Geography* 18 (1999): 309–339.

33. Thom Hartmann, *Unequal Protection: The Rise of Corporate Dominance and the Theft of Human Rights* (Emmaus, PA: Rodale, 2002).

34. Elizabeth Sanders, "Industrial Concentration, Sectional Competition, and Antitrust Politics in the United States, 1880–1980." *Studies in American Political Development* 1 (1986): 142–214.

35. Ron Chernow, *The House of Morgan: An American Banking Dynasty and the Rise of Modern Finance* (New York: Atlantic Press, 1990).

36. Alfred D. Chandler, "The Growth of the Transnational Industrial Firm in the United States and United Kingdom: A Comparative Analysis." *Economic History Review* 33 (1980): 396–410.

37. Mira Wilkins, *The Emergence of Multinational Enterprise: American Business Abroad from the Colonial Era to 1914* (Cambridge, MA: Harvard University Press, 1970).

38. Chandler, "The Growth of the Transnational Industrial Firm," 399.

39. Peter Trubowitz, *Defining the National Interest: Conflict and Change in American Foreign Policy* (Chicago: University of Chicago Press, 1998).

40. Frederick Jackson Turner, "The Problem of the West." *Atlantic Monthly* 78 (1896), 289.

41. Mary Ann Heiss, "The Evolution of the Imperial Idea and U.S. National Identity." *Diplomatic History*, 26 (2002): 511–540.

42. Agnew, *The United States in the World Economy*; Thomas W. Zeiler, "Just Do IT! Globalization for Diplomatic Historians." *Diplomatic History* 25 (2001): 529–551.

43. Emily S. Rosenberg, *Spreading the American Dream: American Economic and Cultural Expansion, 1890–1945* (New York: Hill and Wang, 1983), 37.

44. David Campbell, *Writing Security: United States Foreign Policy and the Politics of Identity* (Minneapolis: University of Minnesota Press, 1992).

45. Frederick Dolan, *Allegories of America: Narratives-Metaphysics-Politics* (Ithaca, NY: Cornell University Press, 1994).

46. Louis Hartz, *The Liberal Tradition in America: An Interpretation of American Political Thought since the Revolution* (New York: Harcourt Brace World, 1955).

47. Michael J. Shapiro, *Violent Cartographies: Mapping Cultures of War* (Minneapolis: University of Minnesota Press, 1997).

48. See. e.g., Richard Slotkin, *Gunfighter Nation: The Myth of the Frontier in Twentieth-Century America* (New York: Atheneum, 1992).

49. Gary Cross, *An All-Consuming Century: Why Commercialism Won in Modern America* (New York: Columbia University Press, 2000).

50. Walter W. Rostow, *The Stages of Economic Growth: A Non-Communist Manifesto* (Cambridge, England: Cambridge University Press, 1960).

51. Karl Marx, *Capital, Volume I* (London: Lawrence and Wishart edn., [1887] 1974), 720, my emphasis.

52. Meghnad Desai, *Marx's Revenge: The Resurgence of Capitalism and the Death of Statist Socialism* (London: Verso, 2002), 142.

53. Desai, *Marx's Revenge*, 142.

54. Mike Davis, *Prisoners of the American Dream: Politics and Economy in the History of the U.S. Working Class* (London: Verso, 1986), 5. On the geographically complex form that this fratricide took and the critical role in it of the skilled/unskilled distinction, see, e.g., Sari Bennett and Carville Earle, "Socialism in America: A Geographical Interpretation of its Failure." *Political Geography Quarterly*, 2 (1983): 31–55.

55. Alfred D. Chandler and James W. Cortada, ed., *A Nation Transformed by Information: How Information Has Shaped the United States from Colonial Times to the Present* (New York: Oxford University Press, 2000).

56. The language is that of Albert Hirschman, *Exit, Voice, and Loyalty* (Cambridge, MA: Harvard University Press, 1970).

57. Dick Howard, *The Specter of Democracy* (New York: Columbia University Press, 2002), 232, my emphasis.

58. Howard, *The Specter of Democracy*, 232. The revival of American Christian Fundamentalism since the 1970s has involved a fusion between Americanism and Christianity that is difficult for foreign commentators to understand. It is often put down entirely to paranoia and xenophobia about race and cultural change, when it also reflects a theological interpretation of the United States as both the "Last Great Hope of Mankind" (as manifested in its material abundance) and the Good Side in a Manichean Millennialism always about to occur with the Evil Side, represented by whomever is the current Enemy of the United States government. On the origins of the recent fundamentalist revival in the United States, see, e.g., Joel A. Carpenter, *Revive Us Again: The Reawakening of American Fundamentalism* (New York: Oxford University Press, 1997), and on some of its major theological and geopolitical ideas, see Philip Melling, *Fundamentalism in America: Millennialism, Identity and Militant Religion* (Edinburgh: Edinburgh University Press, 1999).

59. Peter N. Stearns, *Consumerism in World History: The Global Transformation of Desire* (London: Routledge, 2001), 53.

60. Thomas Frank, *The Conquest of Cool: Business Culture, Counterculture, and the Rise of Hip Consumerism* (Chicago: University of Chicago Press, 1997).

61. Thomas Frank, *One Market under God: Extreme Capitalism, Market Populism, and the End of Economic Democracy* (New York: Random House, 2000).

62. Nicholas Lemann, "The New American Consensus: Government of, by, and for the Comfortable." *New York Times Magazine*, November 1, 1998, 68.

63. Garry Wills, *A Necessary Evil: A History of American Distrust of Government* (New York: Simon and Schuster, 1999), 320.

64. Frank, *One Market under God*; Charles McGovern, "Consumption and Citizenship in the United States, 1900–1940," in *Getting and Spending: European and American Consumer Societies in the Twentieth Century*, ed. Susan Strasser, Charles McGovern, and Matthias Judt (Cambridge, England: Cambridge University Press, 1998).

65. Lizabeth Cohen, "The New Deal State and the Making of Citizen Consumers," in *Getting and Spending: European and American Consumer Societies in the Twentieth Century*, ed. Susan Strasser, Charles McGovern, and Matthias Judt (Cambridge, England: Cambridge University Press, 1998).

66. Cohen, "The New Deal State and the Making of Consumers Citizen," 125.

67. Richard Wightman Fox and T. J. Jackson Lears, "Introduction," in *The Culture of Consumption: Critical Essays in American History, 1880–1980*, ed. Richard Wightman Fox and T. J. Jackson Lears, xii (New York: Pantheon, 1983). More generally, see Jeffrey L. Decker, *Made in America: Self-Styled Success from Horatio Alger to Oprah Winfrey* (Minneapolis: University of Minnesota Press, 1997).

68. Lizabeth Cohen, *A Consumers' Republic: The Politics of Mass Consumption in Postwar America* (New York: Random House, 2003).

Chapter Five

1. Philip Bobbitt, *The Shield of Achilles: War, Peace, and the Course of History* (New York: Knopf, 2002).

2. Bobbitt, *The Shield of Achilles*, 410.

3. Samuel P. Huntington, *Political Order in Changing Societies* (New Haven, CT: Yale University Press, 1968), 93.

4. See, e.g., Joseph M. Lynch, *Negotiating the Constitution: The Earliest Debates over Original Intent* (Ithaca, NY: Cornell University Press, 1999) for a cogent examination of interpretive disputes over the U.S. Constitution in the early years of U.S. independence and their continuing importance down to the present.

5. William H. Riker, "Federalism," in *A Companion to Political Philosophy*, ed. Robert E. Goodin and Philip Pettit (Oxford: Blackwell, 1993), 509.

6. Compare Garry Wills, *A Necessary Evil: A History of American Distrust of Government* (New York: Simon and Schuster, 1999) with Max M. Edling, *A Revolution in Favor of Government: Origins of the U.S. Constitution and the Making of the American State* (New York: Oxford University Press, 2003).

7. It also encourages partisan gerrymandering by focusing efforts on drawing electoral districts that maximize advantage to one party over others. In multimember districts with proportional representation there is no such incentive. More generally, see, e.g., Bhikhu Parekh, "The Cultural Particularity of Liberal Democracy," in *Prospects for Democracy: North, South, East, West*, ed. David Held (Stanford, CA: Stanford University Press, 1993).

8. U.K. Preuss, "The Political Meaning of Constitutionalism," in *Constitutionalism, Democracy and Sovereignty: American and European Perspectives*, ed. Richard Bellamy (Aldershot, England: Avebury, 1996).

9. See, e.g., Kevin P. Phillips, *Arrogant Capital: Washington, Wall Street, and the Frustration of American Politics* (Boston: Little, Brown, 1994).

10. Jennifer Nedelsky, *Private Property and the Limits of American Constitutionalism: The Madisonian Framework and its Legacy* (Chicago: University of Chicago Press, 1990).

11. John G. A. Pocock, *The Machiavellian Moment: Florentine Political Thought and the Atlantic Republican Tradition* (Princeton: Princeton University Press, 1975).

12. *Pace* Robert Kagan, *Of Paradise and Power: America and Europe in the New World Order* (New York: Knopf, 2003).

13. Marcel Gauchet, "Tocqueville," in *New French Thought: Political Philosophy*, ed. Mark Lilla (Princeton: Princeton University Press, 1994).

14. Potentially, this is one of the main causes of the low voter turnouts in American elections. The range of choice among political positions is remarkably constrained in the United States compared to many other democratic countries. On this, see the magisterial research of Walter Dean Burnham, *The Current Crisis in American Politics* (New York: Oxford University Press, 1982).

15. Michael Hardt and Antonio Negri, *Empire* (Cambridge, MA: Harvard University Press, 2000).

16. Martin Morris, "The Critique of Transcendence: Poststructuralism and the Political." *Political Theory*, 32 (2004): 121–132.

17. Hardt and Negri, *Empire*, 333, their emphasis.

18. Hardt and Negri, *Empire*, 314.

19. William I. Robinson, *Promoting Polyarchy: Globalization, U.S. Intervention, and Hegemony* (Cambridge, England: Cambridge University Press, 1996).

20. Daniel Lazare, *Frozen Republic: How the Constitution Is Paralyzing Democracy* (New York: Harcourt Brace, 1996).

21. Gauchet, "Tocqueville"; Larry Siedentop, *Tocqueville* (Oxford: Oxford University Press, 1994).

22. Philip Schmitter, "Federalism and the Euro-Polity." *Journal of Democracy* 11 (2000): 41. Siedentop, *Tocqueville*, might beg to differ.

23. Lazare, *Frozen Republic*, pp. 145–146.

24. Bruce Ackerman, "The New Separation of Powers." *Harvard Law Review* 113 (2000): 641.

25. See, e.g., John Zvesper, "The Separation of Powers in American Politics: Why We Fail to Accentuate the Positive." *Government and Opposition* 34 (1999): 3–23.

26. In Woodrow Wilson, *Congressional Government: A Study in American Politics* (Boston: Houghton Mifflin, 1885). Arguably, the separation of powers has allowed organized interest groups, particularly corporate ones, to provide an unofficial national coordinating role through campaign contributions and lobbying that the Constitution disallows for any formal institution. Interestingly, this began in earnest at the very time when U.S. economic interests were expanding externally and the U.S. government became more active in world politics—between 1890 and 1920 (see, e.g., Daniel J. Tichenor and Richard A. Harris, "Organized Interests and American Political Development." *Political Science Quarterly* 117 [2002–03]: 587–612).

27. Gauchet, "Tocqueville," 98.

28. Larry Siedentop, *Democracy in Europe* (London: Allen Lane, 2000).

29. Gauchet, "Tocqueville," 101–102.

30. K. Neunreither, "Governance without Opposition: The Case of the European Union." *Government and Opposition* 33 (1998): 419–441; Michael Newman, "Reconceptualising Democracy in the European Union," in *Transnational Democracy: Political Spaces and Border Crossings*, ed. James Anderson (London: Routledge, 2002).

31. Barbara Arneil, *The Defense of English Colonialism* (New York: Oxford University Press, 1996).

32. Anders Stephanson, *Manifest Destiny: American Expansion and the Empire of Right* (New York: Hill and Wang, 1995), 18–20.

33. J. Nicholas Entrikin, "Political Community, Identity, and the Cosmopolitan Place." *International Sociology* 14 (1999): 269–282.

34. David P. Calleo, *The Imperious Economy* (Cambridge, MA: Harvard University Press, 1982), 193–194.

35. Carville Earle, *The American Way: A Geographical History of Crisis and Recovery* (Lanham, MD: Rowman and Littlefield, 2003), 185–205.

36. Philip Cerny, "Political Entropy and American Decline." *Millennium* 18 (1989): 47–63.

37. Cerny, "Political Entropy and American Decline," 54.

38. The "imperial presidency" has had a major weakness, as Theodore J. Lowi has pointed out (in *The Personal President: Power Invested, Promise Unfulfilled* [Ithaca, NY: Cornell University Press, 1985]), in that it has lacked any system of collective responsibility or checks-and-balances *within* the executive branch and hence has been subject to all manner of abuses as revealed in the Watergate, Contra, and other scandals.

39. Howard Gillman, *The Votes that Counted: How the Court Decided the 2000 Presidential Election* (Chicago: University of Chicago Press, 2001).

40. Partisan gerrymandering of election districts is one of the main ways in which incumbency is institutionalized to the extent that, as of 2003, only about 15 percent of the seats in the U.S. House of Representatives are actually competitive. Increasingly, therefore, most seats are controlled through party primaries in which a tiny percentage of the electorate (with the Republicans, an increasingly conservative one) determines who is elected.

41. Peter Gowan, *The Global Gamble: Washington's Bid for World Dominance* (London: Verso, 1999).

42. John T. Noonan, Jr., *Narrowing the Nation's Power: The Supreme Court Sides with the States* (Berkeley: University of California Press, 2002).

43. D. Lasher, "Golden—and Global—in California." *Los Angeles Times*, January 8, 1998: A1, 22.

44. Cerny, "Political Entropy and American Decline," 59.

Chapter Six

1. On the first see, in particular, David Harvey, *The Condition of Postmodernity* (Oxford: Blackwell, 1989); on the second, see Roland Robertson, *Globalization: Social Theory and Global Culture* (London: Sage, 1992); and on the third, see Henk Overbeek, ed., *Restructuring Hegemony in the Global Political Economy: The Rise of Transnational Neo-Liberalism in the 1980s* (London: Routledge, 1993), and Meghnad

Desai, *Marx's Revenge: The Resurgence of Capitalism and the Death of Statist Socialism* (London: Verso, 2002).

2. See, e.g., Brian W. Blouet, *Geopolitics and Globalization in the Twentieth Century* (London: Reaktion Books, 2001).

3. President Calvin Coolidge, quoted in Arthur M. Schlesinger, Jr., *The Age of Roosevelt, Volume I* (Boston: Houghton Mifflin, 1956), 57.

4. David M. Kennedy, *Freedom from Fear: The American People in Depression and War, 1929–1945* (New York: Oxford University Press, 1999), 155.

5. Kennedy, *Freedom from Fear*, 159.

6. Kennedy, *Freedom from Fear*, 390.

7. See, e.g., Stephan Haggard, "The Institutional Foundations of Hegemony: Explaining the Reciprocal Trade Agreements Act of 1934." *International Organization* 42 (1988): 91–119. An apparently modest law with restrictions on how and for how long negotiations could go on, the RTAA granted the president authority to negotiate tariff reductions with foreign governments independent of congressional action. Thus, "access to American markets could be exchanged for entry into foreign markets, and American businesses that wished to export would have the incentive to lobby as a counterbalance to those seeking protection" (John M. Rothgeb, Jr., *U.S. Trade Policy: Balancing Economic Dreams and Political Realities* [Washington, DC: CQ Press, 2001], 45).

8. Robert J. Art, "A Defensible Defense: America's Grand Strategy after the Cold War." *International Security* 15 (1991): 5–53.

9. Howard Wachtel, *The Money Mandarins: The Making of a Supranational Economic Order* (New York: Pantheon, 1986).

10. Charles S. Maier, "The Politics of Productivity: Foundations of American International Economic Policy after World War II," in *Between Power and Plenty*, ed. Peter J. Katzenstein (Madison: University of Wisconsin Press, 1978); and Mark E. Rupert, "Producing Hegemony: State/Society Relations and the Politics of Productivity in the United States." *International Studies Quarterly* 34 (1990): 427–456.

11. John G. Ruggie, "International Regimes, Transactions, and Change: Embedded Liberalism in the Postwar Economic Order," in *International Regimes*, ed. Stephen D. Krasner (Ithaca, NY: Cornell University Press, 1983). A good overview of the political-economic convergence between the United States and Western Europe and how much this may have owed to U.S. government actions is provided in John Killick, *The United States and European Reconstruction, 1945–1960* (Edinburgh: Keele University Press, distributed by Edinburgh University Press, 1997).

12. Desai, *Marx's Revenge*, 220.

13. John Agnew, *The United States in the World Economy: A Regional Geography* (Cambridge, England: Cambridge University Press, 1987), Chapter 4.

14. Giovanni Arrighi, "The Three Hegemonies of Historical Capitalism." *Review* 13 (1990): 403.

15. Henry R. Nau, *The Myth of America's Decline: Leading the World Economy into the 1990s* (New York: Oxford University Press, 1990).

16. Marie-Laure Djelic, *Exporting the American Model: The Postwar Transformation of European Business* (Oxford: Oxford University Press, 1998); John Agnew and J. Nicholas Entrikin, ed., *The Marshall Plan Today* (London: Routledge, 2004).

17. Nau, *The Myth of America's Decline*, 48–49.

18. G. John Ikenberry and Charles A. Kupchan, "Socialization and Hegemonic Power." *International Organization* 44 (1990): 283–315. For an excellent case study, see Wyatt Wells, *Antitrust and the Formation of the Postwar World* (New York: Columbia University Press, 2002).

19. Qingxin Ken Wang, "Hegemony and Socialisation of the Mass Public: The Case of Postwar Japan's Cooperation with the United States on China Policy." *Review of International Studies* 29 (2003): 99–119.

20. R. Wood, *From Marshall Plan to Debt Crisis: Foreign Aid and Development Choices in the World Economy* (Berkeley: University of California Press, 1986).

21. Nau, *The Myth of America's Decline.*

22. Desai, *Marx's Revenge,* 217.

23. David P. Calleo, *Beyond American Hegemony: The Future of the Western Alliance* (New York: Basic Books, 1987), 147.

24. John O'Loughlin, "World-Power Competition and Local Conflicts in the Third World," in *A World in Crisis?* ed. R. J. Johnston and Peter J. Taylor (Oxford: Blackwell, 1989).

25. Fraser J. Harbutt, *The Cold War Era* (Oxford: Blackwell, 2002), 324.

26. Robert M. Collins, *More: The Politics of Economic Growth in Postwar America* (New York: Oxford University Press, 2000).

27. Eric Helleiner, *States and Reemergence of Global Finance: From Bretton Woods to the 1990s* (Ithaca, NY: Cornell University Press, 1994), 82.

28. Agnew, *The United States in the World Economy,* Chapter 4.

29. Thomas Engelhardt, *The End of Victory Culture: Cold War America and the Disillusioning of a Generation* (New York: Basic Books, 1995).

30. See, e.g., Susan Jeffords, *The Remasculinization of America: Gender and the Vietnam War* (Bloomington: Indiana University Press, 1989); Cynthia Enloe, *The Morning After: Sexual Politics at the End of the Cold War* (Berkeley: University of California Press, 1993); and James W. Gibson, *Warrior Dreams: Violence and Manhood in Post-Vietnam America* (New York: Hill and Wang, 1994).

31. Susan Strange, *Casino Capitalism* (Oxford: Blackwell, 1986).

32. See, e.g., R. Edmonds, *Soviet Foreign Policy: The Brezhnev Years* (New York: Oxford University Press, 1983), and Andrew Cockburn, *The Threat: Inside the Soviet Military Machine* (New York: Random House, 1983).

33. Peter Kornbluh, ed., *The Pinochet File: A Declassified Dossier on Atrocity and Accountability* (New York: New Press, 2003).

34. Allen J. Matusow, *Nixon's Economy: Boom, Bust, Dollars, and Votes* (Lawrence, KS: University Press of Kansas, 1998), 5.

35. Collins, *More,* 109.

36. Jonathan Schell, *Observing the Nixon Years* (New York: Random House, 1989).

37. Robert Triffin, *Gold and the Dollar Crisis* (New Haven, CT: Yale University Press, 1960); and A. W. Cafruny, "A Gramscian Concept of Declining Hegemony: Stages of U.S. Power and the Evolution of International Economic Relations," in *World Leadership and Hegemony,* ed. David P. Rapkin (Boulder, CO: Lynne Rienner, 1990).

38. Joanne S. Gowa, *Closing the Gold Window: Domestic Politics and the End of Bretton Woods* (Ithaca, NY: Cornell University Press, 1983), 23.

39. Stephen Gill, *American Hegemony and the Trilateral Commission* (Cambridge, England: Cambridge University Press, 1990).

40. Frances Fitzgerald, *Way Out There in the Blue: Reagan, Star Wars and the End of the Cold War* (New York: Simon and Schuster, 2000) shows how Reagan was able to obtain billions of dollars in funding for a program that was technologically impossible through his ability to read American popular fear of nuclear war and appeal to Americans' belief in technical "fixes" that would not require them to change how they or their government behave.

41. William Greider, *Secrets of the Temple: How the Federal Reserve Runs the Country* (New York: Simon and Schuster, 1987), Part Three.

42. This list makes the Reagan policies seem much more internally coherent than they really were, if the insider account by David A. Stockman, *The Triumph of Politics: The Inside Story of the Reagan Revolution* (New York: Harper and Row, 1986) is to be believed. Stockman, director of the White House Office of Management and the Budget in the first Reagan administration, reveals that lowering taxes became the be and end all of the "Reagan Revolution," notwithstanding that financing tax cuts required sustaining expanded federal government expenditures by borrowing and thus expanding the federal deficit. But in the early Reagan years all sorts of madcap ideas seem to have circulated without the President really understanding what they meant and how they might work at cross purposes. One, for example, concerned whether the Federal Reserve Bank was "really necessary" (Letter, Gordon C. Luce to Ronald Reagan, July 23, 1981; Letter, Ronald Reagan to Gordon C. Luce, July 30, 1981, FG 143, WHORM Subject File, Ronald Reagan Library). Although the radical advocates of tax cuts as the panacea of public finance, like Jude Wanniski and Jack Kemp, thought of themselves as sidelined during the early Reagan years because monetarist doctrines tended to dominate under the influence of Federal Reserve Chairman Paul Volcker, they provided the rationale for cutting taxes without reducing expenditures that has become the leitmotif of the Reagan years (Folder 1008, WHORM Subject File, Ronald Reagan Library). In the belief that the tax cuts would so stimulate the economy that revenues would explode, Reagan bequeathed a poisonous legacy embraced enthusiastically by the administration of George W. Bush: that federal deficits do not matter to either the United States or the world economies. Of course, if the deficits were acquired because of productivity-enhancing investment that would be one thing. But that they are the product of a failure to match tax-take to current expenditures by substituting borrowing (mainly from foreigners) is something else entirely.

43. Arguments were also made to the effect that government intervention can be perverse, futile, and jeopardize "liberty." Indeed, the rich were seen as an "embattled minority" subject to punitive taxation that not only constrained their "animal spirits" as potential investors but also undermined their liberty to do with their money as they pleased. These classic reactionary claims have been cogently examined in Albert O. Hirschman, *The Rhetoric of Reaction: Perversity, Futility, Jeopardy* (Cambridge, MA: Belknap Press of Harvard University Press, 1991). At the same time, the market was construed as representing a return to an older (pre–New Deal) America in which: "One achieves good by refusing to intend it or plan it. All the individual's actions are good as long as they are not interfered with. The Market

thus produces a happy outcome from endless miseries, a sinless product of count-less sins and inadvertencies. Eden was lost by free choice in the Fall of Man. It rises again, unbidden, by the automatic engineerings of the Market" (Garry Wills, *Reagan's America: Innocents at Home* [New York: Doubleday, 1987], 384).

44. Joel Krieger, *Reagan, Thatcher, and the Politics of Decline* (Cambridge, England: Polity Press, 1986), for example, overstates the parallels. The letters between President Reagan and Prime Minister Thatcher declassified under the Free-dom of Information Act (FOIA) at the Ronald Reagan Library in Simi Valley, California, are typically focused on a specific issue (e.g., Ronald Reagan to Margaret Thatcher, October 17, 1982, asking that the planned Williamsburg G7 Summit be more informal than previous summits; Ronald Reagan to Margaret Thatcher, June 15, 1983, praising Thatcher's economic policies and congratulating her on her elec-tion landslide victory; and Ronald Reagan to Margaret Thatcher, January 16, 1984, sharing the gist of a speech on U.S.-Soviet relations before he presented it, FOIA [12/11/97] Thatcher, Ronald Reagan Library). The letters are friendly but not ef-fusively so. Many of the letters to the Prime Minister are in fact replicas of the letters sent to other leaders, such as President Mitterrand of France. Most of the Prime Minister's replies came indirectly through the British embassy in Washington rather than "person to person." The letter traffic between the two leaders during the second Reagan administration has not yet been declassified. It might reveal a deeper relationship over substantive economic issues, as might access to telephone records.

45. Mike Davis, *Prisoners of the American Dream* (London: Verso, 1986), Chapter 6.

46. Benjamin Friedman, *Day of Reckoning: The Consequences of American Economic Policy* (New York: Random House, 1988), 233–270.

47. Friedman, *Day of Reckoning*, 209–232.

48. Kevin Phillips, *The Politics of Rich and Poor* (New York: Harper Collins, 1990).

49. Overbeek, *Restructuring Hegemony in the Global Political Economy*; Helleiner, *States and the Reemergence of Global Finance*, Chapter 7.

50. Collins, *More*, 214–232.

51. Some basic sources would include, *inter alia*, Michael Piore and Charles Sabel, *The Second Industrial Divide* (New York: Basic Books, 1984); Peter F. Cowhey and Jonathan D. Aronson, *Managing the World Economy: The Consequences of Corporate Alliances* (New York: Council on Foreign Relations Press, 1993); Michael Storper, "The New Industrial Geography." *Urban Geography* 8 (1987): 585–598; and Peter Dicken et al., "Chains and Networks, Territories and Scales: Towards a Relational Framework for Analysing the Global Economy." *Global Networks* 1 (2001): 89–112.

52. Dicken et al., "Chains and Networks, Territories and Scales."

53. See, e.g., Robert Brenner, *The Boom and the Bubble: The U.S. in the World Economy* (London: Verso, 2002).

54. Andrew Glyn et al., "The Rise and Fall of the Golden Age," in *The Golden Age of Capitalism: Reinterpreting the Postwar Experience*, ed. Stephen A. Marglin and Juliet B. Schor, 53 (Oxford: Clarendon Press, 1990).

55. Michael J. Webber and David L. Rigby, *The Golden Age Illusion: Rethinking Postwar Capitalism* (New York: Guilford Press, 1996).

56. Webber and Rigby, *The Golden Age Illusion*, 325.

57. On the prospects for harmonization of tax policies across countries and its implications for "statehood," see Roland Paris, "The Globalization of Taxation: Electronic Commerce and the Transformation of the State." *International Studies Quarterly*, 47 (2003): 153–182.

58. Cowhey and Aronson, *Managing the World Economy*.

59. Joe S. Bain, *Industrial Organization* (New York: John Wiley and Sons, 1959).

60. Peter Dicken, *Global Shift: Transforming the Global Economy*, Third Edition (New York: Guilford Press, 1998); John H. Dunning, "Globalization and the New Geography of Foreign Direct Investment," in *The Political Economy of Globalization*, ed. Ngaire Woods (London: Palgrave, 2000). By way of example, in 2001 fully one-quarter of the profits of U.S. companies came from abroad (Martin Wolf, "The Dependent Superpower: How Will the U.S. Cope with the Global Integration its Policies Unleashed?" *Financial Times* [December 18, 2003]: 11).

61. Robert B. Reich, *The Work of Nations: Preparing Ourselves for Twenty first Century Capitalism* (New York: Vintage, 1996).

62. DeAnne Julius, *Global Companies and Public Policy: The Growing Challenge of Foreign Direct Investment* (New York: Council on Foreign Relations, 1990).

63. Richard Lipsey and Irving Kravis, "The Competitiveness and Comparative Advantage of U.S. Multinationals, 1957–1984." *Banca Nazionale del Lavoro Quarterly Review*, 161 (1987): 147–165.

64. Robert B. Reich, "Who Do We Think They Are?" *American Prospect*, 4 (1991): 49–53.

65. Allen J. Scott and Michael Storper, "Regions, Globalization, Development." *Regional Studies* 37 (2003): 579–593.

66. See, e.g., Robert Wade, "The Coming Fight over Capital Flows." *Foreign Policy*, 113 (1998–1999): 41–54; and George Soros, "Capitalism's Last Chance?" *Foreign Policy*, 113 (1998–1999): 55–66.

67. Robert T. Kudrle, "Hegemony Strikes Out: The U.S. Global Role in Antitrust, Tax Evasion, and Illegal Immigration." Paper presented at the March 22–26, 2002 Meeting of the International Studies Association, New Orleans.

68. Compare, e.g., John Agnew and Stuart Corbridge, *Mastering Space: Hegemony, Territory, and International Political Economy* (London: Routledge, 1995), Chapters 7 and 8, with Michael Hardt and Antonio Negri, *Empire* (Cambridge, MA: Harvard University Press, 2000).

69. Though see, e.g., James N. Rosenau, *Distant Proximities: Dynamics Beyond Globalization* (Princeton, NJ: Princeton University Press, 2003). Rosenau, however, cannot envisage any place for regions and localities because his view of geography reduces to a two-sided either/or of presumably territorial states or placeless networks. This polarity plagues much writing about globalization as if it were synonymous with deterritorialization and that together both represent the "end of geography" tout court.

70. Isabelle Grunberg, "Exploring the 'Myth' of Hegemonic Stability." *International Organization* 44 (1990): 431–477.

71. Richard Rosecrance, *The Rise of the Trading State: Commerce and Conquest in the Modern World* (New York: Basic Books, 1986), 67.

72. David Morley, *Home Territories: Media, Mobility and Identity* (London: Routledge, 2000).

73. Ronald Rogowski, *Commerce and Coalitions: How Trade Affects Domestic Political Alignments* (Princeton, NJ: Princeton University Press, 1989), 88.

74. Rosecrance, *The Rise of the Trading State.*

75. Davis, *Prisoners of the American Dream*, Chapter 6.

76. Lipsey and Kravis, "The Competitiveness and Comparative Advantage of U.S. Multinationals."

77. Louis Uchitelle, "Small Companies Go Global." *New York Times*, November 29, 1989: 1–5.

78. Martin Wolf, "The Dependent Superpower," 11.

79. C. Higashi and G. P Lauter, *The Internationalization of the Japanese Economy* (Boston: Kluwer, 1987).

80. Gill, *American Hegemony and the Trilateral Commission.*

81. For a particularly prescient analysis, see Richard L. Sklar, "Postimperialism: A Class Analysis of Multinational Corporate Expansion." *Comparative Politics* 9 (1976): 75–92.

82. See, e.g., David Newman, ed., *Boundaries, Territory and Postmodernity* (London: Frank Cass, 1998); Malcolm Anderson and Eberhart Bort, *The Irish Border: History, Politics, Culture* (Liverpool: University of Liverpool Press, 1999).

83. Allen J. Scott, *Regions and the World Economy* (Oxford: Oxford University Press, 1998).

84. Guntram H. Herb and David H. Kaplan, eds., *Nested Identities: Nationalism, Territory, and Scale* (Lanham, MD: Rowman and Littlefield, 1999).

85. Andrés Rodríguez-Pose and Nicholas Gill, "The Global Trend Towards Devolution and Its Implications." *Environment and Planning C: Government and Policy* 21 (2003): 333–351; Darel E. Paul, "Re-scaling IPE: Subnational States and the Regulation of the Global Political Economy." *Review of International Political Economy*, 9 (2002): 465–489.

Chapter Seven

1. David Harvey, *The Condition of Postmodernity* (Oxford: Blackwell, 1989).

2. Marie Françoise Durand et al., *Le Monde: Espaces et systèmes* (Paris: Dalloz, 1993).

3. Michael Mann, *The Sources of Social Power. Vol. II: The Rise of Classes and Nation-States, 1760–1914* (Cambridge, England: Cambridge University Press, 1993); John Allen, *Hidden Geographies of Power* (Oxford: Blackwell, 2003).

4. Bond rating agencies (Standard and Poor's, etc.) are one example. See, e.g., Timothy J. Sinclair, "Reinventing Authority: Embedded Knowledge Networks and the New Global Finance." *Environment and Planning C: Government and Policy*, 18 (2000): 487–502.

5. Hannah Arendt, *The Human Condition* (Chicago: University of Chicago Press, 1958).

6. See, e.g., Stephen Gill, *American Hegemony and the Trilateral Commission* (Cambridge, England: Cambridge University Press, 1990); Leslie Sklair, *The*

Transnational Capitalist Class (Oxford: Blackwell, 2001) for a clear focus on the denationalization of capitalist elites.

7. Peter Dicken, "Placing Firms: Grounding the Debate on the 'Global' Corporation," in *Remaking the Global Economy: Economic-Geographical Perspectives*, ed. Jamie Peck and Henry Wai-chung Yeung (London: Sage, 2003).

8. William K. Carroll and Colin Carson, "Forging a New Hegemony? The Role of Transnational Policy Groups in the Network and Discourses of Global Corporate Governance." *Journal of World-Systems Research*, 9 (2003): 67–102.

9. Harvey, *The Condition of Postmodernity*.

10. Harvey, *The Condition of Postmodernity*, 294.

11. See, e.g., Henri Lefebvre, *The Production of Space* (Oxford: Blackwell, 1991); Edward W. Soja, *Postmodern Geographies: The Reassertion of Space in Critical Social Theory* (London: Verso 1989); Edward W. Soja, *Thirdspace: Journeys to Los Angeles and Other Real-and-Imagined Places* (Oxford: Blackwell, 1996); Edward W. Soja, "Thirdspace: Expanding the Scope of the Geographical Imagination," in *Human Geography Today*, ed. Doreen Massey et al. (Cambridge, England: Polity Press, 1999).

12. Soja, "Thirdspace," 277.

13. Robert A. Dodgshon, "Human Geography at the End of Time? Some Thoughts on the Idea of Time-Space Compression." *Society and Space*, 17 (1999): 607–620.

14. See, e.g., Peter J. Taylor et al., "On the Nation-State, the Global, and Social Science." *Environment and Planning A*, 28 (1996): 1917–1995.

15. Timothy W. Luke and Gearoid Ó Tuathail, "Global Flowmations, Local Fundamentalisms, and Fast Geopolitics: 'America' in an Accelerating World Order," in *An Unruly World? Globalization, Governance and Geography*, ed. Andrew Herod et al. (London: Routledge, 1998), 72.

16. Paul Virilio, *Speed and Politics* (New York: Semiotext[e], 1986).

17. Luke and Ó Tuathail, "Global Flowmations," 76.

18. Luke and Ó Tuathail, "Global Flowmations," 76.

19. Mackenzie Wark, *Virtual Geography: Living with Global Media Events* (Bloomington: Indiana University Press, 1994), 93.

20. Michael Storper, "Territories, Flows and Hierarchies in the Global Economy," in *Spaces of Globalization: Reasserting the Power of the Local*, ed. Kevin R. Cox (New York: Guilford Press, 1997), 31.

21. Storper, "Territories, Flows, and Hierarchies," 35.

22. Kevin R. Cox, "Introduction: Globalization and Its Politics in Question," in *Spaces of Globalization: Reasserting the Power of the Local*, ed. Kevin R. Cox (New York: Guilford Press, 1997), 16.

23. Neil Brenner, "'Glocalization' as a State Spatial Strategy: Urban Entrepreneurialism and the New Politics of Uneven Development in Western Europe," in *Remaking the Global Economy: Economic-Geographical Perspectives*, ed. Jamie Peck and Henry Wai-chung Yeung (London: Sage, 2003).

24. See, e.g., Jefferey M. Sellers, *Governing from Below: Urban Regions and the Global Economy* (Cambridge, England: Cambridge University Press, 2002); Andrés Rodríguez-Pose and Nicholas Gill, "The Global Trend Towards Devolution and Its Implications." *Environment and Planning C: Government and Policy* 21 (2003): 333–351.

25. Allen J. Scott, "Regional Motors of the Global Economy." *Futures* 28 (1996): 391–411.

26. Giovanni Arrighi and Beverly J. Silver, *Chaos and Governance in the Modern World-System* (Minneapolis: University of Minnesota Press, 1999).

27. See Chapter 6.

28. John Agnew, "The United States and American Hegemony," in *The Political Geography of the Twentieth Century*, ed. Peter J. Taylor (London: Belhaven Press, 1993).

29. See, e.g., Robert C. Feenstra, "Integration of Trade and Disintegration of Production in the Global Economy." *Journal of Economic Perspectives* 12 (1998): 31–50; Richard Kozul-Wright and Robert Rowthorn, "Spoilt for Choice? Multinational Corporations and the Geography of International Production." *Oxford Review of Economic Policy* 14 (1998): 74–92; Jörn Kleinart, "Growing Trade in Intermediate Goods: Outsourcing, Global Sourcing, or Increasing Importance of MNE Networks?" *Review of International Economics* 11 (2003): 464–482.

30. See Chapter 6 on market-access capitalism.

31. Peter J. Taylor, *World City Network: A Global Urban Analysis* (London: Routledge, 2004).

32. Bruce Robbins, "Actually Existing Cosmopolitanism," in *Cosmopolitics*, ed. P. Cheah and Bruce Robbins (Minneapolis: University of Minnesota Press, 1998), 1.

33. Ulf Hannerz, *Transnational Connections* (London: Routledge, 1996), Chapter 4.

34. Richard Wilk, "Learning to Be Local in Belize," in *Worlds Apart*, ed. Daniel Miller, 111 (London: Routledge, 1997), quoted in David Morley, *Home Territories: Media, Mobility, Identity* (London: Routledge, 2000), 11.

35. James L. Watson et al., ed., *Golden Arches East: McDonald's in East Asia* (Stanford, CA: Stanford University Press, 1997).

36. Theodore C. Bestor, "Supply-Side Sushi: Commodity, Market, and the Global City." *American Anthropologist* 103 (2001): 76–95.

37. Bestor, "Supply-Side Sushi," 83.

38. John Agnew and Stuart Corbridge, *Mastering Space: Hegemony, Territory, and International Political Economy* (London: Routledge, 1995), 167–168.

39. Taylor, *World City Network*.

40. UNCTAD *World Investment Report* (New York: United Nations, 2001), 13.

41. James K. Galbraith, "A Perfect Crime: Inequality in the Age of Globalization." *Daedalus* (Winter, 2002): 11–25.

42. Lant Pritchett, "Divergence, Big Time." *Journal of Economic Perspectives*, 11 (1997): 3–17.

43. Pritchett, "Divergence: Big Time," 5, 13; based on Angus Maddison, *Monitoring the World Economy, 1820–1992* (Paris: OECD, 1995).

44. Pritchett, "Divergence: Big Time," 11. The lower bound is based on the annual average per capita incomes found today in the poorest countries projected back into the nineteenth century. Actual incomes were probably lower.

45. Galbraith, "A Perfect Crime."

46. As claimed by Paul Bairoch, *Economics and World History: Myths and Paradoxes* (Chicago: University of Chicago Press, 1993).

47. World Bank, *World Development Report: Attacking World Poverty* (New York: Oxford University Press, 2001).

48. R. Summers and A. Heston, "The Penn World Tables (Mark 5): An Expanded Set of International Comparisons, 1950–88." *Quarterly Journal of Economics*, 106 (1991): 327–368.

49. Pritchett, "Divergence: Big Time," 14.

50. Presciently, the late David Gordon offered a similar set of categories. See David Gordon, "The Global Economy: New Edifice or Crumbling Foundations?" *New Left Review*, 168 (1988): 57.

51. Xavier Sala-i-Martin, *The World Distribution of Income* (Cambridge, MA: National Bureau of Economic Research, 2002).

52. The editor of *The Economist*, Bill Emmott, makes this inference: "Radical Thoughts on our 160th Birthday." *The Economist*, June 28, 2003, 5.

53. Surjit S. Bhalla, *Imagine There's No Country: Poverty, Inequality, and Growth in the Era of Globalization* (Washington, DC: Institute for International Economics, 2002).

54. Bhalla, *Imagine There's No Country*, 184.

55. Stanley Fischer, "Globalization and Its Challenges." *American Economic Review*, 93 (2003): 984.

56. "Follow the Yellow BRIC Road: Welcome to Tomorrow's Economic Giants," *The Economist*, October 11, 2003: 74.

57. Glenn Firebaugh, *The New Geography of Income Inequality* (Cambridge, MA: Harvard University Press, 2003), 6–12.

58. Firebaugh, *The New Geography of Global Income Inequality*.

59. Firebaugh, *The New Geography of Global Income Inequality*.

60. Firebaugh, *The New Geography of Global Income Inequality*, 130.

61. Firebaugh, *The New Geography of Global Income Inequality*, 160–161.

62. Firebaugh, *The New Geography of Global Income Inequality*, 187–203.

63. Bhalla, *Imagine There's No Country*; Firebaugh, *The New Geography of Global Income Inequality*.

64. Richard McGregor, "GM Hitches a Ride on the Chinese Expressway: Carmaker Expects China to Become Largest Market by 2025." *Financial Times*, October 17, 2003: 18.

65. Azizur Rahman Khan and Carl Riskin, *Inequality and Poverty in China in the Age of Globalization* (New York: Oxford University Press, 2001).

66. Pritchett, "Divergence: Big Time."

67. Bruce Cumings, "The Origins and Development of the Northeast Asian Political Economy: Industrial Sectors, Product Cycles, and Political Consequences." *International Organization* 38 (1984): 1–40.

68. Cumings, "The Origins and Development of the Northeast Asian Political Economy."

69. "Global Capitalism: Can It Be Made to Work Better?" *Business Week*, Special Issue, 2000: 98.

70. Richard Grant and John Agnew, "Representing Africa: The Geography of Africa in World Trade, 1960-1992." *Annals of the Association of American Geographers*, 86 (1996): 729–744.

71. Grant and Agnew, "Representing Africa."

72. Firebaugh, *The New Geography of Global Income Inequality*.

73. In GDP by purchasing power parity, China accounted for 25 percent of global GDP growth between 1995 and 2002, compared to 20 percent for the United States and 18 percent for the rest of Asia (excluding Japan). In these terms, China, and not the United States, is the "engine" of the world economy (see "Steaming." *Economist*, November 15, 2003: 67–68).

74. Bruce Cumings, "Still the American Century?" *Review of International Studies*, 25, Special Issue (1999): 287.

75. Cumings, "Still the American Century?" 294.

Chapter Eight

1. See, e.g., Erik Brynjolffson and Loren Hilt, "Beyond Computation: Information Technology, Organizational Transformation, and Business Performance." *Journal of Economic Perspectives* 14 (2000): 23–48; Dale Jorgenson and Kevin Stiroh, "Raising the Speed Limit: U.S. Economic Growth in the Information Age." *Brookings Papers on Economic Activity* 1 (2000): 125–211; Steven Oliner and Daniel Sichel, "The Resurgence of Growth in the Late 1990s: Is Information Technology the Story?" *Journal of Economic Perspectives* 14 (2000): 3–22.

2. Optimists include J. Bradford DeLong, "Productivity Growth in the 2000s" (unpublished paper, Department of Economics, University of California, Berkeley, June 2002). Susanto Basu et al., "Productivity Growth in the 1990s: Technology, Utilization, or Adjustment" (Cambridge, MA: National Bureau of Economic Research, 2000) provide evidence that the rate of technological change picked up dramatically after 1995 but are agnostic about its sustainability. The McKinsey Global Institute, "U.S. Productivity Growth, 1995–2000" (New York: McKinsey and Company, 2001), and Stephen S. Roach, "The Productivity Paradox." *New York Times*, November 30, 2003: op-ed, 9, are somewhat more pessimistic that (a) reported productivity increases are real and (b) that technology is largely responsible for the reported increases.

3. "Desperately Seeking a Perfect Model." *The Economist*, April 8, 1999: 10; Lawrence Mishel et al., *The State of Working America* (Ithaca, NY: ILR Press, 2003), chapter 7.

4. D. Lee, "L.A. County Jobs Surge Since '93, but Not Wages." *Los Angeles Times*, July 26, 1999: A1, A10.

5. Mishel et al., *The State of Working America*, 430–432. For a thorough discussion of how to make U.S.-Europe income and productivity comparisons, see Robert Gordon, "Two Centuries of Economic Growth: Europe Chasing the American Frontier." Available at: http://faculty-web.at.northwestern.edu/economics/gordon/355.pdf.

6. "Yes, the '90s Were Unusual but Not Because of Economic Growth." *Business Week*, April 24, 2000: 32; Austan Goolsbee, "The Unemployment Myth." *New York Times*, November 30, 2003: op-ed, 9.

7. "Desperately Seeking a Perfect Model." *The Economist*.

8. William Wolman and Anne Colamosca, *The Judas Economy: The Triumph of Capital and the Betrayal of Work* (Reading, MA: Addison-Wesley, 1997), 76–77.

9. See, e.g., Alan S. Blinder and Richard E. Quandt, "The Computer and the Economy." *The Atlantic Monthly* (December 1997): 26–32. On the limited effect of technology on productivity and the greater importance of increases in hours worked, see Lawrence Mishel et al., *The State of Working America*, 203–212, 238–243.

10. Daniel Drache, "From Keynes to K-Mart: Competitiveness in a Corporate Age," in *States Against Markets: The Limits of Globalization*, ed. Robert Boyer and Daniel Drache, 31–61 (London: Routledge, 1996).

11. Dani Rodrik, *Has Globalization Gone Too Far?* (Washington, DC: Institute for International Economics, 1997).

12. John Dumbrell, "Varieties of Post-Cold War American Isolationism." *Government and Opposition* 34 (1999): 24–43.

13. Kenneth F. Scheve and Matthew J. Slaughter, *Globalization and the Perceptions of American Workers* (Washington, DC: Institute for International Economics, 2001), 90. An excellent recent empirical survey of the benefits and costs of globalization across U.S. industries and social groups is provided in J. David Richardson, *Global Forces, American Faces: U.S. Economic Globalization at the Grass Roots* (Washington, DC: Institute for International Economics, 2003).

14. C. Fred Bergsten, "The United States and the World Economy." *Annals of the American Academy of Arts and Sciences* 460 (1982): 13.

15. John Agnew, *The United States in the World Economy: A Regional Geography* (Cambridge, England: Cambridge University Press, 1987), Chapter 4.

16. See, e.g., Peter Gowan, *The Global Gamble: Washington's Faustian Bid for Global Dominance* (London: Verso, 1999); and Robert Hunter Wade, "The Invisible Hand of the American Empire." *Ethics and International Affairs* 17 (2003): 77–88.

17. Robert Rowthorn and R. Ramaswamy, "Growth, Trade and Deindustrialization." *IMF Staff Working Papers* 46 (1999): 18–41.

18. Bob Jessop, *The Future of the Capitalist State* (Cambridge, England: Polity Press, 2002), 105.

19. Mishel et al., "The State of Working America," 189–196, show a consistent premium across wages and benefits to belonging to a labor union. The pity is that fewer and fewer American workers belong to unions, falling from 29 percent in 1977 to around 14 percent in 2001. Also, see Robert E. Baldwin, *The Decline of U.S. Labor Unions and the Role of Trade* (Washington, DC: Institute for International Economics, 2003).

20. See, e.g., John O'Loughlin, "Economic Globalization and Income Inequality in the United States," in *State Restructuring in America: Implications for a Diverse Society*, ed. Lynn Staeheli, Janet Kodras, and Colin Flint (Thousand Oaks, CA: Sage, 1997).

21. "A New Economy but No New Deal: More Full-Time Workers Are Poor." *Business Week*, July 10, 2000: 34.

22. Robert Brenner, "New Boom or New Bubble? The Trajectory of the U.S. Economy." *New Left Review*, 25 (2004): 57–100.

23. See K. M. Dudley, *The End of the Line: Lost Jobs, New Lives in Postindustrial America* (Chicago: University of Chicago Press, 1994); and Katherine Newman, *Declining Fortunes: The Withering of the American Dream* (New York: Basic Books, 1993). On the even higher and increasing concentration of assets or wealth than that of income in the United States, see Edward N. Wolff, "Recent Trends in the

Size Distribution of Household Wealth." *Journal of Economic Perspectives* 12 (1998): 131–150.

24. Sharon Zukin, *Point of Purchase: How Shopping Changed American Culture* (New York: Routledge, 2003).

25. Louis Uchitelle, "Why Americans Must Keep Spending." *New York Times*, December 1, 2003: A1, A4.

26. Brenner, "New Boom or New Bubble?" 77.

27. Thomas Frank, *One Market Under God: Extreme Capitalism, Market Populism, and the End of Economic Democracy* (New York: Random House, 2000). That the true electoral geography is much more variegated and localized, see Thomas Frank, "Lie Down for America: How the Republican Party Sows Ruin on the Great Plains." *Harper's Magazine* (April 2004): 33–46; and Philip A. Klinkner, "Red and Blue Scare: The Continuing Diversity of the American Electoral Landscape." *The Forum* 2 (2004), article 2, http://www.bepress.com/forum.

28. Neil Fligstein and Taekjin Shin, "The Shareholder Value Society: A Review of Changes in Working Conditions in the U.S., 1976–2000," in *The New Inequalities*, ed. K. Neckerman (New York: Russell Sage Foundation, 2004), show that focusing on shareholder value led the managers of U.S. businesses to pay more attention to profits and stock price and less to employees and communities.

29. Harvey S. Perloff et al., *Regions, Resources, and Economic Growth* (Lincoln, NE: University of Nebraska Press, 1960).

30. Agnew, *The United States in the World Economy*, Chapter 3.

31. Janet E. Kodras, "'With Liberty and Justice for All': Negotiating Freedom and Fairness in the American Income Distribution," in *American Space/American Place: Geographies of the Contemporary United States*, ed. John A. Agnew and Jonathan Smith (Edinburgh: Edinburgh University Press, 2002).

32. Iain Wallace, "Manufacturing in North America," in *North America: A Geographical Mosaic*, ed. Frederick W. Boal and Stephen A. Royle (London: Arnold, 1999); William B. Beyers, "The Service Economy," in *North America: A Geographical Mosaic*, ed. Frederick W. Boal and Stephen A. Royle (London: Arnold, 1999); David L. Rigby, "Urban and Regional Restructuring in the Second Half of the Twentieth Century," in *American Space/American Place: Geographies of the Contemporary United States*, ed. John A. Agnew and Jonathan Smith (Edinburgh: Edinburgh University Press, 2002).

33. "Whose Economy Will Prosper? How America's 50 States Stack Up." *Business Week*, July 27, 2000: 20; "Where Venture Capital Ventures: To Just a Few States and Industries." *Business Week*, February 7, 2000: 30.

34. Edward Alden, "Crusader Urges 'Unfair Trade' Crackdown." *Financial Times*, August 22, 2003: 2.

35. Alan Beattie and Christopher Swann, "Gains in Productivity Leave Jobs Market Lagging Behind Recovery." *Financial Times*, October 2, 2003: 2.

36. Simon Head, *The New Ruthless Economy: Work and Power in the Digital Age* (New York: Oxford University Press, 2003), 188, points out, "The link between higher productivity and higher real wages and benefits breaks down when technology is used in ways that deskill most workers, undermine their security in the workplace, and leave them vulnerable to employers possessed of overwhelming power."

37. Stephen Cecchetti, "America's Job Gap Will Be Difficult to Close." *Financial Times*, October 2, 2003: 13.

38. See, e.g., Peter J. Taylor, *World City Network: A Global Urban Analysis* (London: Routledge, 2004).

39. Taylor, *World City Network*, 204.

40. Manuel Castells, *The Rise of Network Society* (Oxford: Blackwell, 1996), 148–149.

41. Larry S. Bourne, "The North American Urban System: The Macro-Geography of Uneven Development," in *North America: A Geographical Mosaic*, ed. Frederick W. Boal and Stephen A. Royle (London: Arnold, 1999). For the 1990s I have drawn on U.S. Bureau of the Census, Table 5: Metropolitan Areas Ranked by Percent Population Change, 1990–2000 (Census 2000 PHC-T-3) (Washington, DC: Bureau of the Census, 2001). Between 1980 and 2000 the population of Las Vegas, Nevada increased by a staggering 237.6 percent. Only Orlando, Florida (134.9 percent) and Austin, Texas (132.7 percent) came close.

42. Although with dropping oil prices in the 1990s they proved adept at catering to the American taste for massive vehicles in the form of the SUV (sport utility vehicle) craze. Japanese firms quickly followed suit as consumers demanded "bigger and better" SUVs that were much more status goods than efficient (or safer) people movers. On this trend, see the devastating indictment of Keith Bradsher, *High and Mighty: The Dangerous Rise of the SUV* (New York: Public Affairs, 2002).

43. Barry Lynn, "Unmade in America: The True Cost of the Global Assembly Line." *Harper's Magazine* (June 2002): 33–41; Micheline Maynard, *The End of Detroit: How the Big Three Lost Their Grip on the American Market* (New York: Doubleday, 2003); Jeremy Grant, "Toyota Nudges Ford Motors out of Second Slot." *Financial Times*, November 11, 2003: 22.

44. Lydia Polgreen, "As Jobs Vanish, the Sweet Talk Could Turn Tough." *New York Times*, October 12, 2003: 26.

45. Evelyn Iritani and Marla Dickerson, "Tech Jobs Become State's Unwanted Big Export." *Los Angeles Times*, December 12, 2002: 1, 46; Andrew Pollack and David Leonhardt, "Economy Worries Californians, but It's Not That Bad." *Los Angeles Times*, October 12, 2003: 21.

46. Kevin Phillips, *The Politics of Rich and Poor* (New York: Random House, 1991).

47. Ronald Rogowski, "Trade and Representation: How Diminishing Geographic Concentration Augments Protectionist Pressure in the U.S. House of Representatives," in *Shaped by War and Trade: International Influences on American Political Development*, ed. Ira Katznelson and Martin Shefter, 204 (Princeton, NJ: Princeton University Press, 2002).

48. Catherine L. Mann, "Perspectives on the U.S. Current Account Deficit and Sustainability." *Journal of Economic Perspectives* 16 (2002): 131–152.

49. "Another Hangover in the Making? America's Spurt in Growth Is Being Fuelled by a Dangerous Cocktail." *The Economist*, November 9, 2003: 71–72.

50. But the continuing role of the U.S. dollar in this capacity is not guaranteed, particularly if central banks in China and elsewhere decide to float their currencies against a "basket" of foreign currencies (other than just the U.S. dollar) and declines in the value of the dollar against the Euro and other currencies encourage such a

diversification (see "A Central Question: How Long Will Central Banks Outside America Keep Buying Greenbacks?" *The Economist*, December 13, 2003: 75–76.

51. See, e.g., Wade, "The Invisible Hand of the American Empire."

52. Ka Zeng, "Trade Structure and the Effectiveness of America's 'Aggressively Unilateral' Trade Policy." *International Studies Quarterly* 46 (2002): 93–115.

Chapter Nine

1. It was first in the United States and now as a result of American hegemony elsewhere that capitalism has truly globalized. The perspective of this book emphasizes the priority to capitalism of circulation through consumption. As Marx (in *Grundrisse*, Notebook IV [London: Penguin, 1993, 420–421]) put it: "What precisely distinguishes capital from the master-slave relation is that the worker confronts him as consumer and possessor of exchange values, and that in the form of the possessor of money, in the form of money he becomes a simple center of circulation—one of its infinitely many centers, in which his specificity as a worker is extinguished." From this viewpoint, there is no easy way out of capitalism when workers are fundamentally involved in its very production and reproduction. Consequently, only through their social position as consumers can workers collectively remake the system (Kojin Karatani, *Transcritique: On Kant and Marx* [Cambridge, MA: MIT Press, 2003]).

2. James A. Camilleri and James Falk, *The End of Sovereignty? The Politics of a Shrinking and Fragmenting World* (Aldershot: Edward Elgar, 1992), 238.

3. Dani Rodrik, *Has Globalization Gone Too Far?* (Washington, DC: Institute of International Economics, 1997).

4. Somewhat more sanguine about state capacity under globalization is Geoffrey Garrett, "Shrinking States? Globalization and National Autonomy," in *The Political Economy of Globalization*, ed. Ngaire Woods (London: Palgrave, 2000).

5. Robert D. Sack, *Human Territoriality: Its Theory and History* (Cambridge, MA: Cambridge University Press, 1986).

6. Allen J. Scott, *Regions and the World Economy* (Oxford: Oxford University Press, 1998).

7. Bhikhu Parekh, "Reconstituting the Modern State," in *Transnational Democracy: Political Spaces and Border Crossings*, ed. James Anderson (London: Routledge, 2002).

8. Andrew Linklater, *The Transformation of Political Community* (Cambridge, MA: Polity Press, 1998).

9. David P. Calleo, *The Imperious Economy* (Cambridge, MA: Harvard University Press, 1982), 195.

10. Max Horkheimer, *Eclipse of Reason* (New York: Oxford University Press, 1947), 178.

11. Quoted in G. John Ikenberry, "America's Imperial Ambition." *Foreign Affairs* 81 (September/October 2002): 52.

12. Immanuel Wallerstein, *The Decline of American Power* (New York: New Press, 2003), 308.

13. Mary Kaldor, "American Power: From 'Compellance' to Cosmopolitanism?" *International Affairs* 79 (2003): 1–2.

14. David P. Calleo, "Power, Wealth, and Wisdom: The United States and Europe after Iraq." *The National Interest* 72 (2003): 9–10.

15. The interlocking corporate directorships and policy groups operating across state boundaries constitute two of the main foundations for this class (see Chapter 7). Suggestive of how important such groups are becoming in creating a class directorate for a truly global marketplace society, see, e.g., William I. Robinson, "Social Theory and Globalization: The Rise of a Transnational State." *Theory and Society* 30 (2001): 157–200; and Leslie Sklair, *The Transnational Capitalist Class* (Oxford: Blackwell, 2001).

Index